QUICK
ESCAPES®

New York City

31 Weekend Getaways
From the Big Apple

FIFTH EDITION

SUSAN FAREWELL

The
Globe
Pequot
Press

GUILFORD, CONNECTICUT

Photo credits: Pp. 1, 5, 14, 21, 41, 59: New York State Department of Economic Development; p. 29: Carolyn Mendelker; p. 52: Mary Ellen Kretz; p. 77: Homestead Inn; p. 70: The Fire Island Lighthouse Preservation Society, Inc.; p. 88: Keeler Tavern Museum; pp. 98, 112, 120: Connecticut Economic Development; p. 105: Claire White-Peterson; pp. 73, 133, 180: Jim McElholm, Oxford, Mass.; p. 139: Rhode Island Tourism Division; pp. 145, 149, 169: Kindra Clineff, photos courtesy of Massachusetts Office of Travel & Tourism; p. 162: Rockport Chamber of Commerce; p. 215: Digital Vision; p. 203: Vermont Travel Division; p. 223: photo courtesy of The Captain Lord Mansion; pp. 247, 256: Pennsylvania Department of Commerce; pp. 229, 233: New Jersey Division of Travel and Tourism; p. 238: Mid-Atlantic Center for the Arts; p. 271: Virginia Tourism Corporation.

Text design by Casey Shain
Maps by Maryann Dubé © The Globe Pequot Press

ISBN 0-7627-2543-5

Manufactured in the United States of America
Fifth Edition/First Printing

For her unconditional love and supportive friendship,
I dedicate this book to my beautiful sister, Joanne.

CONTENTS

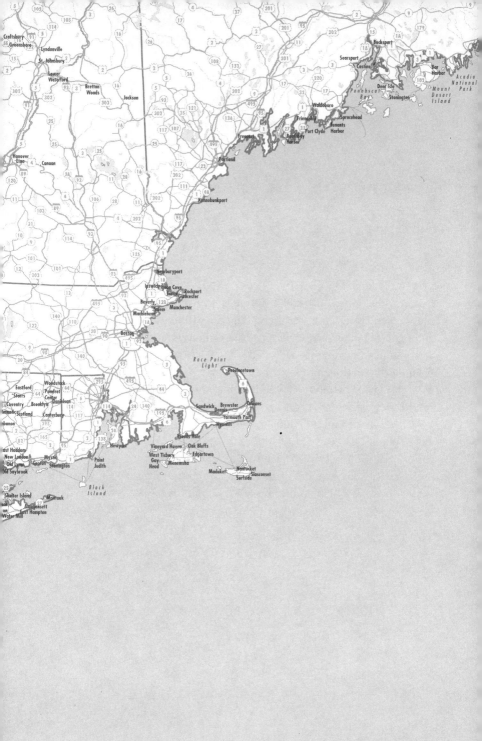

ACKNOWLEDGMENTS

I cannot just rattle off a half a dozen or so names of people who helped me with the research of this book. The list would go on and on for pages and include innkeepers, chefs, historians, curators, and tourism officials in all the states I covered. It would also include many of my colleagues and friends who are forever recommending places to visit and a large number of anonymous contributors whom I can only remember as "the blond boy on the bicycle in Nantucket" or "the couple on the ferry to Block Island."

There are several individuals who did, however, make this book actually happen. They include my editor, Laura Strom, who was unflaggingly patient with me, my many friends who accompanied me on trips or provided day-to-day support throughout the writing of it, and my parents, who kept asking, "Have you finished that book yet?"

INTRODUCTION

Have you ever gone away for the weekend without knowing precisely what places to visit (and the easiest way to get there), where to stay, and what to see and do once you have arrived? What should or could have been a little vacation can very often turn into a big disappointment. You find yourself saying things like "There must be some place we could just get a sandwich" or "Well, it cost only $5.00 to get in, not a major loss." Perhaps the most frequently uttered words of all, however, are "Next time." "Next time we'll stay at the inn on the water." "Next time we'll have brunch at that little restaurant in town." "Next time we'll leave enough time to hike to the summit." Unfortunately the "next time" may not happen very soon, if at all. It's hard enough finding the time to get away; the last thing you need is to have regrets.

It is precisely with those concerns in mind that I've compiled the thirty-one quick escapes that follow. They range in length from one to three nights and take you to some well-known and some hardly known destinations in New York State, New Jersey, Connecticut, Massachusetts, Rhode Island, Pennsylvania, Virginia, Washington, D.C., Vermont, New Hampshire, and Maine. For those of you who aren't traveling by car, I've included four trips you can make by using public transportation. Keep in mind, however, that several of the Quick Escapes can be done without a car.

Whether you're an out-of-towner visiting the New York area, a newcomer, or a longtime resident, this guide will help you find the places I've been lucky to have discovered or have had pointed out to me over the years as a child growing up in New York State, as a longtime resident of Connecticut, and as a travel writer.

Each escape is designed to be a little vacation in itself, offering you a combination platter of things to do and taking in the area's most noteworthy attractions. The itineraries are meant to be used as guides only, so feel free to improvise as you go along. If you see a road that looks compelling, by all means, follow it. Making your own discoveries can be lots of fun. You won't be able to fit in everything I suggest, so choose the things that most appeal to you and, if you have more time, consider combining trips.

In most of the locales, I've suggested restaurants (or great picnic spots) for all meals during your stay. In most cases there are several other eating places worthy of inclusion, some of which are listed under **Other Recommended Restaurants and Lodgings** at the end of the itinerary. Nevertheless there are still others, and to list them all would probably double the length of this book. For a complete list of restaurants and accommodations, contact the tourist offices listed under **For More Information** at the end of each escape.

In the resort areas, be sure to make restaurant reservations. Otherwise, you can wait for hours. If it's a holiday weekend, reservations are a must.

I've avoided listing prices because they change so often and, in the case of hotels, can vary from season to season. The restaurants and accommodations I have included are generally moderately priced or on the splurgey side. My thinking was that you don't need this guide to locate the chain hotels and motels. The places I have selected generally are either full of character or otherwise special in some way, which, in many cases, translates into more money.

It's always a good idea to make lodging reservations as far in advance as possible, especially for shore destinations in summer and ski destinations in winter. Some inns are booked up a year in advance. Many of the island inns (and resort town inns) require a minimum two- or three-night stay for a summer weekend. For destinations all over the area, 99 percent of the time you'll be asked to give an advance deposit with your credit card or to send in a check to guarantee your room. Check-in time is generally between 2:00 and 3:00 in the afternoon; checkout is usually somewhere around noon.

Following each itinerary are lists of additional things to do in the area (from outlet shopping to horseback riding), special annual events, and contact numbers and addresses for more information.

To make your trip go as smoothly as possible, be prepared. Use the following as a checklist before setting out.

Getting the Car Ready

Start by making sure that all important car documents are up to date and tucked away in the glove compartment. Be sure to do the following:

- Make sure that all lights are working properly. Walk around the car while someone tests the turn signals, the brake lights, the backup lights, and the emergency flashers.

- Test the horn.
- Check the wiper blades. If they're starting to show signs of wear and tear, replace them.
- Make sure that there is enough windshield-washing solution.
- Inspect the tires for cuts, bulges, or bald patches. Make sure that they have the recommended pressure.
- Check the engine oil level while the engine is off and the vehicle is parked on level ground.
- If you haven't had your car serviced in a while, it's a good idea to do so before any long trip.

Other things to check or have checked:
- Engine-coolant level
- Brake-fluid level
- Power-steering-fluid level
- Automatic-transmission-fluid level
- Battery-electrolyte (water) level
- All belts and hoses

Handy Take-Alongs

Comfort on the road is important for you and your traveling companions. In addition to dressing comfortably, in loose-fitting layers, consider taking these items along:
- Plastic water bottle that can be refilled along the way and/or a supply of nonalcoholic liquids (in cans, plastic bottles, pouches, or a thermos)
- Snacks (preferably dry or nonjuicy fruits, crackers, raw veggies, trail mix)
- Pillow and blanket for passenger(s)
- Sunglasses
- Reading material for passenger(s)
- Good map or atlas
- Umbrella
- Large box of tissues

- Pocket knife (with corkscrew)
- Camera (with film and extra batteries)
- Binoculars

For auto emergencies be sure to have these items:

- A cellular phone
- Coins for pay phone calls
- Flares or reflector triangles
- Jumper cables
- Empty gas can
- Fire extinguisher
- Blanket
- Flashlight (and extra batteries)
- First-aid kit

If you're traveling with children:

- Crayons and coloring books
- Storybooks
- Games (remember that small pieces get lost easily)
- Wipes to clean up messes and sticky hands

If you're traveling with pets:

- Water dish and water supply
- Dry snacks
- Favorite toys
- Leash and/or pet carrier

If you're traveling in winter:

- Ice scraper
- Collapsible shovel
- Traction mats
- Sand

Suggested Clothing and Footwear

What to pack for a trip outside New York City depends entirely on what time of year you go, since the weather varies so dramatically. Nevertheless, there are some items that may come in handy year-round. They include:

- A jacket and tie for men
- At least one dressy outfit for women
- Hiking boots
- A pair of sneakers or comfortable walking shoes
- A raincoat or poncho
- A robe (especially if you're staying at a bed and breakfast with the bathroom down the hall)
- A sweater (even in summer months)

And don't forget:

- Any prescriptions or medications
- A travel alarm

Getting In and Out of the City

Getting caught in rush-hour traffic going out of or coming into Manhattan can put a real damper on a weekend getaway. Do yourself a huge favor and rearrange work schedules or any other responsibilities so you avoid heavy traffic completely. During the warm-weather months (especially in the height of summer), traffic heading out to Long Island, to New Jersey, and to virtually all points north and east of the city starts getting thick right around lunchtime on Friday afternoons. Same thing late Sunday afternoon returning to the city. Otherwise, the customary rush hours (roughly 7:00 to 10:00 A.M. and 4:00 to 7:00 P.M.) should be avoided. Also, keep your eyes and ears open for events taking place. Something like the marathon or a presidential visit can keep you stalled in traffic for hours. A good radio station to tune into for these sorts of announcements is WINS (1010 on your AM dial).

As you venture out and discover places along the routes in this guide, feel free to send your findings to my attention at Globe Pequot.

Enjoy!

Help Us Keep This Guide Up to Date

Every effort has been made by the authors and editors to make this guide as accurate and useful as possible. However, many things can change after a guide is published—establishments close, phone numbers change, facilities come under new management, etc.

We would love to hear from you concerning your experiences with this guide and how you feel it could be improved and kept up to date. While we may not be able to respond to all comments and suggestions, we'll take them to heart and we'll also make certain to share them with the author. Please send your comments and suggestions to the following address:

The Globe Pequot Press
Reader Response/Editorial Department
P.O. Box 480
Guilford, CT 06437

Or you may e-mail us at:
editorial@globe-pequot.com

Thanks for your input, and happy travels!

NEW YORK
ESCAPES

The East Bank

1 Night

As a major waterway, the Hudson River, which was first explored by Henry Hudson in 1609, is rich with history. Scattered along its banks there are historic riverfront towns and stately old mansions (built by the rich and famous) surrounded by thick woods and spectacular scenery.

☐ River estates

☐ Historic houses

☐ Rural countryside

☐ Farms

☐ Shaker Museum

☐ Antiques shops

☐ FDR's Home

☐ Culinary Institute of America

You could easily make several trips to the Hudson Valley region and not retrace your steps. For this particular escape we take you north and east of the river through several rural towns and hamlets and then follow the river down along its eastern banks through some of the area's most historically interesting towns. This trip can be combined with the Hudson River Valley II and/or Hudson River Valley III escapes, which follow.

Day 1 / Morning

From Manhattan take the Henry Hudson Parkway north to the Saw Mill River Parkway to the Taconic State Parkway. At Route 44 turn east toward **Millbrook.** Home to many farms, Millbrook and the surrounding hamlets are well known among the horsey set. There are several worthwhile attractions in the Millbrook area including **Wing's Castle** (on Bangall Road, off Route 44; Millbrook, NY 12545; 845–677–9085), built by artists Peter and Toni Wing. The castle, which is made from salvaged materials from antique buildings, took them more than twenty-five years to complete. In the summer months, hours are noon to 4:30 P.M. Wednesday through Sunday. During the fall, the castle is open Saturday and Sunday only, from noon to 5:00 P.M. The **Institute of**

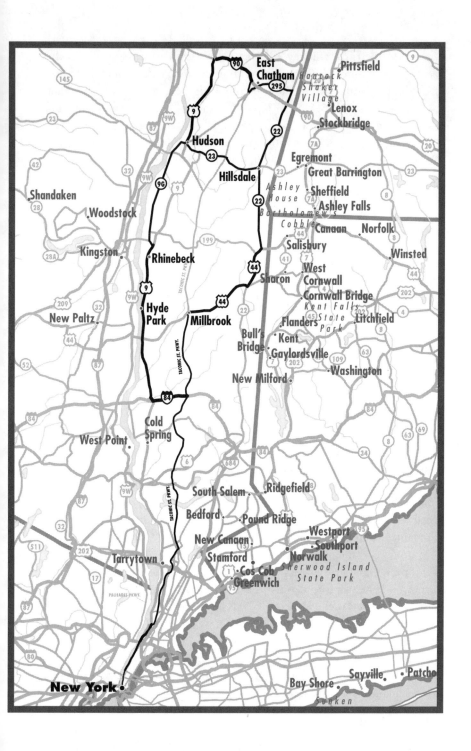

Ecosystem Studies Mary Flagler Cary Arboretum (on the northern side of Route 44A, 1 mile from the junction with Route 44 to the west and 2 miles from the junction with Route 44 to the east, Millbrook, NY 12545; 845–677–5343) is an ecological research and education center with nature trails, a perennial garden, a fern glen, a greenhouse, and a gift and plant shop. Hours vary seasonally, so do call ahead. When you reach Route 22 at Millerton, take a left and head north. You'll soon reach **Taconic State Park** and **Copake Falls.** Follow the signs to **Bash Bish Falls** if you want to do a little hiking in an entrancingly beautiful valley that has 50-foot falls as its centerpiece. From the parking lot it's about a mile-long (or twenty-minute) walk.

Afterward return to Route 22 and head north for a couple of miles until you reach Route 23. Turn right and follow signs for the Catamount Ski Area, Hillsdale, NY (518–325–3200), where you can pause to have lunch.

LUNCH: The **Swiss Hutte,** adjacent to the ski area (P.O. Box 357, Hillsdale, NY 12529; 518–325–3333), is a good lunch choice. It has everything from chef salad and burgers to filet of sole plus a pretty view of Catamount Mountain.

Afternoon

Continue north on Route 22 to Route 295 and turn left. Follow Route 295 for about 6 miles into East Chatham. Then go right on the Albany Turnpike for about 3 miles to **Old Chatham.** In Old Chatham turn left onto County Route 13 and follow that for about a mile. On the right you'll see the **Shaker Museum and Library,** 88 Shaker Museum Road, Old Chatham, NY 12136 (518–794–9100), which showcases an unparalleled collection of Shaker furnishings in several farm buildings. The museum and library are open between late May and October from 10:00 A.M. to 5:00 P.M. daily, except Tuesdays.

From Old Chatham it's a short drive to **Kinderhook** (follow 9H South), where you'll find three historic houses open to the public. The **James Vanderpoel House,** on Route US 9 (16 Broad Street, Kinderhook, NY 12106; 518–758–9265), is a Federal mansion that was built around 1820. The **Luykas Van Alen House,** south of town on Route 9H, Kinderhook, NY 12106 (518–758–9265), was built in 1737 and is now a museum of eighteenth-century Dutch domestic culture. Both are maintained by the Columbia County Historical Society and are open Thursday through Saturday from 11:00 A.M. to 5:00 P.M. and Sunday from

Lindenwald, Martin Van Buren's retirement home, is open for touring.

1:00 to 5:00 P.M. from Memorial Day weekend through Labor Day weekend. A ticket bought at one house is good for visits to both of them.

Drive south another mile or so and you'll reach **Lindenwald,** which is also known as the **Martin Van Buren National Historic Site,** about 2 miles south of Kinderhook on Route 9H, Kinderhook, NY 12106 (518–758–9689). This was the retirement home of the eighth president of the United States. The mansion and grounds are open for touring from 9:00 A.M. to 4:30 P.M. from late May through early December.

From Lindenwald continue south on Route 9H and then head east on Route 23 to Hillsdale, where you can settle in for the night and a memorable meal.

DINNER: Aubergine, at the junction of Routes 22 and 23, Hillsdale, NY 12529 (518–325–3412), has a French-inspired menu with lots of contemporary accents. One of chef-owner David Lawson's signature dishes is Seared Maine Scallop Cakes with shiitakes, scallions, bean sprouts, and Ponzu sauce.

LODGING: You can stay in one of four guest rooms at Aubergine, which is run by Stacy Lawson, wife of the chef at Aubergine's restaurant. Each room is decorated in a French Country style and has its own bathroom.

Day 2 / Morning

BREAKFAST: Start with complimentary coffee at the inn and then head over for a classic American breakfast at **The Dutch Treat** (1843 State Route 23, Craryville, NY; 518–325–5107), which is about two minutes away.

Head west on Route 23 to the former whaling town of **Hudson.** Here you'll find several antiques shops as well as a fine collection of beautifully restored Federal, Greek Revival, and Victorian houses that were built in the eighteenth century. Detailed walking-tour maps are available in most of the shops. There's a fire-fighting museum in town, the **American Museum of Fire Fighting,** 117 Harry Howard Avenue, Hudson, NY 12534 (518–828–7695), which is filled with antique fire-fighting equipment including a 1725 fire engine. The museum is open daily year-round, from 9:00 A.M. to 4:30 P.M.

Head south of town on NY 9G and you'll come to **Olana State Historic Site,** about 5 miles south of Hudson on Route 9G, Hudson, NY 12534 (518–828–0135). This was the home of the nineteenth-century landscape artist Frederic Edwin Church. He built Olana, a five-story Persian-style villa atop a bluff overlooking the Hudson, in the 1870s. There are forty-five-minute tours of the first floor from the beginning of April until the end of December.

Continue south on Route 9G and then west on Route 6 to **Clermont State Historic Site/Museum,** 1 Clermont Avenue, Germantown, NY 12526; (518–537–4240). Clermont was the home of Robert R. Livingston (and seven generations of his family), one of five men elected to draft the Declaration of Independence. He also was Chancellor of New York and administered the oath of office to George Washington. The house is open for touring (April through October, Tuesday through Sunday 11:00 A.M. to 5:00 P.M. and November 1 through December 15, Saturday and Sunday 11:00 A.M. to 4:00 P.M.); the grounds are open year-round for hiking, riding, cross-country skiing, and picnicking.

A little farther south is **Rhinebeck,** which has a museum devoted to vintage airplanes, WWI aircraft, and other early craft. The **Old Rhinebeck Aerodrome,** off Route 9 at 42 Stone Church Road, Rhinebeck, NY 12572 (845–752–3200), is open from May 15 through October 31, daily, from 10:00 A.M. to 5:00 P.M. Air shows are on Saturdays and Sundays from mid-June through mid-October.

LUNCH: Schemmy's Restaurant and Ice Cream Parlor, 19 East Market Street, Rhinebeck, NY 12572 (845–876–6215) is a local favorite serving delicious sandwiches on a variety of breads, gourmet pizzas (try the Texas BBQ chicken), charbroiled burgers, and several house specialties.

Afternoon

After lunch spend a little time checking out the shops in Rhinebeck and then head south again on Route 9. In Staatsburg (between Rhinebeck and Hyde Park), take time out to see **Mills Mansion,** in Mills-Norrie State Park, off Route 9, Staatsburgh, NY 12580 (845–889–8851). The Beaux Arts estate of Ogden and Ruth Livington Mills is set on 900 acres. There are hiking trails, guided tours, and beautiful river views. It's open Wednesday through Saturday from 10:00 A.M. to 4:00 P.M. and Sunday from noon to 4:00 P.M. Just before you reach Hyde Park, you'll come to the **Vanderbilt Mansion,** Hyde Park, NY 12538 (845–229–9115). This fifty-four-room Beaux Arts mansion was designed by McKim, Mead & White for Frederick Vanderbilt. After a tour of the house, be sure to wander around the grounds. The view of the Hudson from here is nonpareil. The house is open 9:00 A.M. to 5:00 P.M. daily year-round; grounds are open daily from 7:00 A.M. until sunset.

Hyde Park, which is well known as the site of FDR's home, is next on the itinerary. You could easily spend an entire day (or more) here, especially if you're a history buff. Start with the **Home of Franklin D. Roosevelt National Historic Site,** 1 mile south of town on US 9, Hyde Park, NY 12538 (845–229–9115). This estate, known as Springwood, was the president's birthplace and lifelong residence. It's open daily 9:00 A.M. to 5:00 P.M. year-round; grounds are open daily from 7:00 A.M. until sunset. Adjacent is the **FDR Museum and Library,** which is filled with memorabilia, letters, documents, and photographs. It's open daily. Two miles east of the estate is the **Eleanor Roosevelt National Historic Site,** Hyde Park, NY 12538, which is open daily from May through October and on Saturday and Sunday only from November through April. For information on all three places, call (845) 229–9115.

Once you've had your fill of presidential history, you can complete your journey with a wonderful meal at the Culinary Institute of America.

DINNER: The **Culinary Institute of America,** Route 9, Hyde Park, NY 12538 (845–471–6608). Be sure to call ahead for reservations at this highly esteemed cooking school. There are four student-staffed restaurants on the 150-acre campus: St. Andrew's Cafe offers contemporary dishes, the Caterina de Medici Dining Room features regional Italian cuisine, the Escoffier Restaurant serves French cuisine, and the American Bounty Restaurant specializes in American food. The Apple Pie Bakery Café showcases the talents of the school's baking and pastry arts students and faculty.

It's about a ninety-minute trip back to New York City from here. Take Route 9 south to 84 east and then pick up the Taconic heading south.

There's More

Hiking. Poet's Walk, County Road 103, north of the Rhinecliff-Kingston Bridge, Red Hook, NY 12571; (845) 473–4440. A 120-acre park with trails for hiking and benches scattered about.

Historic Houses. Montgomery Place, River Road, Annandale-on-Hudson, NY 12504; (845) 758–5461. This nineteenth-century estate is set on hundreds of acres overlooking the Hudson River and the Catskill Mountains. There are gardens, a greenhouse, nature trails, and pick-your-own-fruit orchards.

Shopping. Hammertown Barn, Route 199, Pine Plains, NY 12567; (518) 398–7075. Here you'll find nineteenth-century English and American antiques, quilts, woven wool Navajo blankets, birdhouses, handcrafted jewelry, and much more. The barn is 1 mile east of the village of Pine Plains, which is north of Millbrook.

Vineyards. Cascade Mountain Winery, 835 Cascade Mountain Road, Amenia, NY 12501; (845) 373–9021. Tours and tastings offered. There's also a cafe and picnic area. Open year-round, daily, from 10:00 A.M. to 6:00 P.M.

Millbrook Vineyards and Winery, Wing Road and Shunpike Road, Millbrook, NY 12545; (845) 677–8383. Tours and tastings. Open year-round, daily, from noon to 7:00 P.M.

Special Events

May. Rhinebeck Antiques Fair. Held at the Dutchess County Fairgrounds, Rhinebeck, NY 12572; (845) 876–1989.

June. Crafts at Rhinebeck. A juried show of more than 350 exhibitors. Held at the Dutchess County Fairgrounds, Rhinebeck, NY 12572; (845) 876–4001.

August. Annual Shaker Museum Antiques Festival, Shaker Museum, Old Chatham, NY 12136; (518) 794–9100. More than one hundred dealers.

September. Annual Radio Control Jamboree. An air show and other aerial events at the Old Rhinebeck Aerodrome, Rhinebeck, NY 12572; (845) 229–2371.

October. Crafts at Rhinebeck Fall Festival. More than 200 exhibitors plus harvest-related activities. At the Dutchess County Fairgrounds, Rhinebeck, NY 12572; (845) 876–4001.

Rhinebeck Antiques Fair. Dealers from all over New England show furniture, folk art, paintings, etc. At the Dutchess County Fairgrounds, Rhinebeck, NY 12572; (845) 876–1989.

Other Recommended Restaurants and Lodgings

Amenia

Cascade Mountain Winery and Restaurant, 835 Cascade Mountain Road, Amenia, NY 12501; (845) 373–9021. Thursday through Sunday, lovely lunches made with ultrafresh ingredients are served.

Troutbeck, Leedsville Road, Amenia, NY 12501; (845) 373–9681. This 1920s-era stone manor house on a Dutchess County estate has a split personality. During the week it's an executive retreat for conferences, and on weekends, it's a romantic country inn. Troutbeck is exquisitely furnished with antiques throughout. Its dining room is a great find, serving contemporary American cuisine.

Dover Plains

Old Drovers Inn, Old Post Road (Route 22 near Millbrook), Dover Plains, NY 12522; (845) 832–9311. This old inn (it's been welcoming visitors for more than 250 years!) is a member of the elite Relais and Châteaux hotel group. It's full of old-fashioned charm and has a respectable restaurant specializing in innovative American cuisine. There are only four guest rooms, so be sure to make reservations in advance.

Rhinebeck

Belvedere Mansion, 10 Old Route 9, Rhinebeck, NY 12572; (845) 889–8000. This is both a bed and breakfast and a restaurant that serves exquisite American cuisine made from many local products. Many of its cooks and wait staff are alumni and students of the Culinary Institute.

Foster's Coach House, 9193 Montgomery Street (Route 9), Rhinebeck, NY 12572; (845) 876–8052. If you're in the mood for a burger, a sandwich, or something else simple and American, you can't go wrong with Foster's.

For More Information

Historic Hudson Valley, 150 White Plains Road, Tarrytown, NY 10591; (914) 631–8200.

Hudson Valley Tourism, P.O. Box 2840, Salt Point, NY 12578; (800) 232–4782.

Columbia County Office of Tourism, 401 State Street, Hudson, NY 12534; (518) 828–3375 or (800) 724–1846.

Dutchess County Tourism Promotion Agency, 3 Neptune Road, Poughkeepsie, NY 12601; (845) 463–4000 or (800) 445–3131.

New York Department of Economic Development, Division of Tourism, One Commerce Plaza, Albany, NY 12245; (518) 474–4116 or (800) 225–5697.

Hudson River Valley II

The Lower Hudson

1 Night

Both the east and west banks of the Lower Hudson are liberally sprinkled with historic, contemporary, and natural attractions. To take in the highlights of the area, we suggest driving up the eastern shore, crossing over on I–84, and then returning on the western banks. This trip can be combined with Hudson River Valley I escape and/or Hudson River Valley III escape.

- ☐ Riverside towns and scenery
- ☐ Woodlands
- ☐ Hiking
- ☐ Restaurants
- ☐ Antiques and crafts shops
- ☐ Historic houses
- ☐ Museums •
- ☐ United States Military Academy

Day 1 / Morning

Head north out of New York on the Henry Hudson Parkway to the Saw Mill River Parkway. Then jog over to US 9 in Hastings, an exit off the Saw Mill River Parkway. Route 9 roughly follows the Hudson shoreline, taking you through a string of historic towns and attractions.

Make your first destination **Tarrytown,** a riverside town that was settled by the Dutch in the mid-1600s and later made famous by the writings of Washington Irving, particularly "The Legend of Sleepy Hollow." There are several noteworthy attractions in the area including **Lyndhurst,** 635 South Broadway, Tarrytown, NY 10591 (914–631–4481), a Gothic Revival estate that was the former home of financier Jay Gould. It's open for touring Tuesday through Sunday from 10:00 A.M. to 5:00 P.M. between mid-April and October and on Saturday and Sunday only from November through April. You can visit Irving's Hudson River estate **Sunnyside,** on West Sunnyside Lane, Tarrytown, NY 10591 (914–591–8763), which is open daily between April and December. This estate, along with several of the other properties that follow, is under the care of Historic Hudson

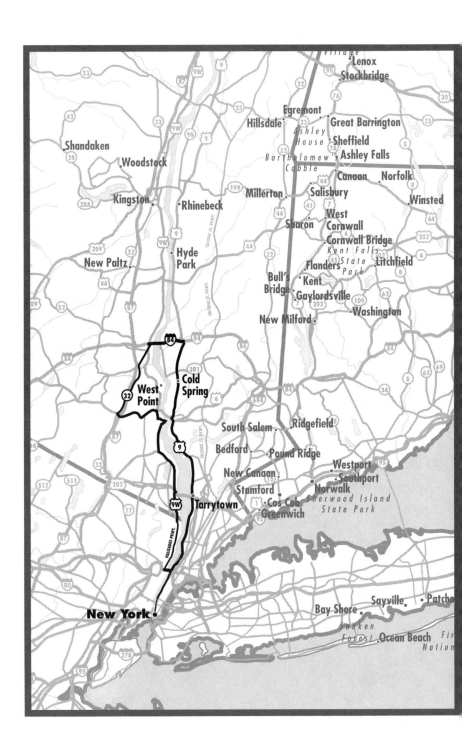

Valley, a nonprofit organization, which will gladly provide you with more information (see address and telephone number under "For More Information"). In nearby North Tarrytown you'll find **Philipsburg Manor,** on US 9, Sleepy Hollow, NY 10591-3660 (914–631–8200), a beautifully restored seventeenth-century manor house with a mill and millpond. It's also open daily year-round. Also in North Tarrytown is **Kykuit,** (It's pronounced "kye-kit.") a Rockefeller estate in Sleepy Hollow, NY 10591-3660 (accessible by shuttle bus from Philipsburg Manor) (914–631–9491), which has been opened for public viewing. It's a forty-room Colonial Revival mansion, on eighty-seven lush acres, dotted with sculpture by modern masters including Alexander Calder, Henry Moore, and Lois Nevelson. Nearby you'll find **Union Church of Pocantico Hills,** with stained-glass windows by Marc Chagall and Henri Matisse. It was commissioned by members of the Rockefeller family; tours are offered from April through December.

Continue up Route 9 to **Van Cortlandt Manor,** in **Croton-on-Hudson** (914–271–8981), which is a restored baronial manor offering insight into the life of a wealthy family in the early 1800s.

From there carry on to **Garrison,** which is home to **Boscobel,** (NY 9D, Garrison, NY 10524; 845–265–3638), an early-eighteenth-century country home open for touring. It's an acclaimed example of Federal architecture. There are guided tours indoors and gardened grounds outside overlooking the Hudson River.

Just to the north is the village of **Cold Spring,** where you can settle in for a wonderful lunch, a relaxing afternoon, and the night. The town is filled with historic nineteenth-century buildings.

LUNCH: Plumbush Inn, 1656 Route 9D; Cold Spring, NY 10516 (845–265–3904), is a beautiful Victorian restaurant on five woodland acres. Lunch is a bit of a splurge, but worth it. The cuisine is largely continental. Open Wednesday through Sunday.

Afternoon

Spend the afternoon poking around the many antiques and crafts shops in Cold Spring and check out the **Foundry School Museum,** 63 Chestnut Street, Cold Spring, NY 10516 (845–265–4010), which displays Hudson River School paintings. The museum is open March through December, Tuesday and Wednesday from 10:00 A.M. to 4:00 P.M., Thursday from 1:00 to 4:00 P.M., and Sunday from 2:00 to 5:00 P.M.

Views of the Hudson River from Bear Mountain are sensational.

DINNER: Bird & Bottle Inn, 1123 Old Albany Road, Garrison, NY 10524 (845–424–3000), serves traditional American and continental dishes in a tavern that dates from 1761.

LODGING: Hudson House, 2 Main Street, Cold Spring, NY 10516 (845–265–9355), is an attractive twelve-room country inn on the banks of the Hudson River.

Day 2 / Morning

BREAKFAST: On Saturday and Sunday mornings, a full breakfast is included in the room price at Hudson House. During the week a continental breakfast is served.

After breakfast drive north via Route 301 from Cold Spring to Route 9 north and then take I–84 west over the river and head into **Newburgh** to see **Washington's Headquarters,** Liberty and Washington Streets (84

Liberty Street, Newburgh, NY 12551; 845–562–1195). From here Washington commanded his troops from 1781 to 1782. The headquarters are open between April and October, Wednesday through Saturday from 10:00 A.M. to 5:00 P.M. and Sunday from 1:00 to 5:00 P.M.

From Newburgh head south on Route 32 about 7 miles or so until you see a sign for the **Storm King Art Center,** One Pleasant Hill Road, Mountainville, NY 10953 (845–534–3115). Plan to spend several hours here: Storm King is the leading outdoor sculpture park and museum in the United States. It sprawls over 400 acres of lawns, terraces, fields, and woods. Visiting hours are from 11:00 A.M. to 5:30 P.M. daily from April 1 through late October and 11:00 A.M. to 5:00 P.M. from late October through November 15.

LUNCH: On weekends from May through October, you can picnic on the grounds. Drinks and snacks are available in vending machines.

Afternoon

After lunch continue south to **West Point,** home of the **United States Military Academy.** Founded in 1802, this spectacularly situated academy (it crowns a bluff high above the Hudson) has turned out many prominent leaders including Robert E. Lee, Ulysses S. Grant, and George S. Patton. The best time to visit is during spring or fall when the cadets parade or a sporting event takes place. There's a museum devoted to military history. The Visitors Center is located at 2107 New South Post Road, West Point, NY 10996; (845) 938–2638. The Visitors Center is open daily (with the exception of Thanksgiving, Christmas, and New Year's Day), from 9:00 A.M. to 4:45 P.M.

From West Point take Route 9W South and get off at the Haverstraw exit to reach **Bear Mountain State Park** (845–786–2701), a 5,067-acre park that extends westward from the Hudson. Here you'll find an excellent **Trailside Museum,** which consists of several small museums including a reptile museum, a nature-study museum, a geology museum, and a history museum. There are also hiking trails, picnic areas, a mountaintop observatory, and a breathtakingly beautiful drive up the mountain—called **Perkins Memorial Drive.**

Once you've soaked up the serenity of the park, you can head back into Manhattan (which is a mere 45 miles away), taking the dramatically scenic Palisades Parkway south to the George Washington Bridge.

There's More

Hiking. Hudson Highland State Park, just north of Cold Spring, has lots of trails to wander along, as does the Manitoga Nature Preserve, south of Garrison. In nearby Carmel the Appalachian Trail cuts right through Clarence Fahnestock State Park.

Fahnestock State Park is off the Taconic State Parkway on Route 301 in Cold Spring. Extra challenging is Breakneck Ridge, a hike just north of Cold Spring. The first half mile is straight up (though it's not really rock climbing, you do have to use your hands sometimes to hold onto rocks), but it's well worth it. The views—up and down the Hudson and inland a bit—are astonishingly beautiful. If you have time (you'll need a total of two or three hours), do the entire loop trip. You'll sleep well afterward. Also check out Croton Point Park, off Route 9 in Croton-on-Hudson.

Horse racing. Yonkers Raceway, Yonkers Avenue and Central Avenue in Yonkers, on I–87, between exits 2 and 4 (914) 968–4200. Harness racing.

Hudson River History. The Hudson River Museum of Westchester, 511 Warburton Avenue in nearby Yonkers, NY 10701; (914) 963–4550. This museum includes Glenview Mansion, a Hudson River house overlooking the Palisades; a planetarium; and regional art, history, and science exhibits.

Special Events

Early October. Autumn Crafts & Tasks Festival, Van Cortlandt Manor, Croton. Demonstrations of house and farm labor in the 1700s.

October. Annual Arts and Crafts Festival, Bear Mountain State Park. A juried indoor and outdoor show.

December. Candlelight Tours at Sunnyside, Philipsburg Manor, and Van Cortlandt Manor. English Christmas celebration.

Other Recommended Restaurants and Lodgings

Bear Mountain

Old Bear Mountain Inn, Bear Mountain State Park, Bear Mountain, NY

10911; (845) 786–2731. Built in 1915, this rustic, sixty-room hunting lodge has its charms. You can stay overnight or grab a simple meal.

Cold Spring

Pig Hill Inn, 73 Main Street; (845) 265–9247. The antiques throughout this three-story inn can be purchased. There are nine guest rooms, five with private baths. Pssst . . . the breakfasts alone make it worth staying here.

Stormville

Harrald's, Route 52, Stormville, NY 12582; (845) 878–6595. This restaurant is northeast of Cold Spring (about 5½ miles east of the Taconic Parkway) but well worth the detour. It serves international and continental cuisines.

For More Information

Hudson Valley Tourism, P.O. Box 2840, Salt Point, NY 12578; (800) 232–4782.

Historic Hudson Valley, 150 White Plains Road, Tarrytown, NY 10591; (914) 631–8200.

Westchester Convention & Visitors Bureau, Ltd., 222 Mamaroneck Avenue, White Plains, NY 10605; (800) 833–9282.

Orange County Tourism, 20 Matthews Street, Suite III, Goshen, NY 10924; (800) 762–8687.

New York Department of Economic Development, Division of Tourism, One Commerce Plaza, Albany, NY 12245; (518) 474–4116 or (800) 225–5697.

Hudson River Valley III

The West Bank

2 Nights

Back in 1820 author and historian Washington Irving wrote the tale of "Rip Van Winkle," in which Rip joins a party of gnomes in the Catskill Mountains and falls asleep for twenty years. These modest but magical mountains, which can have a calming effect on anyone who visits them, can be reached in less than two hours from Manhattan.

☐ Mountain scenery

☐ Wineries

☐ Hiking

☐ Horseback riding

☐ Sports resorts

☐ Skiing (downhill and cross-country)

☐ International cuisines

☐ Antiques shops

Though the real magnet of the area is **Catskill Park,** which covers 705,500 acres, there are several river towns just to the east and south that are not only gateways to the park but attractions in themselves.

For this trip we suggest you start just south of the park, exploring the countryside around New Paltz, then head north to Kingston, which, back in 1777, was New York State's first capital. From there we take you into the Catskill Forest, to Shandaken in the mountains and Woodstock, which is the Catskills' most famous town.

Day 1 / Morning

Take the Henry Hudson Parkway up to the George Washington Bridge and cross over to the Palisades Interstate Parkway. Take that to the New York State Thruway north up to exit 18, which is **New Paltz.**

Head right for the Mohonk Mountain House, a National Historic Landmark and your home for the night, where you'll have a chance to wander about its wooded trails and feast your eyes on the lake for which

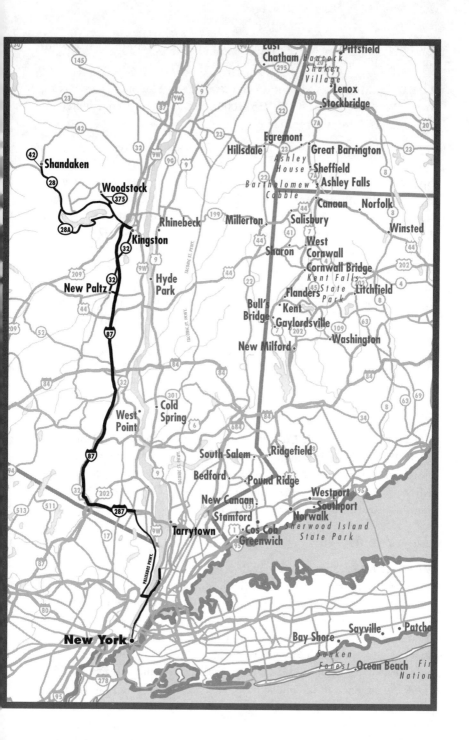

the resort is named (*mohonk* means "lake in the sky"). For the best view of all, climb the cliff-top observation tower.

LUNCH: Mohonk Mountain House, 1000 Mountain Rest Road, New Paltz, NY 12561 (845–255–1000), has a hot and cold buffet for lunch (included in the room rate).

Afternoon

Spend the afternoon visiting the wineries and other attractions along the **Shawangunk Wine Trail,** a 30-mile loop (well marked with signs) that includes several Ulster County wineries including Applewood Winery, 82 Four Corners Road, Warwick, NY 10990 (845–988–9292); Adair Vineyards, 52 Allhusen Road, New Paltz, NY 12561 (845–255–1377), and many others. Bear in mind that you could make an entire day out of this, so the sooner you head out after lunch, the better. Visiting hours vary from vineyard to vineyard, but generally the vineyards are open during summer months until 5:00 P.M. Maps are available at the individual vineyards and tourism offices.

DINNER: Mohonk Mountain House, 1000 Mountain Rest Road, New Paltz, NY 12561 (845–255–1000). Dinners in the dining room (included in the room rate) are usually traditional American dishes, though there are often other choices featured as daily specials.

LODGING: Mohonk Mountain House, 1000 Mountain Rest Road, New Paltz, NY 12561 (845–255–1000), is a big old-fashioned country hotel surrounded by the arrestingly beautiful scenery of the Shawangunk Mountains (right next to the Catskill Mountains). There's golf, tennis, hiking, and horseback riding—you name it.

Day 2 / Morning

BREAKFAST: Start the day with a big traditional American breakfast (included in the room rate) at Mohonk House.

After breakfast head into town to see **Huguenot Street,** which is the oldest street in the United States where original buildings still stand. New Paltz was founded back in 1678 by half a dozen Huguenots who were granted land by the Colonial governor of New York. Huguenot Street is lined with several stone houses and a church, which were built between 1692 and 1799. All are open to the public for guided tours only from May 1 through

Ulster County is home to several wineries open for tours and tastings.

October 31. Contact the Huguenot Historical Society (18 Broadhead Avenue, New Paltz, NY 12561; 845–255–1660) for more information.

From New Paltz head north on Route 32 toward **Kingston.** Along the way consider stopping in at **Apple Hill Farm,** 141 Route 32 South, New Paltz, NY 12561 (845–255–0917), where you can pick your own apples and pumpkins during the fall season.

Kingston is an old river port that was founded in 1652 as a Dutch trading settlement and became New York State's first capital in 1777. Many of its early buildings still stand today and are open to the public including the **Old Dutch Church,** 272 Wall Street, Kingston, NY 12401 (845–338–6759), and the **Senate House,** 312 Fair Street, Kingston, NY 12401 (845–338–2786). All tour sites are either in or adjacent to the historic district, which is known as the Stockade because of the walls that used to surround it. Other Kingston attractions include the **Hudson**

River Maritime Museum and Rondout Lighthouse, One Rondout Landing (845–338–0071), Kingston, NY 12401, which is devoted to the maritime history of the area (daily, May 1 through October 31, from 11:00 A.M. to 5:00 P.M.), and the **Trolley Museum of New York,** 89 East Strand, Kingston, NY 12401 (845–331–3399), which showcases old trolley cars. The Trolley Museum is open between Memorial Day and Columbus Day on Saturdays, Sundays, and holidays. Also worthwhile is the **Volunteer Firemen's Hall and Museum of Kingston,** 265 Fair Street, Kingston, NY 12401 (845–331–0866).

LUNCH: **Le Canard Enchaine,** 276 Fair Street, Kingston, NY 12401 (845–339–2003) has a nice selection of healthy sandwiches as well as a selection of French entrees that vary daily.

Afternoon

Once you've had a look around Kingston, head west on Route 28 (this route takes you right into the **Catskill Forest Preserve,** which is a large part of the Catskills under the protection of the government), then turn north on Route 42 to reach **Shandaken,** a township that includes several mountain hamlets and is home to **Slide Mountain,** the highest peak in the Catskills.

DINNER: This part of the Catskills has several fine eateries featuring French cuisine and, in fact, is known as "the French Catskills." One of the best is **Auberge des 4 Saisons,** ½ mile north of Shandaken on NY 42, Shandaken, NY 12480 (845–688–2223), which specializes in duck.

LODGING: You can also stay at the **Auberge des 4 Saisons,** NY 42, Shandaken, NY 12480 (845–688–2223), in a simple lodge room with a jaw-droppingly beautiful mountain view.

Day 3 / Morning

BREAKFAST: Breakfast is included in the room rate at Auberge des 4 Saisons.

After breakfast head back onto Route 28, detouring on Route 28A for some more beautiful scenery around the 12-mile-long Asholkan reservoir, and then follow Route 375 into **Woodstock,** where the famed rock concert took place in 1969. Here you can spend hours browsing through shops and galleries before heading back to New York City. Don't miss the **Woodstock Artists Association Gallery,** 28 Tinker Street at

Village Green, Woodstock, NY 12498 (845–679–2940). It has been the center of the community since 1920, featuring works by both local and nationally known artists.

LUNCH: Joshua's, 51 Tinker Street, Woodstock, NY 12498 (845–679–5533), is right in town and offers a good selection of sandwiches and vegetarian dishes, plus some Middle Eastern dishes as well.

From Woodstock it's a short drive east to Route 87, which you take south back to the New York metropolitan area.

There's More

Biking. Mountain and road bikes can be rented at Bicycle Depot, 15 Main Street, New Paltz, NY 12561 (845–255–3859) and at Overlook Mountain Bikes, 93 Tinker Street, Woodstock, NY 12498 (845–679–2122).

Bird-watching. Slide Mountain is an especially good place for bird-watching. Among its many inhabitants are wild turkeys, ruffed grouse, pileated woodpeckers, yellow-bellied sapsuckers, and several different warblers and thrushes.

Game farm. Catskill Game Farm, off Route 32, near Catskill, NY 12414; (518) 678–9595. This game farm is in the neighborhood where Rip Van Winkle is said to have slept. Kids can feed tame deer, llamas, and other animals. Open daily from late April through October 31, 9:00 A.M. to 6:00 P.M.

Golf. Mohonk Mountain House in New Paltz, NY 12561 (845–255–1000) and Green Acres Golf Club in Kingston (845–331–2283).

Hudson River boat tours. In Kingston several boat companies offer river trips. Among them are Hudson River Cruises (845–255–6515), which has music and dinner cruises, North River Cruises (845–679–8205), and the Great Hudson Sailing Center (845–429–1557), which offers sailing trips.

Parks and preserves. Cohotate Preserve, Greene County Environmental Education Center, Route 385, north of the Rip Van Winkle Bridge, near Athens, NY 12015; (518) 622–3620.

Four Mile Point Preserve, Route 385, Four Mile Point Road, near Coxsackie, NY 12051; (845) 473–4440 (Scenic Hudson).

Ramshorn-Livington Sanctuary, off Route 9W, Grandview Avenue, Catskill, NY 12414; (845) 473–4440 (Scenic Hudson). A tidal swamp with more than 480 acres operated by the North Catskills Audubon Society.

Skiing. For downhill and cross-country skiing, there's Belleayre Mountain Ski Center, Route 28, Highmount (845–254–5600); for cross-country only, Lake Mohonk in New Paltz (845–255–1000).

Special Events

August. Ulster County Fair, an annual event at the Fairgrounds, 2 miles southwest of New Paltz on Libertyville Road.

September. Hudson Valley Food Festival, uptown Kingston, Wall Street area. Includes music, tastings, and demonstrations.

Hudson Valley Garlic Festival, Cantine Field (exit 20 off the Governor Thomas E. Dewey Thruway), Saugerties. Food, cooking demonstrations, lectures, crafts, and entertainment.

Harvest Moon Festival at the Hudson River Maritime Museum, Rondout Landing, Kingston. Seasonal foods, music, exhibits.

Other Recommended Restaurants and Lodgings

High Falls

Depuy Canal House, Route 213, High Falls, NY 12440; (845) 687–7700. This very special restaurant is in a landmark historic stone building that used to be a tavern (back in 1797). The menu—some seafood, some meat dishes—changes frequently.

Highland

Rocking Horse Ranch Resort, Highland, NY 12528; (845) 691–2927. A great choice for families, this resort is a dude ranch complete with horseback riding, all-you-can-eat chuck-wagon cuisine, and a whole "alphabet of activities."

New Paltz

Locust Tree Inn, 215 Huguenot Street, New Paltz, NY 12561; (845) 255–7888. An attractive restaurant serving chicken, lamb, and fish dishes. It overlooks a golf course.

For More Information

Ulster County Public Information, P.O. Box 1800, Kingston, NY 12401; (800) 342–5826.

New Paltz Chamber of Commerce, 124 Main Street, New Paltz, NY 12561; (845) 255–0243.

Woodstock Chamber of Commerce, Box 36, Woodstock, NY 12498; (845) 679–6234.

New York Department of Economic Development, Division of Tourism, One Commerce Plaza, Albany, NY 12245; (518) 474–4116 or (800) 225–5697.

Northern Westchester County

Horse Country

2 Nights

If you thought you had to drive for five or six (well, at least three) hours to get to someplace that's very New England, you'll be pleasantly surprised to discover this little chunk of the world.

Just a little over an hour's drive from Manhattan, there are at least half a dozen little towns or hamlets (including Bedford, Katonah, North and South Salem, and Pound Ridge) that could easily pass for New England. They're small, they're home to antiques shops, galleries, and little bistros selling fragrant soups on chilly days, and they're surrounded by woods and streams and lakes that really do sparkle. Drive down Main Street in South Salem on an autumn day, and yes, you will think you took a wrong turn somewhere and ended up in New Hampshire.

- ☐ Horse farms
- ☐ Colonial houses
- ☐ Hiking
- ☐ Rural countryside
- ☐ Antiques shops
- ☐ Fine dining
- ☐ Galleries and museums
- ☐ Concerts

This little corner of southeastern New York, right on the border of Connecticut, is not only scenic but also culturally very active. There are several museums and galleries, music festivals, and some restaurants that, on their own, warrant a trip to the area. On top of that, however, there are some diversions you can find only in rural areas, including pick-your-own orchards, horse shows at sprawling farms, and hundreds of acres of woodland preserved for public use.

Unfortunately, there are really no places to stay, aside from a Holiday Inn in nearby Mt. Kisco. Nevertheless, Ridgefield, Connecticut, which is home to a couple of country inns, is just over the border from both North and South Salem, and New Canaan, Connecticut, is just beyond Pound

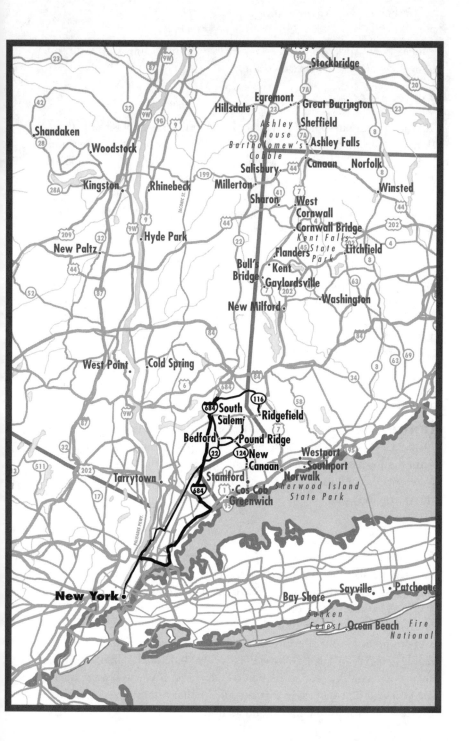

Ridge, New York. You can very easily combine this trip with our Ridgefield and New Canaan escape.

Day 1 / Morning

To reach the area head north on either I–684 or the Saw Mill River Parkway. Both will get you to the Bedford/Katonah exits in just about an hour's time. In fact the Saw Mill River Parkway merges with I–684, where you should exit (exit 6, Katonah/Cross River). Turn right onto Route 35, take it to the first stoplight, and then turn right onto Route 22. About half a mile or so up on the left, you'll see the signs for the **Katonah Museum of Art,** Route 22 East at Jay Street, Katonah, NY 10536 (914–232–9555), your first stop of the day.

Firmly ensconced in local history, this museum, which originally occupied a small room in the Katonah Village Library, showcases between eight and ten exhibitions a year from a variety of periods, cultures, and mediums, many of which have received national recognition. There's also a sculpture garden. Open Tuesday, Thursday, Friday, and Saturday from 10:00 A.M. to 5:00 P.M., Wednesday from 10:00 A.M. to 8:00 P.M., and Sunday from noon to 5:00 P.M.

Right across from the museum, you'll see Jay Street, which takes you right into the town of Katonah, where you can pause for lunch and a look around some artsy shops.

LUNCH: The **Baker's Cafe,** 17 Katonah Avenue, Katonah, NY 10536 (914–232–8030), is a busy little bistro always packed with locals. The food is on the healthful side (sprouts and such), and the breads and desserts are baked on the premises. There are tables outside for eating alfresco when the weather's good.

Afternoon

From town retrace your steps on Jay Street back to Route 22, where you'll turn right. Follow Route 22 for a little more than a mile and you'll see the **John Jay Homestead State Historic Site,** Route 22, Katonah, NY 10536 (914–232–5651), on the left. This large farmhouse, built in 1787, housed the Jay family up until the 1960s. Costumed hostesses take visitors around, pointing out the furnishings that belonged to John Jay and the family generations that followed. Hours and dates the house is open change through the year, so it's best to call ahead. If you're visiting during the year-end holidays, there are scheduled holiday house tours and marionette shows for both children and adults.

Northern Westchester County's Caramoor Center for Music and the Arts

Just beyond the homestead turn left onto Girdle Ridge Road at the concrete dividers. About half a mile down on the right is the **Caramoor Center for Music and the Arts,** Katonah, NY 10536 (914–232–5035), which contains both a house museum and a Venetian theater surrounded by formal gardens. The house, a Mediterranean-style villa painted pink, was originally the country home of Walter Tower Rosen, a lawyer and invest-ment banker. It's filled with artwork and antiques that he and his wife col-lected from palaces throughout Europe. Entire rooms, in fact, were brought over, including a library from a French château and a pine-paneled room from a home in England. Performances, which include those by concert pianists, chamber groups, and opera companies, are held during the summer months. For a schedule write Caramoor Center for Music and the Arts, Box R, Katonah, NY 10536 or call (914) 232–5035. The house is open for tour-ing Wednesday through Sunday from 1:00 to 4:00 P.M. from May through October and between November and April by appointment only.

One of Bedford's most scenic roads, **Hook Road,** is right behind Caramoor. Well worn by the hooves of horses, the dirt route takes you past big old houses surrounded by woods and gardens and through countryside that feels a million miles away from the concrete chasms of New York City.

Follow Hook Road to the end and you'll be back on Route 22 (called Cantitoe Street here). Turn left and it'll take you right into **Bedford Village,** a treasure box of a town with impeccably cared for Colonial houses and historic buildings and a flawless green. Bedford Village was settled back in 1680 and became a popular country retreat for wealthy families in the mid-1800s, when the railroad made access to the area very easy. Many of the buildings were built after the Revolution (since most were burned by the British in 1779) and are lovingly preserved by the Bedford Historical Society. These include the 1787 Court House (the oldest public building in Westchester County) and the one-room schoolhouse, which are open for touring from May to October. Other historic buildings and sites include the old burial ground, the general store (1838), and the Bedford Free Library (1807). For more information, call (914) 234–9751.

If you're antiquing, allow yourself some time to poke around the shops on the main street. Antiques hunters customarily go from Bedford Village on to Scotts Corners in **Pound Ridge,** which has not only several antiques shops but also quite a few antiques fairs and sidewalk sales. Many people call Pound Ridge the arts and antiques capital of Westchester. There are more than twenty shops and galleries, all within half a mile of one another. To reach Pound Ridge, follow Route 172 east out of Bedford Village, then turn right onto Route 137, then left onto Westchester Avenue. It'll take you right into Scotts Corners, a one-street village center usually lined with Mercedes-Benzes, BMWs, or limousines-in-waiting. Quite a few celebrities (including Christopher Reeves and Ralph Lauren) have homes tucked away in the dense woods that ramble off in every direction around here.

DINNER: The **Inn at Pound Ridge,** Route 137, Pound Ridge, NY 10576 (914–764–5779), is high on most people's pre- or post-Caramoor list. Formerly Emily Shaw's Inn, it is an old inn in a magnificent country setting with a long history of favorable restaurant reviews. The food is traditional American, and the price might be considered a bit of a splurge. If you're not up for spending the money, head into nearby New Canaan for a softer-on-the-wallet meal (burgers, big salads, light American cuisine) at **Gates Restaurant,** 10 Forest Street, New Canaan, CT 06840; (203) 966–8666.

LODGING: The **Roger Sherman Inn,** 195 Oenoke Ridge, New Canaan, CT 06840 (203–966–4541), sits on a lovely stretch of country road just outside the center of New Canaan (not quite a ten-minute drive from Scotts Corners; just follow Route 124). It's a small seven-room inn (some with fireplaces) that dates from circa 1740.

Day 2 / Morning

BREAKFAST: A continental breakfast comes with the room at the Roger Sherman Inn.

From New Canaan backtrack through Scotts Corners and follow Route 124 to **South Salem.** South Salem is the kind of community where you may find yourself asking directions to the center of town, only to be told, "You're in it." It's made up of a post office, a library, a town hall, a police barracks, a flower shop, a market, two churches, and some beautiful old houses. To reach the center, take a right onto Route 35, and then turn left onto Spring Street. Spring Street runs right into Main Street, which is where "everything" is. Chances are good that you'll pass some horseback riders en route. There are several horse farms in South Salem, and all the roads are used for riding.

In nearby Cross River (which is about 2 or 3 miles west of South Salem, via Route 35), you'll find two of Northern Westchester's most delightful attractions, the Yellow Monkey Village and Ward Pound Ridge Reservation. **Yellow Monkey Village** is a little cluster of eighteenth-century buildings colonized by chic shops selling everything from penny candy to highly valued antiques. Shops include the Cheshire Tree (for unique and unusual dried and fresh flowers), Panache (fine gifts and linens), M. A. Jackson and Co. (home furnishings and interior design), and Yellow Monkey Antiques (emphasis is on English and Irish country pieces). The village shops are open Tuesday through Sunday from 10:00 A.M. to 5:30 P.M.

LUNCH: If the weather's good, take a picnic to Ward Pound Ridge Reservation. Turn right when you pull out of the Yellow Monkey Village driveway and immediately turn right into the Fifth Division, a little market/deli where you can gather picnic provisions.

Afternoon

Directly opposite the Fifth Division is Route 121. Right after you turn onto Route 121, you'll see a sign at the entrance of **Ward Pound Ridge**

Reservation, a 4,700-acre nature preserve. Do yourself a big favor here and stick to the posted speed limit of a mere 15 mph—you will not drive away unticketed if you don't. You can take your pick of places to park and wander the park's trails. They cut through meadows and woodlands and run alongside streams, up hillsides, through deep hemlock ravines, over marsh swamps, by cliffs—you name it. "The Reservation," as the locals refer to it, is rife with birds and other wildlife. There's a small museum called the Trailside Museum with taxidermic mounts, a weather station, and Indian artifacts. Out back there's a wildflower garden. Any time of year is a beautiful time to visit the Reservation. In winter you can cross-country ski or go sleigh riding or tobogganing. Admission is $8.00 a car or $4.00 if you have a Westchester County Park Pass (open dawn to dusk). A map is provided.

After at least a couple of hours of fresh air, head back toward South Salem, turning left onto Mead Street (about 2 miles east of the Fifth Division) to go into **Waccabuc,** a very exclusive community with a country club as its centerpiece. As you drive up Mead, you'll pass one exquisite home after another. If you can't get enough of the beautiful homes, detour down Schoolhouse Road and you'll see more, though foliage hides a lot during the warm-weather months. Then continue back on Mead Street past the **Mead Street Chapel,** which is beautifully tucked away in a corner of the woods, practically blending into the scenery. To the right you'll spot Lake Waccabuc, which has private access only. Mead Street eventually runs into Hawley Road (which is also known as the Mountain Road). Turn left and then turn right onto 121. You are now in **North Salem,** which seems to have more horses than people. Everywhere you look you see farms, with jump-studded pastures and big old barns. You'll see Auberge Maxime (the restaurant we've chosen for dinner) on the right, at the corner of Route 116. Turn right there and follow Route 116 into Ridgefield, Connecticut, where you can settle into your home for the night. It's just a short drive back to North Salem for dinner and for touring the next day.

DINNER: Auberge Maxime, at the junction of Routes 116 and 121, North Salem, NY 10560; (914) 669–5450. A meal here is worth the trip alone. French chef/owner Bernard Le Bris and his wife, Heidi, have been attracting gourmets from around the world since the early 1980s. Not only is the food unfailingly good, but the setting could be the French countryside. When the weather's good, you can dine outdoors. The *spécialité de la maison* (specialty of the house) is duck, which is prepared in more than a dozen delicious ways.

LODGING: Elms Inn, 500 Main Street, Ridgefield, CT 06877; (203) 438–2541. A historic inn, built in the 1760s. Guest rooms are furnished with some antiques and four-poster beds. Consider having a meal here as well, though reservations in advance are a must. The kitchen is run by Brendan Walsh, a former chef of Arizona 206.

Day 3 / Morning

BREAKFAST: Complimentary continental breakfast is served at the Elms Inn.

Return to North Salem, via Route 116, and you can fill several hours just taking in all the bucolic scenery. Be sure to stop and take a quizzical look at **Balanced Rock** (on Route 116, about a quarter of a mile away from Auberge Maxime), which was left behind from the Ice Age. At the intersection of Routes 116 and 124, go straight on Titicus Road and then turn left onto Mill's Road, which takes you through beautiful countryside that looks more like something you'd expect to find in northern Vermont. At some point you can either turn around or carry on to Purdy's and then follow Titicus Road around the reservoir back to North Salem.

At Salem Center turn left and then turn right onto Deveau Road, which takes you up to the **Hammond Museum and Japanese Stroll Garden,** Deveau Road, North Salem, NY 10560 (914–669–5033). The museum, which was founded by Natalie Hays Hammond in 1957, has a schedule of changing exhibits and activities, many focusing on the Far East. Out back there's a Japanese Stroll Garden. The Hammond and its garden are open from 12:00 to 4:00 P.M. Wednesday through Saturday, and Sundays in July and August, from 11:00 A.M. to 3:00 P.M.

LUNCH: The **Silk Tree Café** at the Hammond Museum, Deveau Road, North Salem, NY 10560 (914–669–6777) serves lunch on an elegant tree-lined courtyard from noon to 3:00 P.M. Wednesday through Saturday. Reservations are strongly recommended.

Afternoon

Return to Route 124 and turn right. For more stunning scenery take the next right onto Baxter Road, which is one of North Salem's most scenic roads. Along the way you can park and walk (or ski or go horse-back riding) on what is called the Open Land Foundation, which is open to the public.

Afterward, return to Route 124, turn right, and you'll soon come to the **Old Salem Farm** on the left. This enormous farm (which used to be owned by Paul Newman) is famed in the equestrian world for its shows, and it attracts horse lovers from around the country. For information on horse shows, call (914) 669–5610. Visitors are welcome year-round to walk through the stables and have a look around.

When you pull out of the farm, turn left onto Route 124 and follow it for a couple of miles until you come to Guinea Road on the left. Turn and follow that until you reach **Salinger's Orchard,** Guinea Road, Brewster, NY 10509 (845–277–3521). You'll know when you're close when you start seeing apple trees on both sides of the road. Apples, however, are just part of the picture at Salinger's. Here you can get fresh-baked breads and pies, doughnuts, peanut butter, honey, pasta, and scores of other wonderful treats. Be forewarned, however, that during fall weekends the place is packed. The orchard is open from 9:00 A.M. to 5:30 P.M. year-round.

From Salinger's backtrack to Route 124 and follow it back to Hardscrabble Road on the right. A short distance in, on the left, is the **North Salem Vineyard,** North Salem, NY 10560 (914–669–5518). Free tours and tastings are offered year-round, Saturday and Sunday from 1:00 to 5:00 P.M. The vineyard will prepare a basket lunch, which you can eat indoors or out.

From the vineyard you can very easily hop back on I–684, heading south toward New York City. You'll find the entrance by turning left out of the vineyard and following Hardscrabble Road, which crosses right over I–684.

There's More

See Southern New England Escape Two, Ridgefield and New Canaan.

Animal farm. Muscoot Farm, Route 100, Somers, NY; (914) 232–7118. This is a turn-of-the-century interpretive farm owned and operated by the Westchester County Department of Parks, Recreation, and Conservation. From Katonah go west on Route 35 to Route 100 and turn right. The farm is 1.5 miles down on the right.

Bicycling. Many of the roads in this area are great cycling routes, though quite hilly. Consider taking your bicycle along. An especially good biking area is Ward Pound Ridge Reservation.

Hiking. In addition to some of the hiking places already described, this part of Westchester has several wildlife preserves with nature trails. In Mount Kisco there are two sanctuaries worth seeking out. The Butler-Meyer Sanctuary is a 604-acre preserve with self-guiding trails and a resident naturalist. This sanctuary is popular for birders; in fact, there is a hawk watch station. To reach Butler: At Bedford Village, bear left on Route 172 for 1 mile to the Shell station and the blinker (still on Route 172) and go 2 miles, under Route 684; carry on another ⁹⁄₁₀ of a mile up the hill, and just before you reach the top of the hill, turn left onto Chestnut Road; go 1.5 miles and you'll see the entrance on the right. Westmoreland Sanctuary (which is opposite Butler), offers 150 acres with 15 miles of trails to explore. There are also a museum, nature programs, naturalists, and guided walks. Another worthwhile preserve is Halle Ravine, on Trinity Pass in Pound Ridge.

Skiing. During the winter months you can cross-country ski in Ward Pound Ridge Reservation and on the Open Land Foundation property in North Salem.

Special Events

May. Horse Show, Old Salem Farm, Route 124, North Salem, NY 10560; (914) 669–5610. Though there are horse shows throughout the year, this one is the biggest. It usually takes place the last two weeks in May. In addition to all the competitions, there are food stalls and vendors selling everything from curry combs to saddles and great Western wear.

Other Recommended Restaurants and Lodgings

Banksville

La Crémaillère, 46 Bedford–Banksville Road, Banksville, NY 10506; (914) 234–9647. This French Provincial restaurant—just a couple miles down the road from Bedford Village—is beautifully situated in a 1750s "Widow Brush House." It offers a wonderfully romantic atmosphere with brick fireplaces and murals throughout, as well as unfailingly good dishes such as its cassoulet of escargots, ravioli au fromage, roast duckling, and coquilles St. Jacques.

Bedford Village

Bistro Twenty-Two, Route 22, Bedford, NY 10506; (914) 234–7333. An expensive but very sophisticated bistro.

Katonah

Blue Dolphin Diner, 175 Katonah Avenue, Katonah, NY 10536; (914) 232–4791. On a summer weekend evening, the sidewalk in front of this diner becomes an open-air cocktail party, with loyal regulars willing to wait as long as it takes for dinner. Inside it's far from a diner. The cuisine, from Capri and the Amalfi Coast, is consistently and astoundingly good.

New Canaan

Maples Inn, 179 Oenoke Ridge, New Canaan, CT 06840; (203) 966–2927. This twenty-five-room inn is right next to the Roger Sherman we previously recommended. It has a beautiful wraparound porch.

Tequila Mockingbird, 6 Forest Street, New Canaan, CT 06840; (203) 966–2222. Here you'll find one of the most authentic Mexican restaurants in the Westchester–Fairfield County areas. In addition to wonderfully fresh South-of-the-Border fare, you'll find splashy colors, paintings, and folk art.

Ridgefield

Bernard's Inn at Ridgefield, 20 West Lane, Ridgefield, CT 06877; (203) 438–8282. This small inn was purchased and completely refurbished by the dynamic cooking team, chefs Bernard and Sarah Bouissou. Their nonpareil French cuisine can be enjoyed inside elegant dining rooms or—during the summer months—in the Victorian patio gardens.

Elms Inn, 500 Main Street, Ridgefield, CT 06877; (203) 438–9206. Owned by highly regarded American chef Brendan Walsh (the original chef of New York City's Arizona Cafe), the Elms Inn has earned itself a wonderful reputation. There are several small dining rooms, always abuzz with contented diners. Among the menu offerings: Connecticut Seafood Stew, Grilled Loin of Cervena Venison, and Thyme Roasted Pheasant.

South Salem

Le Château, Route 35; (914) 533–6631. Some people have never heard of

South Salem, but they've heard about Le Château. The castle itself, built in 1907 by J. P. Morgan, is on thirty-two woodland acres. The classic French cuisine is reliably good.

For More Information

Westchester County Office of Tourism, 222 Mamaroneck Avenue, White Plains, NY 10605; (914) 995–8500.

New York Department of Economic Development, Division of Tourism, One Commerce Plaza, Albany, NY 12245; (518) 474–4116 or (800) 225–5697.

Montauk and the Hamptons

Long Island Beaches

2 Nights

Sun-bleached beaches. Platters piled high with spanking fresh lobster. Sea-breeze-swept verandas. These are just some of the images that come to mind when you mention Montauk or the Hamptons to most New Yorkers. This strip of Atlantic coast on Long Island's eastern end has long been a favorite summer escape for city residents.

Though sharing the same stretch of beach (it goes on for miles and miles), the Hamptons and Montauk are actually very different. The Hamptons, which include Westhampton, Hampton Bays, Southampton, Bridgehampton, and East Hampton, are very upscale, with huge houses surrounded by well-coiffed hedges. They are also very social, attracting celebrities and other boldfaced names from all over. Many New Yorkers either rent, own, or take shares in summer houses and spend a good chunk of their time party hopping or playing tennis with clients. Montauk, on the other hand, is more laid back in both appearance and attitude.

For this escape we combine a visit to both the Hamptons and Montauk. If you'd rather spend more time beaching, consider cutting the journey in half, visiting either just the Hamptons or just Montauk.

By the way, traffic can be painfully uncomfortable, especially going

- ☐ Ocean beaches and views
- ☐ Farms
- ☐ Fresh seafood
- ☐ Chic boutiques
- ☐ Art galleries
- ☐ Estates
- ☐ Wineries
- ☐ Museums
- ☐ Boating
- ☐ Wildlife
- ☐ Spa
- ☐ Tennis

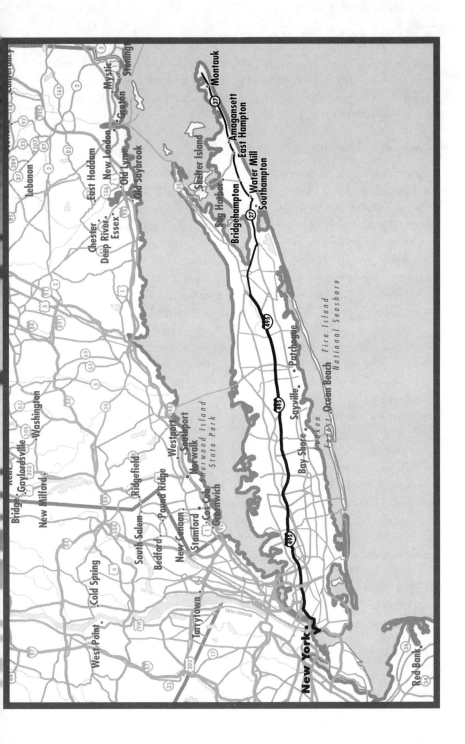

out on Friday afternoons and evenings and returning to the city on Sunday afternoons and evenings. Do yourself a big favor and get a jump start on your trip. Leave early in the morning or midweek. Also, bear in mind that many inns have a three-night minimum, and some have a one-week minimum during July and August.

Day 1 / Morning

Start by taking the Midtown Tunnel from Manhattan under the East River and follow the Long Island Expressway (I–495) east to exit 70. Follow the signs for Route 27 and then turn left. Route 27, the Sunrise Highway, takes you to the five towns known as "The Hamptons" and on to Montauk at the island's easternmost point.

All five of the Hampton towns have long been a haven for writers, artists, and other celebrities in addition to summer visitors. The main attraction is the beach, which, backed by rolling dunes, stretches out for miles, offering plenty of opportunity for undisturbed sunning.

As you hopscotch from town to town, you'll find that a popular Hampton activity is browsing through the boutiques and galleries; in fact, sometimes it's hard to tell the difference. Here, a perfect ear of corn can be discussed as if it were an objet d'art, filling the better part of a dinner-party conversation. You'll find all sorts of one-of-a-kind must-haves such as heavy pasta bowls and conversation-piece sweaters that you'll figure out how to clean later. If you're here for the shopping, your best bet is to just pull over wherever you spot a parking place in a town. Chances are there will be enough shops to keep you happily amused.

Otherwise make your first stop in **Southampton** at the **Old Halsey House,** 21 South Main Street, Southampton, NY 11968 (631–283–3527). This is the oldest English frame house in New York State. There's also a Colonial herb garden. The house has summer and off-season hours. Call in advance. Also worth seeing is the **Southampton Historical Museum,** 17 Meeting House Lane, off Main Street, Southampton, NY 11968 (631–283–2494). The main building, which was formerly a whaling captain's home (1843) is filled with period furnishings. There's also a one-room schoolhouse and a carriage house plus a nineteenth-century village street with more than a dozen restored shops.

Southampton's most famous shopping area is **Job's Lane,** where you'll find pricey boutiques competing for your credit card signature. As riveting as shopping can be, don't miss the **Parrish Art Museum,** also on Job's Lane at

The beaches in Montauk are washed by powerful Atlantic waves.

25 Job's Lane, Southampton, NY 11968 (631–283–2118), which has a good collection of nineteenth- and twentieth-century American paintings along with other changing exhibits. During the summer it's open Monday through Saturday from 11:00 A.M. to 5:00 P.M. and Sunday from 1:00 to 5:00 P.M.; closed Tuesday and Wednesday from mid-September. Closed some holidays.

After a look around the Parrish and a bit of shop hopping, take time out to gape at the town's legendary megamansions. As with most affluent oceanfront areas, the biggest and the best homes are on the roads that run parallel to the ocean or intersect them. You can feast your eyes by driving down Meadow, Gin, Halsey Neck, Copper's Neck, and First Neck Lanes.

LUNCH: One of Long Island's most popular restaurants, **George Martin** (56 Nugent Street, Southampton, NY 11968; 631–204–8700) has recently opened a branch in Southampton. The cuisine is contemporary American and includes a variety of steaks and seafood dishes.

Afternoon

Even if you're not a hard-core beach person, consider taking time out to plop down on the beach for an hour or so. There's a wonderful public beach right on Meadow Lane.

Afterward, continue east on Route 27, stopping at shops in the villages of **Water Mill** and **Bridgehampton.** Water Mill is named for its gristmill, which is now a museum called the **Water Mill Museum,** Old Mill Road, Bridgehampton, NY 11932 (631–726–4625). It's open from Memorial Day through mid-September.

The destination for the day is **East Hampton,** which has an impressive collection of old houses that have been declared historic landmarks. The best way to enjoy them is to stop by the Chamber of Commerce, 79A Main Street, East Hampton, NY 11937 (631–324–0362), and pick up a free walking-tour map. Some of the highlights include the oldest houses, some of which can be found on James Lane, which borders the eastern edge of the South End Burying Ground. Most famous of them is the 1680 **"Home Sweet Home" House,** 14 James Lane, East Hampton, NY 11937 (631–324–0713), which was the childhood home of John Howard Payne, the composer of the song of the same title. It's open to visitors April through December, 10:00 A.M. to 4:00 P.M. Monday through Saturday and 2:00 to 4:00 P.M. Sunday from April through September and Saturday and Sunday only in October and November. There's also a windmill that was built in 1804 out back. **Historic Mulford Farm,** circa 1680, is also on James Lane, East Hampton, NY 11937 (631–324–6850). It's a living-history museum with summer hours only (call ahead).

On Main Street you'll find the **Guild Hall Museum,** 158 Main Street, East Hampton, NY 11937 (631–324–0806), which is an art museum and the cultural center of East Hampton. During the summer, it's open Monday through Saturday from 11:00 A.M. to 5:00 P.M. and Sunday from noon to 5:00 P.M. In the winter, hours are Thursday through Saturday from 11:00 A.M. to 5:00 P.M. and Sunday from noon to 5:00 P.M. Close by you'll find **Clinton Academy,** 151 Main Street, East Hampton, NY 11937 (631–324–6850), the first prep school in New York State. It's now a museum exhibiting a collection of eastern Long Island artifacts. Call ahead; hours vary.

At the end of town on North Main Street stands **Hook Mill,** a wind-powered gristmill, next to a burial ground with tombstones dating from 1650. There are tours of the mill through the summer.

Before leaving East Hampton take a drive down Lily Pond Lane to see more magnificent homes.

DINNER: Nick & Toni's, 136 North Main Street, East Hampton, NY 11937 (631–324–3550), prides itself on its wood-burning oven specials. The cuisine is contemporary American with lots of fresh fish offerings.

LODGING: The **Maidstone Arms Inn and Restaurant,** 207 Main Street (631– 324–5006), is a nineteen-room inn across from the green in East Hampton. It's open year-round.

Day 2 / Morning

BREAKFAST: During the summer months, a full breakfast (included in the room rate) is served at the Maidstone Arms Inn and Restaurant. The rest of the year, a continental breakfast is available.

Amagansett has more shops to explore plus the **Town Marine Museum,** on Bluff Road, ½ mile south of Route 27 on the ocean, Amagansett, NY 11930 (631–267–6544), with shipwreck and undersea exhibits. There are also several town beaches on which to spread your blanket out.

From Amagansett carry on east to **Montauk,** which is truly land's end. Though just 120 miles from the chasms and towers of Manhattan, it honestly feels a million miles away. You'll start to feel the difference just after Amagansett, when the shops trickle out.

There's not a long list of things to do in Montauk. The best pastime is to wander along the beach looking for shells or birds, or maybe go for a trail ride on a pair of mares at the **Deep Hollow Ranch,** located on Route 27 (3 miles east of Montauk), Montauk, NY 11954 (631–668–2744).

The one big sight-seeing attraction is the **Montauk Point Lighthouse** in **Montauk State Park,** 6 miles east of town on Route 27 (631–668–2544), which has stood poised atop an ocean bluff for about two hundred years. It was built in 1795 by order of George Washington.

LUNCH: Gosman's Dock, West Lake Drive at the entrance to Montauk Harbor, Montauk, NY 11954 (631–668–5330), is famed for its generous servings of ultrafresh seafood (you can watch them unload catches right on the dock). Try the broiled fluke; it's hard to find elsewhere. You'll find a take-out counter and some picnic tables outside in addition to the restaurant dining rooms inside. (Gosman's is closed during the winter.)

Afternoon

Spend the afternoon exploring the trails of nearby **Hither Hills State Park,** 3 miles west on Route 27 (631–668–2461). The park is open year-round, sunrise to sunset.

DINNER: Dave's Grill, Flamingo Road on Montauk Harbor, Montauk, NY 11954; (631) 668–9190. This formerly run-down fishermen's haunt is now a sophisticated bistro. Order the fish of the day or try the Provençal fisherman's stew out on the waterside patio.

LODGING: Peri's Bed & Breakfast, 206 Essex Street, Montauk, NY 11954 (631–668-1394), is a historic Carl Fisher Tudor home within easy reach of the beach. There are just three guest rooms, one with a Moroccan theme, one done in art deco, and the other featuring French design.

Day 3 / Morning

BREAKFAST: A buffet breakfast is set up and open to the public at the **Montauk Yacht Club Resort and Marina,** Star Island, Montauk, NY 11954 (631–668–3100), when they're open (between April and November). The buffet starts early, at 7:00 A.M.

After breakfast consider spending the day being pampered at **Gurney's Inn Resort & Spa,** Old Montauk Highway, Montauk, NY 11954 (631–668–2345), before heading back to Manhattan.

To return to the city, retrace your steps by following Route 27 west and turning north at Eastport to reach the Long Island Expressway (Route 495), which will take you back to the Midtown Tunnel.

There's More

Biking. Amagansett Beach & Bicycle, at the light in Amagansett, 624 Montauk Highway, Amagansett, NY (631–267–6325), has all types of bikes (kids' cruisers, hybrids, mountain bikes, and tandems) for rent. Locks and helmets are included.

Birding. Montauk Point State Park is a good spot to take your binoculars.

Cruises to Block Island. The *Viking Starliner* takes passengers on 1½-hour-long cruises to Block Island and back. The trips leave at 9:00 A.M. July through October.

Fishing. In Montauk charter boats will take anglers out to fight for blues, marlin, swordfish, and even sharks.

Horseback riding. Deep Hollow Ranch in Montauk offers horseback riding through 4,000 acres of trails to the beach. For more information call (631) 668–2744.

Spa. Gurney's Inn Resort & Spa, Old Montauk Highway, Montauk, NY 11954; (631) 668–2345. In addition to a long menu of spa treatments (seaweed body wraps, herbal wraps, facials, massages), Gurney's is home to a drop-dead gorgeous beach the likes of which you'd be hard-pressed to find anywhere else.

Special Events

July 4. Southampton's Parade. The town's antique auto museum shows off its classic cars in an annual parade.

Labor Day weekend. Powwow. At the Shinnecock Indian Reservation, just off NY 27A (near Southampton). Dances, ceremonies, displays.

Other Recommended Restaurants and Lodgings

Amagansett

Clam Bar, Montauk Highway, Amagansett, NY 11930; (631) 267–6348. Open from May through October, this is the place to go to for fresh seafood. The menu includes the catch of the day whether it's fresh tuna, swordfish, or striped bass. Their menu also features lobster, clam chowder, scallops, fried clams, oysters, and clams on the half shell. Dress is super casual. Diners eat under yellow and white umbrellas outside or at the counter. Service is quick.

Lobster Roll, Montauk Highway (look for flagpole), Amagansett, NY 11930; (631) 267–3740. In summer months this is a must. A no-frills, roadside seafood eatery, its lobster sandwiches and salads are worth every minute you stand in line. There are also wonderful pies for dessert.

East Hampton

Babette's, 66 Newtown Lane, East Hampton, NY 11937; (631) 329–5377. Here you can feast on wonderfully healthy cuisine. Many fitness-minded celebs have dined here, including Gwyneth Paltrow, Jerry Seinfeld, Richard Gere, and Ed Burns.

Della Femina, 99 North Main Street, East Hampton, NY 11937; (631) 329–6666. Popular in the Hamptons since the early 1990s, Della Femina prides itself on its creative New American dishes.

Laundry, 31 Race Lane, East Hampton, NY 11937; (631) 324–3199. Go if only to try the jumbo lump crab cakes with avocado salsa. Laundry is locally famed for its seafood and imaginative American dishes.

Maidstone Arms Inn and Restaurant, 207 Main Street; (516) 324–5006. The food here is contemporary American with a Pacific Rim influence. Among its star-studded clientele are Billy Joel, Alec Baldwin, and Kim Basinger, Steve Guttenberg, and Kevin Costner—just to drop a few names.

Riccardo's Seafood House, 313 Three Mile Harbor Road, East Hampton, NY 11937; (631) 324–0000. Along with dramatic sunsets, the cuisine here is dreamy: Latin seafood specialties. In fact, the ceviche alone is worth the trip.

Montauk

East Deck Motel, Ditch Plains Road, Montauk, NY 11954; (631) 668–2334. Here you can stay in an efficiency studio. Each one sleeps four to six and has basic cable and a full kitchen and dining area. They're perfect for families or couples traveling together. There's a pool and adjacent beach, which has a lifeguard on duty from 10:00 A.M. to 5:00 P.M. The motel is ½ mile east of the plaza on Montauk Highway; go right on Ditch Plains Road. Open mid-June to early September.

Hotel Montauket, 88 Firestone Road, Montauk, NY 11954; (631) 668–5992. Overlooking Gardiner's Bay, this is a basic hotel (no pool, TV, private phones, or air-conditioning, and some guests share bathrooms), but it's friendly, clean, and inexpensive. The bar and restaurant are popular with locals. From the Plaza take Edgemere Street north; make a left on Fleming Road and then a right on Firestone Road.

Montauk Manor, 236 Edgemere Street, Montauk, NY 11954; (631) 668–4400. An English Tudor–style castle, Montauk Manor originally was erected by industrialist Carl Fisher as the centerpiece for what he had hoped to be an elaborate summer-resort community. Unfortunately, the Great Depression squelched his plans. Nevertheless, the building remains, renovated inside to be a modern luxury hotel. Ask for a room with a terrace or patio.

Montauk Yacht Club Resort and Marina, Star Island, Montauk, NY 11954; (631) 668–3100. Now public, the Montauk Yacht Club is a truly deluxe hotel complete with tennis, water sports, spa treatments, and lots more. Back in the twenties and thirties, it was frequented by the Vanderbilts, Astors, and Whitneys.

The Panoramic View, Old Montauk Highway, Montauk, NY 11954 (516–668–3000), lives up to its name. It's spectacularly situated on ten acres with arrestingly beautiful ocean vistas. The rooms are simply but tastefully decorated with maple furniture. They have high, beamed ceilings and knotty-pine paneling; most have balconies.

Shepherds Neck Inn, 90 Second House Road, Montauk Point, NY 11954; (631) 668–2105. Located on Long Island's East End, this country inn is set on eight acres of lush lawns and gardens. There are seventy guest rooms, and it's within easy reach of the beaches.

Southampton

Plaza Café, 61 Hill Street, Southampton, NY 11968; (631) 283–9323. One of the East End's top restaurants, the Plaza specializes in creatively prepared seafood. It's owned by chef Douglas Gulija.

Red Bar Brasserie, 210 Hampton Road, Southampton, NY 11968; (631) 283–0704. An East End favorite, this restaurant serves up French-inspired American fare. The signature dish is pan-seared sea scallops with creamed corn, fava beans, and black trumpet mushrooms.

Southampton Inn, 91 Hill Street, Southampton, NY 11968; (631) 283–6500. An ideal base for exploring the South Fork, this ninety-room inn has the charm of a bed and breakfast but the amenities of a resort.

Village Latch Inn Hotel, 101 Hill Street, Southampton, NY 11968; (631) 283–2160. Steps away from Southampton Village, this sixty-seven-room inn is comprised of charming buildings, both historic and contemporary. It's an easy walk to the area's beaches, shops, restaurants, galleries, and museums.

Westhampton Beach

Tierra Mar Restaurant, 231 Dune Road, Westhampton Beach, NY 11978; (631) 288–2700. Propped up on the dunes in Westhampton Beach, this is one of the few oceanfront restaurants in the Hamptons. The cuisine is New American, imaginatively prepared.

For More Information

East Hampton Chamber of Commerce, 79A Main Street, East Hampton, New York 11937; (631) 324–0362.

Long Island Convention and Visitors Bureau, 330 Motor Parkway, Suite 103, Hauppauge, NY 11788; (631) 951–3440.

Montauk Chamber of Commerce, P.O. Box 5029, Montauk, NY 11954; (631) 668–2428.

New York Department of Economic Development, Division of Tourism, One Commerce Plaza, Albany, NY 12245; (518) 474–4116 or (800) 225–5697.

Shelter Island

A Total Getaway

1 Night

If you want to go someplace for the weekend and just "be" rather than "do," Shelter Island is a good choice. Tucked between the north and south forks on the east end of Long Island, it's reachable only by ferry. About a third of the island is nature preserve (Mashomack Forest), and the rest is beautifully unspoiled, thanks to residents who are committed to keeping it that way.

Some say the name Shelter Island comes from an Indian word; others say it was named by Quakers who were persecuted by the Puritans in New England and sought refuge there. Whatever. There is a monument to the Quakers and a graveyard with seventeenth-century stones if you're interested. That's about it in the way of man-made attractions on the island. The island's real attraction is its natural beauty: miles of white sand beaches, rolling wooded hills, and lots of beautiful views of the water.

☐ Beaches

☐ Seafood

☐ Biking

☐ Peace and quiet

If you want to avoid the summer traffic, plan to head out to the island between May (except Memorial Day weekend) and early June or after Labor Day through October (except for Columbus Day weekend).

Consider combining this trip with a visit to Montauk or the Hamptons (see New York Escape Five).

Day 1 / Morning

From Manhattan take the Midtown Tunnel to the Long Island Expressway (I–495). Follow it out to exit 70 and pick up Route 27 east; turn left in Bridgehampton following signs to Sag Harbor. From downtown Sag Harbor cross the bridge and follow signs to the ferry. Ferries shuttle between North Haven and Shelter Island several times throughout the day. For information call (631) 749–1200. The price for one car with a driver

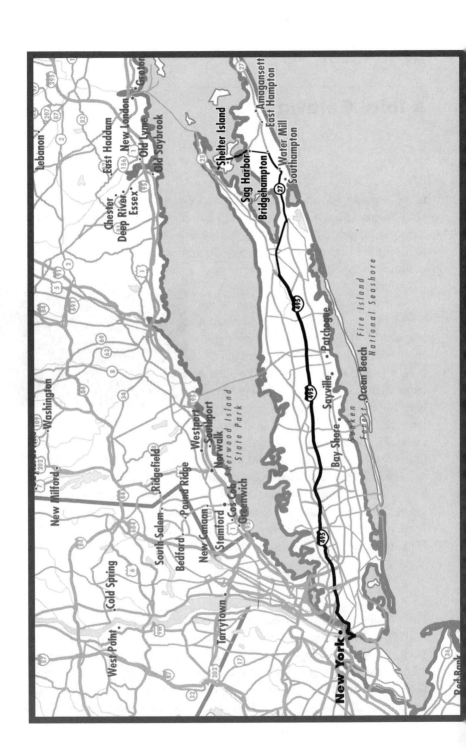

is $7.00 each way plus $1.00 for each additional passenger. Round-trip, same-day tickets are $8.00. There are also ferries from Greenport on the North Fork.

Once you arrive on Shelter Island, follow Route 114 to **Shelter Island Heights,** where you'll find the island's handful of stores and restaurants including the Chequit Inn, where you can take time out for lunch.

LUNCH: Chequit Inn, 23 Grand Avenue, Shelter Island, NY 11964 (631–749–0018), has a terrace from which you can gaze out at sailboats in Dering Harbor. The restaurant specializes in grilled seafood, though lighter fare is available at lunch.

Afternoon

After lunch and maybe a short walk around the Heights, head to the eastern tip of the island, where you'll find a causeway leading to Ram Island, so named because it's shaped like a ram. Check into your hotel and spend the afternoon parked on its private beach or swinging in a hammock under a shady tree in the backyard. If you feel ambitious, the hotel has a tennis court to play on and sailboats to take out. You can also rent bikes (or take along your own) and do some pedaling around this 12-square-mile island.

DINNER: Ram's Head Inn, 108 Ram's Island Drive, Shelter Island, NY 11964; (631) 749–0811. This restaurant, where reservations are a must, alone is worth the trip to Shelter Island. The cuisine is contemporary American, and the setting (it overlooks Coecles Harbor) is dreamy.

LODGING: The **Ram's Head Inn,** 108 Ram's Island Drive, Shelter Island, NY 11964 (631–749–0811), is marvelously situated in a whole little world of its own. All seventeen rooms are nothing extraordinary (though they're perfectly adequate) but are more than compensated for by the setting.

Day 2 / Morning

BREAKFAST: Continental breakfast is included in the room rate.

Enjoy the morning on the beach, then grab a ferry back to **Sag Harbor,** which is an old whaling town filled with nineteenth-century architecture and history. In fact tiny Sag Harbor used to rival New York as an international port. There are a handful of sights to see including the

Summertime is when Dering Harbor on Shelter Island is its liveliest.

Custom House, Garden Street, Sag Harbor, NY 11963 (631–692–4664), which operated as a customhouse and post office during the late eighteenth and early nineteenth centuries. It was actually the first customshouse established by an act of Congress in 1789 and has been restored by the Society for the Preservation of Long Island Antiquities. From June through September it's open daily except Monday. On the corner of Garden Street and Main, you'll find the **Sag Harbor Whaling and Historical Museum,** Garden and Main Streets, Sag Harbor, NY 11963 (631–725–0770), which tells the story of the island's whaling past. The museum is open daily from mid-May through September.

LUNCH: A Sag Harbor must, the **American Hotel,** 25 Main Street, Sag Harbor, NY 11963 (631–725–3535), is renowned for its Old World charm. The food is largely American French.

From Sag Harbor head back to Bridgehampton and retrace your steps back to New York City.

There's More

Bicycling. On Shelter Island you can rent bikes at Piccozzi's, right in the center of the Heights on Bridge Street; (631) 749–0045.

Hiking. The Mashomack Preserve, off Route 114 on Shelter Island, has trails and a visitors center. It's open daily. For more information call (631) 749–1001.

Special Events

Mid-June. Shelter Island 10K Run and Race Walk. This is always an exciting day on Shelter Island, when athletes come from all over to race. It starts in the center of the island near the high school.

Late August. Arts and Crafts Show. Every year the playground near the American Legion in the center of the island turns into a showcase for artists and artisans.

Other Recommended Restaurants and Lodgings

Sag Harbor

The Beacon, 8 West Water Street, Sag Harbor, NY 11963; (631) 725–7088. This is a wonderful spot to settle in and watch the boats glide by. The menu features imaginative salads, the freshest seafood, and perfectly grilled rib-eye steaks.

Oasis Waterfront Restaurant & Bar, 3253 Noyac Road, Sag Harbor, NY 11963; (631) 725–7110. American cuisine with an emphasis on seafood is the fare here. Chef John Donnelly's signature dish is an East End bouillabaisse featuring local seafood in saffron tomato broth.

Shelter Island

Azalea House, 1 Thomas Avenue, Shelter Island, NY 11964; (631) 749–4252. This is a five-room bed and breakfast in the island's center. Thanks to one of its owners, who comes from Finland, it's full of tasteful Finnish touches including light-pine furniture. An extended continental breakfast is included in the room rate.

Beechtree House, 1 South Ferry Road, Shelter Island, NY 11964; (631) 749–4252. Owned by the same people who own the Azalea House, this is a lovely pre-Victorian house with three apartments for guests (two of them have full kitchens). It's named for the monumental beech tree in front, which dominates the yard and is one of the biggest trees on the island.

Shelter Island Heights

The Dory, Route 114, Shelter Island Heights, NY 11965; (631) 749–8871. This is a busy waterfront restaurant (with a dory on top) where the seafood is unfailingly good. It's necessary to have reservations during the summer months.

For More Information

Sag Harbor Chamber of Commerce, 459 Main Street, Sag Harbor, NY 11963; (631) 725–0011.

Shelter Island Chamber of Commerce, Box 577, Shelter Island Heights, NY 11965; (631) 749–0399.

Long Island Convention and Visitors Bureau, 330 Motor Parkway, Suite 203, Hauppauge, NY 11788; (631) 951–3440.

New York Department of Economic Development, Division of Tourism, One Commerce Plaza, Albany, NY 12245; (631) 474–4116 or (800) 225–5697.

The Adirondack Area

Towns and Country

3 Nights

Look at any color map of New York State and you'll see an enormous green area taking up a good chunk of its northern region. That's the Adirondack Park, the largest natural preserve in the East, in fact, covering some six million acres.

You could easily spend weeks here, dividing your time between the different fresh-air activities (including hiking through birch and balsam forests and paddling canoes on lakes) and poking around the attractions near Lake George and in nearby Saratoga Springs, or you could devote an entire week or two to an all-out vacation on a hidden mountain lake.

For this trip we combine a brief visit to Saratoga Springs with a short stay on Lake George and Blue Mountain Lake. All three places could be weekend (or longer) destinations in themselves; we've just mentioned the

- ☐ Backwoods wilderness
- ☐ Lakes
- ☐ Quiet
- ☐ Hiking
- ☐ Canoeing
- ☐ Thoroughbred racing
- ☐ Family amusements
- ☐ Old fort
- ☐ Performing arts

highlights. Keep in mind that in August, when the New York Racing Association has its equine competitions, Saratoga Springs' population swells to two or three times its normal size.

Day 1 / Morning

Take I–87 north to exit 13N. Go left. At the fourth stoplight turn left into **Saratoga Spa State Park** in Saratoga Springs, which is home to your hotel for the night.

Saratoga Springs, a town with a beautiful mixture of Victorian and Greek Revival architecture in the foothills of the Adirondack Mountains, has three major magnets: its thoroughbred racing, its performing arts scene,

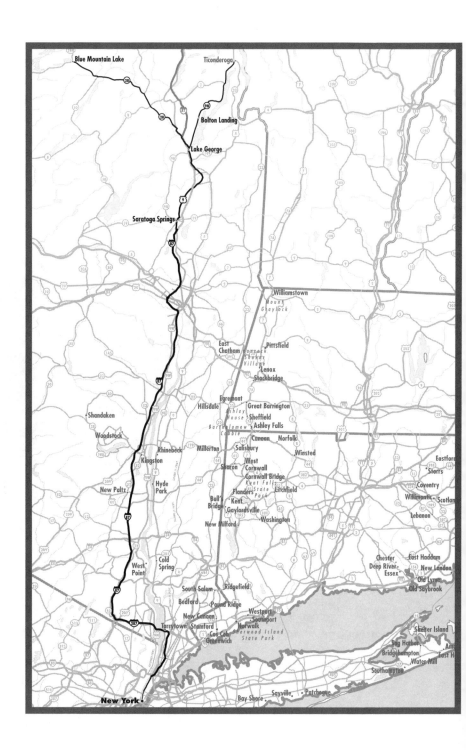

and its mineral baths, for which the town is named. If you'd like to try the latter, you'll find some right in the park—the **Lincoln Mineral Baths** (518–584–2011). Here you can "take the waters" or, more specifically, soak in naturally carbonated water and follow with a half-hour rest on heated sheets on a cot nearby. The experience should leave you feeling relaxed and revived and ready to get out and wander around the town's museums and shops. Hours vary throughout the year; call in advance.

LUNCH: The dining room of the **Gideon Putnam Hotel,** in Saratoga Spa State Park, 24 Gideon Putnam Road, Saratoga Springs, NY 12866 (518–584–3000), is a pleasant spot to have lunch. A large variety of offerings includes burgers, sandwiches, crepes, and the like.

Afternoon

Spend the afternoon checking out the sights and shops in town (follow US 9 north into town from the park). Many of the shops on Broadway are in buildings that have been impeccably restored to their original Victorian appearance. On North Broadway, Circular Street, and Union Avenue, there are many mansions that were originally built in the 1800s. Be sure to wander into **Historic Congress Park,** on Broadway, Saratoga Springs, NY 12866 (518–584–6920), which is home to two worthwhile museums: the Museum of the Historical Society and the Walworth Memorial Museum. They trace the history of the city's growth. From June through October they're open daily; during the rest of the year, they're open afternoons only, Wednesday through Sunday.

If you're interested in the history and highlights of horse racing, be sure to check out the **National Museum of Racing and Thoroughbred Hall of Fame,** 191 Union Avenue, Saratoga Springs, NY 12866 (518–584–0400). It's open Monday through Saturday from 10:00 A.M. to 4:30 P.M. and Sunday from noon to 4:30 P.M. And, of course, the **Saratoga Race Course,** also on Union Avenue, Saratoga Springs, NY 12866, which is the oldest operating thoroughbred racetrack in the country (it was founded in 1863). For information on events call (518) 584–6200.

If you have time, try to visit Saratoga's wonderful dance museum, the **National Museum of Dance,** at 99 South Broadway in Saratoga State Park, Saratoga Springs, NY 12866 (518–584–2225). It's the only museum in the country devoted exclusively to professional American dance. It's open between the end of June and mid-October, Tuesday through Sunday from 10:00 A.M. to 5:00 P.M.

DINNER: **Eartha's Kitchen,** in town at 60 Court Street, Saratoga Springs, NY 12866 (518–583–0602), specializes in sensationally good grilled fare.

LODGING: The **Gideon Putnam Hotel,** in Saratoga Springs State Park, ½ mile south of town on US 9, Saratoga Springs, NY 12866 (518–584–3000 or 800–732–1560), is one of Saratoga Springs' grande dame hotels, surrounded by therapeutic pools, tennis courts, and golf courses. Legendary Sunday brunches take place here in glass-walled rooms overlooking the greens.

Day 2 / Morning

BREAKFAST: A great way to start the morning in Saratoga is by having breakfast at the track (for information call **Breakfast at Saratoga,** 518–584–6200). A buffet is served from 7:00 to 9:30 A.M., during which you can watch the early-morning workouts. A more formal champagne breakfast is offered during racing season in a dining tent called **At the Rail Pavilion** (call 518–584–6200 for restaurant information).

After breakfast head north on I–87 to exit 20 and follow Route 9 north, which will take you through the commercialized town of **Lake George** (shops, entertainment arcades, family attractions) and to **Bolton Landing,** where you can settle in for an all-out relaxing stay at the lakefront **Sagamore** resort. (See "Lodging.") Check-in time is not until 3:00 P.M., but the front desk will hold your bags while you have lunch.

LUNCH: **Mr. Brown's Pub** at the Sagamore, 110 Sagamore Road, Bolton Landing, NY 12814 (518–644–9400), is an informal spot where you'll find soups and salads, sandwiches and burgers.

Afternoon

Spend the afternoon enjoying the resort facilities at the Sagamore or drive up to see **Fort Ticonderoga,** the military fortress and its museum (follow Route 9N to Ticonderoga, NY 12883; 518–585–2821).

Afterward, follow the scenic drive up to the top of **Mount Defiance.**

DINNER: For a splurge make a reservation at the Sagamore's **Trillium,** 110 Sagamore Road, Bolton Landing, NY 12814 (518–664–9400), where you can feast on delicious dishes such as roasted "Broken Arrow Ranch" antelope loin, pomegranate-glazed duck breast, and pan-seared Florida grouper.

During the warm-weather months, Lake George swells with pleasure boats.

LODGING: The **Sagamore,** Bolton Landing, NY 12814; (518) 664–9400 or (800) 358–3585. Established more than one hundred years ago, this Victorian landmark has been described by just about every travel writer as a grande dame hotel. Indeed it is. In addition to one hundred guest rooms and suites in the main building, there are Lakeside Lodges with wood-burning fireplaces and private terraces.

Though you have the six million acres of the Adirondack Park at your fingertips, the Sagamore prides itself on its own combination of sporting activities. Among the offerings are an eighteen-hole course designed by Donald Ross, seven tennis courts (two indoors), a racquetball court, a miniature golf course, an indoor swimming pool, plus walking and jogging trails. There's also a beach where you can swim or take your pick of water sports. There are motorboats for rent, fishing guides, sailboat charters, snorkeling trips, parasailing, and waterskiing, just to name a few. Come winter, there's cross-country skiing right on the grounds, ice skating, and complimentary transportation to nearby Gore Mountain for downhill skiing. On top of all that, there's a spa with a whole menu of services including massage (Swedish, athletic, and aromatherapy body massage), facials, foot reflexology, salt-glos, herbal wraps, seaweed body masks, natural mud body masks, hydrotherapy, and salon services. Also part of the spa is a state-of-the-art fitness center with exercise equipment for strength, endurance, flexibility, and cardiovascular fitness.

Day 3 / Morning

BREAKFAST: A huge buffet is offered at the Sagamore.

To sample some of the Adirondack's most densely scenic landscape, head west on Route 28, making your destination **Blue Mountain Lake,** where there's an outstanding museum devoted to the Adirondacks. Set on the shores of Blue Mountain Lake, the **Adirondack Museum,** Blue Mountain Lake, NY 12812 (518–352–7311), is a complex of twenty-two buildings on thirty acres. One of the most popular exhibits is a display of the successive generations of Adirondack boats. The museum is open daily from 9:30 A.M. to 5:30 P.M. between Memorial Day weekend and mid-October.

Afternoon

LUNCH: Stop in the grocery store in town and get picnic makings to take on a hike up Blue Mountain.

The head of the trail leading to the summit (3,800 feet) is about 1½ miles north of town. The 3-mile-long hike will take you through delicious Adirondack scenery.

DINNER: Big family-style meals, with homemade breads and desserts, are served in the dining room at **Hemlock Hall,** on Route 28N, Blue Mountain Lake, NY 12812 (518–352–7706). Open from Memorial Day through October 16.

LODGING: At **Hemlock Hall** on Route 28N, Blue Mountain Lake, NY 12812 (518–352–7706 or, in winter, 518–359–9065), you can stay in a motel-like unit, a lodge room, or a cabin on the lake. Open from Memorial Day through October 16.

Day 4 / Morning

BREAKFAST: Pancakes, hot cereals, eggs with bacon or sausage—big American breakfasts (included in the room rate) are served in the dining room at Hemlock Hall.

Before heading back to New York City, take time to enjoy the lake and its exquisite scenery. Right at the hotel you can take your pick of canoes, sailboats, paddleboats, and rowboats.

From Blue Mountain Lake retrace your steps back on Route 28 to I–87, heading south.

If you have even more time (another day or two), consider heading farther north up to the **Lake Placid** area. You can visit several Olympic attractions including the Olympic Sports Complex, Ski Jumps, and the **1932 & 1980 Lake Placid Winter Olympic Museum,** Main Street, Lake Placid, NY 12946 (518–523–1655), which includes video highlights of the 1932 and 1980 games, athletes' uniforms, sports equipment, and other Olympic memorabilia. All around the area you'll find lots of hiking and mountain biking trails.

There's More

Mountain biking. High Peaks Cyclery: Mountain Adventure Center, 331 Main Street, Lake Placid, NY 12946; (518) 523–3764. Here you can rent mountain bikes and be sent on your way, choosing anything from an easy 10-mile rolling-hill route to a 75-mile loop with steep ascents. The adventure center can also set you up for in-line skating, skating, camping, and rock climbing.

Performing arts. Saratoga Performing Arts Center, Saratoga Spa State Park, Saratoga Springs, NY 12866; (518) 587–3330. The center hosts a wonderful summer mélange of cultural events including the New York City Opera in June, the New York City Ballet in July, and the Philadelphia Orchestra in August, as well as concerts by a variety of rock, pop, folk, and jazz artists.

Polo matches. Saratoga Polo Association, Saratoga Springs, NY 12866; (518) 584–8108. Matches take place in August.

Scenic flights. Lake Placid Airport, Route 73, Lake Placid, NY 12946; (518) 523–2473. Twenty-minute aerial tours are offered. Passengers can opt for the High Peaks Tour or the Whiteface Mountain Tour; $25 per person (minimum two people).

Skiing. The Adirondacks are home to a dozen alpine ski centers including Lake Placid, which has hosted the winter Olympic Games twice.

Steamboat rides. The Lake George Steamboat Company offers narrated cruises on the lake. For information call (518) 668–5777.

Special Events

June. Lake Placid Horse Show, Lake Placid. This show, combined with the I Love New York Horse Show held the first week of July, make this a popular destination for equestrians.

June. No-Octane Regatta, Blue Mountain Lake. A grand parade of boats. Events include War Canoe Race, Hurry Scurry Race, Guideboat Race, Jousting Competition, Paddling Races, Sailing Canoe Races, and Great Versatility Race.

Mid-July. Ticonderoga Memorial Military Tattoo, Fort Ticonderoga. Eighteenth-century military music in honor of the Scots who served here.

Mid-September. Adirondacks National Car Show, Lake George Village. Hot rods, custom-made cars, and other special-interest cars are paraded here annually at the Fort William Henry Motor Inn.

Other Recommended Restaurants and Lodgings

Blue Mountain Lake

Potter's, on the lake, P.O. Box 279, Blue Mountain Lake, NY 12812; (518) 352–7331. A string of housekeeping cottages, some smack-dab on the water's edge (others just across the street). Though extremely simple and bare-bones, these cottages have charm, especially their front-porch views of the smashingly scenic lake. There's also a motel complex and restaurant plus a tennis court.

Chestertown

Friends Lake Inn, 963 Friends Lake Road, Chestertown, NY 12817; (518) 494–4751. Just across the road from Friends Lake, this is a seventeen-room inn. All rooms are decorated in a country motif; some have four-poster beds. The restaurant is well respected for its sophisticated cuisine and award-winning wine list.

Keene Valley

Noonmark Diner, Route 73, Keene Valley, NY 12943; (518) 576–9737. Though it looks like a regular old house on the outside and a regular diner on the inside, the Noonmark is locally famed for its homemade goodies— sandwich breads, soups, and pies.

Lake Placid

Camp Solitude, Lake Placid, NY 12946; (518) 523–3190. This place is not for everyone. It doesn't have luxury and at-your-beck-and-call service. What it does have is a wonderful atmosphere of relaxed comfort, where you're made to feel like family, and a drop-dead gorgeous setting. Guests are picked up by a launch and zoomed over (there's no direct access by car) to stay in very rustic cabins. The best one by far is the Guest Cottage that stands on top of a hill and has its own gazebo and cobbled fireplace. One of the camp's biggest appeals is that it allows dogs and, in fact, encourages guests to bring their canine friends. It also has a fabulous cook, who turns out dinners that you'd expect to find in a four-star restaurant.

Lake Placid Lodge, Whiteface Inn Road, Lake Placid, NY 12946; (518) 523–2700. Propped up on the shores of forever placid Lake Placid is the rustically elegant Lake Placid Lodge, an Adirondack log-and-stone hotel. Guests can take their pick of a variety of accommodations from lakeside cabins to three-room suites with fireplaces and decks. Absolutely every detail of the Lodge is lovingly tended to, from the outrageously comfortable feather beds that are in every room to local artwork everywhere. Meals are served in the Lake Placid Lodge dining room, which has sweeping views of the lake and Whiteface Mountain. For lunch you can have the dining room prepare a picnic, or during the golf season you can eat at the Whiteface Grill, next to the pro shop. Keep in mind that if you're traveling as a family, children are not welcome.

Mirror Lake Inn, 5 Mirror Lake Drive, Lake Placid, NY 12946; (518) 523–2544. Propped up on the shores of Mirror Lake, this handsome resort and spa is within easy walking distance of the town of Lake Placid's shops, restaurants, and attractions. There are 128 rooms, including some with oversize whirlpool baths, private balconies, and lofts with king-size beds. Year-round there are sporting options, and there is a full-service spa and salon. Mirror Lake itself is a beautiful small lake with a private beach (at the inn) and all sorts of small boats to take out and tool around in.

Saranac Lake

The Point, Beaverwood Road, Saranac Lake, NY 12983; (518) 891–5674 or (800) 255–3530. Located in the northern Adirondacks on an isolated peninsula on Upper Saranac Lake, The Point was built in 1933 as a country getaway for William Avery Rockefeller. Constructed of massive logs and stone, it is a very exclusive retreat with eleven guest rooms, each with a fireplace and museum-quality Adirondack furniture. Extraordinarily good meals are served in the Great Hall, a spectacular high-ceilinged room with hunt trophies adorning the walls.

Saratoga Springs

Adelphi Hotel, 365 Broadway, Saratoga Springs, NY 12866; (518) 587–4688. A grand old Victorian hotel. Complimentary continental breakfast is served in your room.

Inn at Saratoga, 231 Broadway, Saratoga Springs, NY 12866; (518) 583–1890. A very simple, historic hotel within easy reach of Saratoga's attractions.

Olde Bryan Inn, 123 Maple Avenue, Saratoga Springs, NY 12866; (518) 587–2990. This is the place to go to get a big hearty meal for lunch or dinner. You can't go wrong with the stuffed hot turkey sandwich for lunch (in fact, it may be enough to get you by without dinner). You'll also find wonderful soups and appetizers such as Cajun chicken wings, jumbo shrimp wrapped in bacon, and cheddar–bacon potato skins. Dinner offerings include almond-encrusted salmon, Cajun blackened steak, and New Orleans pasta. Don't plan anything too ambitious after your meal.

For More Information

Adirondack Regional Information: 800–487–6867.

Lake George Chamber of Commerce, Route 9, Lake George, NY 12845; (518) 668–5755.

Lake Placid/Essex County Visitors Bureau, 216 Main Street, Lake Placid, NY 12946; (518) 523–2445.

Saratoga Springs Chamber of Commerce, 494 Broadway, Saratoga Springs, NY 12866; (518) 584–3255.

Warren County Tourism, Municipal Center, Lake George, NY 12845; (518) 761–6366 or (800) 365–1050.

New York State Department of Economic Development, Division of Tourism, One Commerce Plaza, Albany, NY 12445; (518) 474–4116 or (800) 225–5697.

Fire Island— With or Without a Car

Life's a Beach

1 Night

Nicknamed New York's Key West, Fire Island has long been known as a carefree, barefoot kind of place, attracting an interesting cross section of humanity. Its occupants are made up of the year-rounders, summer home owners, summer renters, and short-term visitors including day-trippers.

A barrier island stretching 32 miles along the southern side of Long Island and only a quarter-mile wide, Fire Island has a rich social and cultural history. Resort development began here back in the 1890s with the establishment of a Chautauqua Assembly, a movement for Christian betterment through learning and the arts. After that tracts of land were bought up by developers and sold to city folk who were seeking vacation lots. Before long the island became a patchwork of neighborhoods for different communities, often overlapping and coexisting harmoniously, whether involved in boating, fishing, family, and/or gay life.

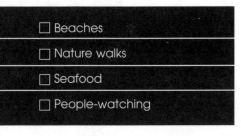

☐ Beaches

☐ Nature walks

☐ Seafood

☐ People-watching

Fortunately, the island hasn't changed much since its early days. No cars were allowed then—or now. The only means of transportation are feet, wagon, bicycle, and boat (golf carts and trucks for contractors). Though only 40 miles from New York City, it is a remote destination with wonderfully wide sandy beaches and unspoiled maritime forests. Most of the land is now protected by the federal government and has been designated the Fire Island National Seashore. Keep in mind that many hotels and restaurants close for the cold-weather months.

There are several ways to reach the island from Manhattan if you don't have a car. You can take either the Long Island Railroad or a jitney to the ferries at Bay Shore, Sayville, or Patchogue. You can also take a taxi from

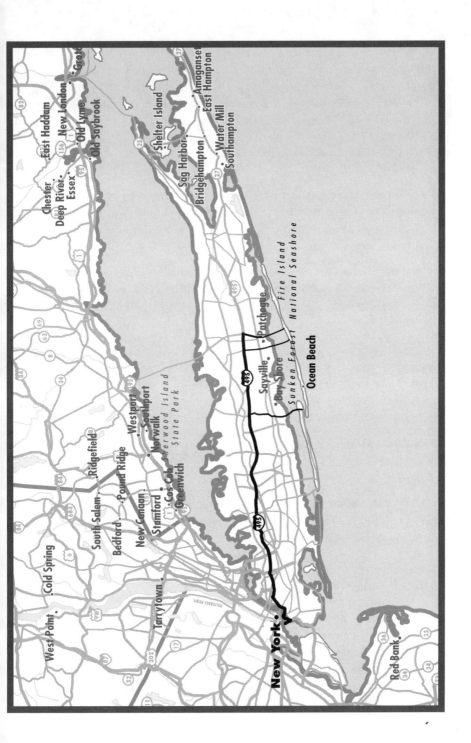

Manhattan (without spending a fortune) to Bay Shore Ferry. If you're driving your own car, take the Long Island Expressway to exit 53 for Bay Shore, exit 59 for Sayville, or exit 63 for Patchogue. There's a parking field at the ferry dock with daily charges. See "For More Information" at the end of this escape for more details.

Day 1 / Morning

Once on the island, you'll find the largest concentration of hotels and restaurants in **Ocean Beach,** Fire Island's de facto capital. Don't, however, wait very long before making hotel reservations on summer weekends. The rooms, especially, fill quickly.

LUNCH: You can have a simple seafood sandwich, a burger, or a salad under an umbrella outside at **Maguires on the Bay** (Bay Number 1, Bungalow Walk, Ocean Beach, Fire Island, NY 11770; 631–583–8800).

Afternoon

After lunch relax a bit on your hotel's beach and then head over (by foot or bike) to take a walk at the **Sunken Forest** (631–589–0810), a National Park Service site in Sailors Haven. The Sunken Forest is truly a sight to behold. It is made up of 36 acres of dense trees and vines and laced with a boardwalk.

DINNER: Mathew's Seafood House (On the bay, east side of Ocean Beach, Fire Island, NY 11770; 631–583–8016) is a good choice for . . . you guessed it! Seafood.

LODGING: Seasons, 468 Denhoff Walk, Ocean Beach, Fire Island, NY 11770; 631–583–8295. This little B&B is open year-round and has eight rooms (with shared baths).

Day 2 / Morning

BREAKFAST: Breakfast (included in room rate) at Seasons.

After breakfast head over by the water taxi to **Watch Hill** (631–597–6455), the island's other National Park Service site, which is about 7 miles east of the Sunken Forest. Situated between the bay and the ocean, Watch Hill is made up of wild salt marsh and dense groves of pitch pine and holly and is lovely to walk around.

Then return to Ocean Beach and plant yourselves on the beach until lunch.

LUNCH: Albatross (Bay Walk, Ocean Beach, Fire Island, NY 11770; 631–583–5697) has patio tables that make great perches for people-watching.

After lunch check out the current exhibit at the **Ocean Beach Historical Society** (Bayview and Cottage Walks, Ocean Beach, Fire Island, NY 11770; 631–583–8972). Hours are Thursday through Monday from 10:00 A.M. to 2:00 P.M. and 7:00 to 10:00 P.M.

Later, after more sun and relaxation or perhaps a bike ride (by the way, the Seasons provides bikes for your use), head back to the mainland and Manhattan.

Special Events

July and August. Beach Apparatus Drills. Every Thursday evening at 7:00 P.M., a group of dedicated volunteers re-enact drills performed by U. S. Lifesaving Service at the turn of the century to rescue shipwreck victims from stranded ships. Takes place in front of the lighthouse. Parking is at Robert Moses Field #5. For information, call (631) 321–7028.

August. Annual Henry Gates "Inn-Side-Out" Clam Shucking Contest takes place between the Inn and the Out restaurants in Kismet. For information, call (631) 666–2026.

There's More

Walking. Besides Watch Hill and the Sunken Forests, there are several wonderful walks on Fire Island. There's a 7-mile walk from Watch Hill east to Smith Point, a 7-mile boardwalk trail at Smith Point, and a 4-mile walk east from Smith Point to Moriches Inlet.

Lighthouse. The Fire Island Lighthouse (Fire Island National Seashore; 631–661–4876) is located on the western end of Fire Island. You can visit the visitors center in the keeper's quarters next to the nineteenth-century lighthouse. Hours vary seasonally.

Fire Island Lighthouse is part of Fire Island's charm.

Other Recommended Restaurants and Lodgings

Ocean Bay Park

The Inn Between, corner of Oneida Street and Bay View Avenue, Ocean Bay Park, Fire Island, NY 11770; (631) 583–0111. An informal restaurant on the bay.

Ocean Beach

Clegg's Hotel, 478 Bayberry Walk, Ocean Beach, Fire Island, NY 11770; (631) 583–5399. Directly across from the ferry dock, this very simple (not luxurious) hotel was built in the 1920s by the grandfather of the current proprietor.

Place in the Sun, 987 Surfview Walk, Ocean Beach, Fire Island, NY 11770; (631) 583–5716. Here you'll find five guest rooms with two shared baths plus an outdoor shower and sauna, open to nonsmokers only.

For More Information

Fire Island National Seashore, 120 Laurel Street, Patchogue, NY 11772; (631) 289–4810. South of Montauk Highway, off West Avenue.

Getting There

By train: The Long Island Railroad provides daily service from Pennsylvania Station to Bay Shore, Sayville, and Patchogue (one-way fares range from $6.00 to $11.00, depending on whether you go peak or off-peak), where you can catch a ferry. The trains leave every thirty to sixty minutes. The ferry terminal at Patchogue is within walking distance of the railroad station, and the ferries at Bay Shore and Sayville are a short taxi ride away. The Long Island Railroad also offers packages that include the train and ferry. For information call (718) 217–5477 or (516) 822– 5477.

By taxi: Tommy's Taxi takes you from a variety of Manhattan locations to the Bay Shore ferry. Departures from Manhattan are from 8:00 A.M. to 9:00 P.M. daily, from April through the end of October. Fares are approximately $17 one-way Monday through Saturday and $20 one-way on Sunday and holidays. For more information call (631) 665–4800.

David's Taxi operates regularly between the Bayshore ferries and 68th Street and Third Avenue in Manhattan. One-way fare is $17 Monday through Saturday and $20 on Sunday. For more information call (631) 665–4384.

By ferry: For current ferry fares and schedules, call Fire Island Ferries, (631) 665–3600.

SOUTHERN
NEW ENGLAND
ESCAPES

Lower Fairfield County

Exploring the Gold Coast

2 Nights

Big old Victorian houses on golf course–like lawns, estates poised on the shores of Long Island Sound, tidal rivers swollen with yachts and sailboats. This little chunk of Connecticut, colonizing the state's southwestern corner, is home to a small galaxy of prosperous towns.

Unfortunately, many would-be visitors skip over the whole area, assuming it's a pocket of bedroom communities. Indeed, thanks to its proximity to New York (most of the towns can be reached in less than an hour), many of its residents commute into the city daily; nevertheless, lower Fairfield County is a good fit for a weekend escape. Within the span of two days, you can hopscotch from town to town (including Greenwich, Norwalk, and Westport), sampling exceptionally good restaurants and discovering truly top-notch museums and shops. On top of that you'll find plenty of opportunities to wander around in gardens, in woodland preserves, and along the shore.

☐ Magnificent homes and estates

☐ Antiques and crafts shops

☐ Tag sales

☐ Beaches

☐ Marine life

Many of the communities along the coast were established in the 1700s, when the area was a thriving commercial center. Most of them are linked by the Boston Post Road (which dates back to the eighteenth century), also known as US Route 1 and frequently referred to as the Boston Post Road, Old Post Road, or simply the Post Road. To confuse visitors even more, US Route 1 has a variety of other names in various communities it passes through on the East Coast between the states of Maine and Florida. Its original purpose—to connect the communities and provide food and lodging for weary travelers along the way—is still very much alive, though in a modern-day version. Along the way you'll pass big-name stores like Staples and Stew Leonard's as well as fast-food chains, gas stations, movie theaters, and the usual assortment of suburban retailers.

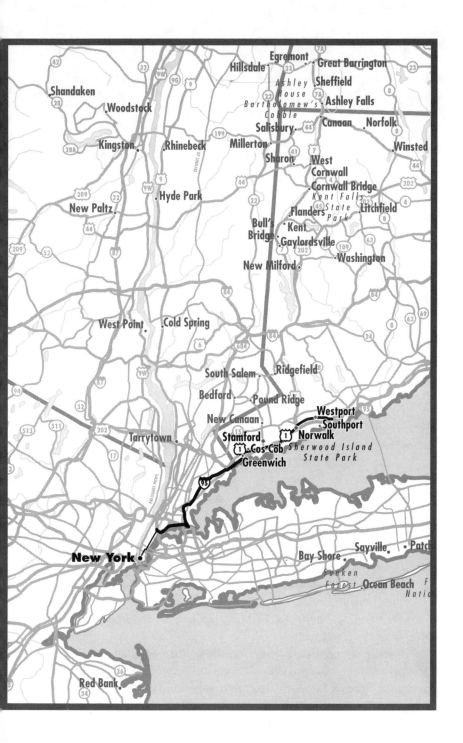

Day 1 / *Afternoon*

If you want to do as the locals do, skip out of Manhattan early on a Friday afternoon to beat the rush-hour traffic. Make your destination **Greenwich** (a mere 28 miles from Times Square, I–95, exit 3), which is the first town you come to when entering the state from the southwest.

DINNER: Chef-owned **Restaurant Jean-Louis,** 61 Lewis Street, between Mason Street and Greenwich Avenue, Greenwich, CT 06830 (203–622–8450), is a splurgey but well-worth-it choice. For gourmets Chef Jean-Louis needs no introduction: He is widely acclaimed for unfailingly good French cuisine, for which he combines both classical and contemporary techniques. Don't even think of not making reservations. To reach the restaurant, turn left off exit 3 onto Arch Street; cross Greenwich Avenue and then turn left onto Mason Street. Lewis Street is the second street down on the left.

LODGING: **The Homestead Inn,** 420 Field Point Road, Greenwich, CT 06830 (203–869–7500), is a fully restored 1799 farmhouse mansion beautifully furnished with country-inn decor and antiques.

Day 2 / *Morning*

BREAKFAST: One of the beauties of setting out on Friday is that you can take your time to greet the day. Consider lounging around on the wraparound porch of the Homestead before having a light breakfast at **Rue de Croissant,** 95 Railroad Avenue, Greenwich, CT 06830 (203–629–1056), a ceramic-tile-floored bistro with fresh-baked breads, muffins, and, of course, croissants.

Devote the morning hours to exploring the town itself, which is centered on Greenwich Avenue, making up an easily strollable historic district complete with wide streets, historic buildings, and stone churches. The shops, of which there are many and all kinds, especially on Greenwich and Putnam Avenues, are on the pricey side (with some exceptions, such as the consignment shops). Take time out to browse around **Just Books,** 19 East Putnam Avenue, Greenwich, CT 06830 (203–869–5023), which purveys titles that appeal to the local clientele (on entertaining, gardening, decorating, and such).

Farther out on East Putnam Avenue is **Putnam Cottage,** 243 East Putnam Avenue, Greenwich, CT 06830 (203–869–9697), which was known as Knapp's Tavern during the Revolutionary War and was a meeting place of leaders including General Israel Putnam. The building itself,

The Homestead Inn in Greenwich is a beautifully restored inn dating from 1799.

which dates from circa 1690, is an attraction (the rare scalloped shingles are especially noteworthy), but indoors there are exhibits as well. It's open Wednesday, Friday, and Sunday from 1:00 to 4:00 P.M.

Afterward consider driving around the so-called country roads of Greenwich, which are punctuated with massive estates, especially along Lake Avenue, North Street, and Round Hill Road. Many peer out from behind high stone walls, crisp white fences, and iron gates.

One former estate open to the public is the **Bruce Museum,** One Museum Drive, Greenwich, CT 06830 (203–869–0376), which had a major renovation. It's a museum of art and science, with exhibits changing about four times a year. The museum is open year-round from 10:00 A.M. to 5:00 P.M. Tuesday through Saturday and 1:00 to 5:00 P.M. Sunday.

In nearby Cos Cob you'll find the **Bush-Holley House,** 39 Strickland Road, Greenwich, CT 06830 (203–869–6899), a National Historic Landmark (1732) that was originally the home of David Bush, a successful farmer and mill owner. Later, from 1890 to 1925, it was a boardinghouse, owned and operated by the Holley family, where writers and artists gathered. Hours vary; call ahead.

LUNCH: Travel east on the Post Road or I–95 to **Stamford** (exit 7), where you can take your pick of cuisines from around the globe (Thai, Indian, Italian, Mexican, German, Chinese, Japanese, French, American— you name it) or join the regulars at **Bull's Head Diner,** 43 High Ridge Road, Stamford, CT 06905 (203–961–1400), which boasts a nine-page menu of mainstream favorites, including lots of Greek specialties.

Afternoon

Stamford is home to more than twenty Fortune 500 corporations, which have colonized its forest of very new-looking office towers. It's also home to several worthwhile attractions such as the **Stamford Museum and Nature Center,** 39 Scofieldtown Road, Stamford, CT 06903 (203– 322–1646), a 118-acre site that includes a New England working farm, trails, galleries, and a planetarium. It's open Monday through Saturday from 9:00 A.M. to 5:00 P.M. and Sunday from 1:00 to 5:00 P.M. Also in Stamford is a unique fish-shaped church designed by Wallace K. Harrison. The **First Presbyterian Church,** 1101 Bedford Street, Stamford, CT 06905 (203– 324–9522), was built in 1958; its stained-glass windows are by Gabriel Loire of Chartres, France. The **Stamford Historical Society Museum,** 1508 High Ridge Road, Stamford, CT 06903 (203–329–1183), has permanent and temporary exhibits, primarily on local history.

One of Stamford's most popular attractions, as well as a one-of-a-kind shopping experience, is **United House Wrecking,** 535 Hope Street, Stamford, CT 06906 (203–348–5371), which purveys the spoils of demolitions and estate sales (antiques, architectural items, old lighting and plumbing fixtures—you have to see this place). It's open year-round, Monday through Saturday from 9:30 A.M. to 5:30 P.M. and Sunday from noon to 5:00 P.M.

Once you've "done" Stamford, hop back on I–95 and take exit 15 to get to **Norwalk.** Norwalk has a very pronounced maritime feel to it. It's home to an exceptionally informative maritime museum, which is called, not surprisingly, the **Maritime Aquarium at Norwalk,** located at 10 North Water Street, Norwalk, CT 06850 (203–852–0700) in SoNo (South Norwalk). Half an hour in this place and you'll have a healthy respect for Long Island Sound and Norwalk's busy harbor life. Among its highlights: an aquarium with sharks and seals, an IMAX theater, a boatbuilding demonstration, and several interactive displays. Walk out the door and you're a couple of blocks away from SoNo's thriving epicenter, which is crammed with funky galleries, boutiques, and a selection of restaurants and bars. SoNo is a revitalized nineteenth-century seaside neighborhood listed on the National Register of Historic Places. Another truly worthwhile attraction in Norwalk is the **Lockwood-Mathews Mansion Museum,** 295 West Avenue, Norwalk, CT 06850 (203–838–9799), a sixty-two-room Victorian mansion built by financier LeGrand Lockwood. Hours are limited, so do call ahead. Sharing the same driveway is the new **Stepping Stones Museum for Children,** 303 West Avenue, Norwalk, CT 06850 (203–899–0606). This museum is a children's dream, with everything from a room where they can do endless water experiments to a full-size helicopter and train car in which they can fiddle with all the knobs and gadgets.

Plan to overnight in **Westport,** a town about which one resident summed up beautifully: "If you live in Westport, you don't have to go away to vacation." Indeed, the town, which is a summer weekend escape for many New Yorkers, has a resorty feel to it, especially in the warm-weather months. The easiest way to reach it from Norwalk (we're talking maybe a ten-minute drive as apposed to taking I–95 which frequently backs up with traffic) is to follow Saugatuck Avenue.

Turn right onto Riverside Avenue and follow for less than half a mile to the Bridge Street Bridge, which is noteworthy only in that it's fabulously redundant. Cross over the Saugatuck River and turn right onto Compo Road South, which puts you in the **Compo Beach** neighborhood. As you approach the water, you'll suddenly begin to feel as if you've been miraculously transported to Nantucket, Martha's Vineyard, or some other idyllic seaside community, especially on a sunny day. You see physically fit people of all ages walking designer dogs, balancing on in-line skates, zipping along (clad in brightly colored Spandex) on bikes, or cruising in antique cars.

Carry on east of Compo Beach to the **Greens Farms** area, which is home to one megahome after another (including one owned by Imus and another by Phil Donahue and Marlo Thomas), especially along Beachside Avenue. By the way, if you have bikes to take along, this is a great biking route. Beachside Avenue takes you right into **Southport,** one of Connecticut's most picturesque communities. It's filled with Federal, Greek Revival, and Victorian houses and a couple of very grand churches. The best way to enjoy it is to park your car by the harbor and just wander around.

DINNER: A great choice is the **Bridge Cafe,** 5 Riverside Avenue, Westport, CT 06880 (203–226–4800). Located on the Saugatuck River, this festively decorated American-Mediterranean restaurant serves fresh seafood, steak, and chicken dishes, as well as a selection of inventive salads. After dinner consider taking in a show at the **Westport Country Playhouse,** 25 Powers Court, Westport, CT 06880 (203–227–4177). This summer theater has had many a name-name on its stage including Bette Davis, Helen Hayes, and Douglas Fairbanks Jr. Its chairwoman is Joanne Woodward, who is helping transform it into a year-round regional theater. The **Westport Arts Center,** 51 Riverside Avenue, Westport, CT 06880 (203–222–7070), showcases the works of Westport artists in its new setting on the banks of the Saugatuck River. It's open from 10:00 A.M. to 4:00 P.M. Monday through Friday and noon to 4:00 P.M. Saturday and Sunday. During the summer months there are shows at the **White Barn Theatre** (Newtown Turnpike, Westport, CT 06880; 203–227–3768), which was founded by Lucille Lortel, and free concerts at the **Levitt Pavilion for the Performing Arts** (off Jesup Road, behind the Westport library; 203–226–7600).

LODGING: The **Inn at National Hall,** Two Post Road West, Westport, CT 06880 (203–221–1351), is a restored historic landmark building (originally built in 1873) right on the shores of the Saugatuck River. There are sixteen truly luxurious, individually designed guest rooms, eight of which are suites. Absolutely every inch of the inn is artistically designed with lots of trompe l'oeil, handcrafted stenciling, and arched ceilings.

Day 3 / Morning

BREAKFAST: If you stay at the Inn at National Hall, a full breakfast is included; otherwise, take your pick of places for coffee and consider brunching later. **Coffee And,** 343 Main Street, Westport, CT 06880 (203– 227– 3808), is locally famed for its homemade doughnuts and muffins (try the chocolate-frosted doughnut), but the coffee's better at the local **Starbucks,** One Parker Harding Plaza, Westport, CT 06880 (203–454–3205).

After breakfast take a walk around the center of town, which has been called a "mall without walls" because of the number of shops—many of them parts of major chains, including Eddie Bauer, J. Crew, Williams-Sonoma, and a sprawling Banana Republic. There are also several one-of-a-kind shops including Uproar, full of innovative home furnishings and accessories. In addition you'll find many antiques shops in this part of town as well as along the Post Road. Westport is also home to the headquarters of the international humanitarian group **Save the Children,** 54 Wilton Road, Westport, CT 06880 (203–221–4000), where you can find all sorts of unique gifts including pottery, musical instruments, and jewelry crafted by children from around the world.

If you're a bird-watcher, consider parking yourself on a bench along the banks of the Saugatuck River by the Westport Public Library. During migration seasons you may see more exotic birds here in half an hour than some people see in a lifetime. You're likely also to see scullers sliding over the water like water spiders and hardworking oarspeople rowing to the commands of a coxswain. Westport is home to the world-class Saugatuck Rowing Club, a training facility for both competitive and recreational rowers.

BRUNCH: A great Sunday brunch choice is **Tavern on Main,** 146 Main Street, Westport, CT 06880 (203–221–7222). It's a bustling little restaurant with a variety of egg dishes, French toast, and other lunch entrees offered for brunch.

After brunch head over to **Sherwood Island State Park** (right off exit 18 on what's called the Sherwood Island Connector; 203–226–6983) or back to Compo Beach for a day at the beach. Sherwood Island State Park is a 238-acre public playground where you'll pay for out-of-state vehicle parking, $8.00 weekdays and $12.00 on weekends, whereas Compo Beach is a more exclusive beach, where parking costs a whopping $30.00 on weekends and holidays, $15.00 on weekdays, and is free during the off season. Or head into town to visit the **Westport Historical Society,** 25 Avery Place, Westport, CT 06880; (203–222–1424). It includes a beautiful Victorian house (circa 1795) with period rooms and exhibit spaces focusing on local history and famous residents over the years. There's also an octagonal-shaped barn in which a walk-around diorama of Westport in the year 1900 is featured. The facility is open from 10:00 A.M. to 4:00 P.M. Tuesday through Friday and noon to 3:00 P.M. Saturday. You might also stop by **Earthplace,** 10 Woodside Lane, Westport, CT 06880 (203–227–7253), a sixty-two-acre wildlife sanctuary with a museum in Westport.

To return, hop back on I–95 to get back to New York City.

There's More

In nearby **Bridgeport,** you'll find the Barnum Museum, (820 Main Street, Bridgeport, CT 06604; 203–331–1104), the Beardsley Zoological Gardens, (1875 Noble Avenue, Bridgeport, CT 06610; 203–394–6565), the Bridgeport Bluefish Ballpark, The Ballpark at Harbor Yard (500 Main Street, Bridgeport, CT 06604; 203–345–4800), the Discovery Museum (4450 Park Avenue, Bridgeport, CT 06604; 203–372–3521) and more—worth extending your trip for.

Nature walks. Look at a map of Fairfield County and you'll see green patches everywhere. It's home to quite a few nature preserves including the following:

Audubon Center of Greenwich, 613 Riversville Road, Greenwich, CT 06831 (Route 15, exit 28; 203–869–5272), is a must for bird-watchers. It's a 522-acre sanctuary with 15 miles of woodland trails.

Barlett Arboretum, at 151 Brookdale Road off High Ridge Road (1 mile north of Route 15, exit 35), in Stamford, CT 06903; (203) 322–6971. Here you'll find sixty-three acres of natural woodland and gardens to explore.

The Nature Conservancy's Devil's Den Preserve, 33 Pent Road, Weston, CT 06883; (203) 226–4991. Wander through 1,746 acres woven with more than 20 miles of well-marked trails through predominantly deciduous forests.

Sheffield Island Lighthouse can be reached by ferry from Hope Dock, which is at the corner of Washington Street and North Water Street in Norwalk. The lighthouse, which dates from 1868, has four levels and ten rooms to explore and is surrounded by three acres of prime picnic grounds. Boat trips and tours are offered between Memorial Day and October. Call (203) 838–9444 for daily ferry service.

Stargazing. Rolnick Observatory, 182 Bayberry Lane, Westport, CT 06880; (203) 227–0925. Two nights a week, Wednesdays and Thursdays (or by appointment), the public can take in a free view of the night sky via a powerful telescope. Operated by Westport Astronomical Society.

Special Events

June. Hidden Garden Tour, Westport. The Westport Historical Society hosts this annual event that allows visitors to tour magnificent gardens. For information, call (203) 222–1424.

Late July–early August. Pequot Library Book Sale, Southport. This is the largest book sale in the state of Connecticut. It features more than ninety thousand volumes in forty-five categories and attracts more than ten thousand people. For more information call (203) 259–0346.

August. SoNo Arts Celebration, Washington Street in South Norwalk. A big block party with food, crafts, arts, and entertainment.

Mid-September. Septemberfest, Greenwich Common, Greenwich. Carnival rides, entertainment, international food festival, a pet show, and more.

Norwalk Oyster Festival, Veterans Park, Norwalk. This annual event celebrates Long Island Sound's seafaring history with entertainment, arts and crafts, boat trips, oyster shucking, and lots of foods.

December. Holiday House Tour, Westport. Every year, five of this community's houses are open for touring. The event is presented by the Westport Historical Society. For information, call (203) 222–1424.

Other Recommended Restaurants and Lodgings

Fairfield

Centro, 1435 Post Road, Fairfield, CT 06430; (203) 255–1210. A great choice for dinner, Centro attracts a beautiful-people crowd who come for the pasta, gourmet pizzas, and other reliably good dishes. You can also count on good, chewy bread and olives for appetizers.

Greenwich

Thomas Henklemann at the Homestead Inn, 420 Field Point Road, Greenwich, CT 06830; (203) 869–7500. This local favorite serves French cuisine with a light flair.

Norwalk

Amberjacks, 99 Washington Street, Norwalk, CT 06854; (203) 853–4332. Here you'll find a spirited atmosphere and excellent seafood.

Barcelona Restaurant and Wine Bar, 63 North Main Street, South Norwalk, CT 06854; (203) 899–0088. Go with friends to this delightful Spanish tapas bar in a former factory.

Meson Galicia, 10 Wall Street, Norwalk, CT 06850; (203) 866–8800. For more formal Spanish dining, this restaurant is a special treat.

Stamford

Beacon Restaurant and Bar, 183 Harbor Drive, Stamford, CT 06901; (203) 327–4600. Dishes—including oysters and lamb chops—are cooked in open-hearth ovens at this lively restaurant overlooking the Stamford Harbor.

Weston

Cobb's Mill Inn, 12 Old Mill Road, Weston, CT 06883; (203) 227–7221. Housed in an eighteenth-century mill, this restaurant draws a large sentimental crowd who have traditionally been coming for holidays, birthdays, anniversaries, and other occasions. Though the food is not remarkable, the view—of the pond and waterfall—and the atmosphere are every bit Fairfield County.

Westport

Arthur Avenue, 539 Riverside Avenue, Westport, CT 06880; (203) 221–1551. A tiny (three-table) restaurant, Arthur's (as the locals know it) is famed for its pasta dishes. Two of its most popular are cavatelli with broccoli rabe and gnocchi with marinara sauce.

Mansion Clam House, 541 Riverside Avenue, Westport, CT 06880; (203) 454–7979. This old Westport restaurant serves some of the freshest and tastiest seafood you'll find. Be sure to try the Cajun popcorn as an appetizer.

Splash, located at the Inn at Longshore, 260 Compo Road South, Westport, CT 06880; (203) 454–7798. Beautifully situated overlooking Long Island Sound, this popular meeting place offers New American dishes with Asian accents.

For More Information

Coastal Fairfield County Convention and Visitors Bureau, 20 Marshall Street, South Norwalk, CT 06854; (203) 840–0770 or (800) 473–4868.

Connecticut Office of Tourism, Department of Economic Development, 505 Hudson Street, Hartford, CT 06067-3405; (860) 270–8080 or (800) 282-6863.

Greenwich Chamber of Commerce, 45 East Putnam Avenue, Greenwich, CT 06830; (203) 869–3500.

Westport/Weston Chamber of Commerce, 60 Church Lane, Westport, CT 06880; (203) 227–9234.

Ridgefield and New Canaan

Two Towns to Tool Around

1 Night

Not too many towns can say they have a gourmet sidewalk hot-dog vendor. Well, **Ridgefield** can. Right in the heart of town, at Chez Leonard's cart, you can take your pick of a variety of gourmet hot dogs including Le Hot Dog Alsacienne (with sauerkraut, French mustard, and caraway seeds), Le Hot Dog Suisse (with Swiss fondue cheese), Le Hot Dog Mexicaine (with chili and Bermuda onions), and Le Hot Dog Excelsior Veneziano (sautéed peppers, onions, olives, tomatoes). Chez Leonard's hot-dog stand is not the only place in town with "good taste," however. The whole village, with its wide Main Street lined with buildings that range from pre-Revolutionary to Victorian, epitomizes good taste. There are no major interstates, parkways, or railroads that take you right there, which may have something to do with the town's wonderful unblemished quality. Nevertheless, as lovely as Ridgefield is, it has been growing quickly; in fact, many longtime residents talk about how beautiful it "used to be."

☐ Historic villages

☐ Stately homes

☐ Antiques and crafts shops

☐ Rural countryside

Less than half an hour's drive away is **New Canaan,** which is also an attractive residential community. The two are just over the New York border, less than 60 miles from Manhattan in the southwest corner of Connecticut. Together they make up a simple but charming weekend getaway with plenty of shops, restaurants, and scenery to keep you happily busy.

Day 1 / Morning

If you start out early in the morning, you'll have the whole day to poke around Ridgefield's shops and galleries. The drive should take no more

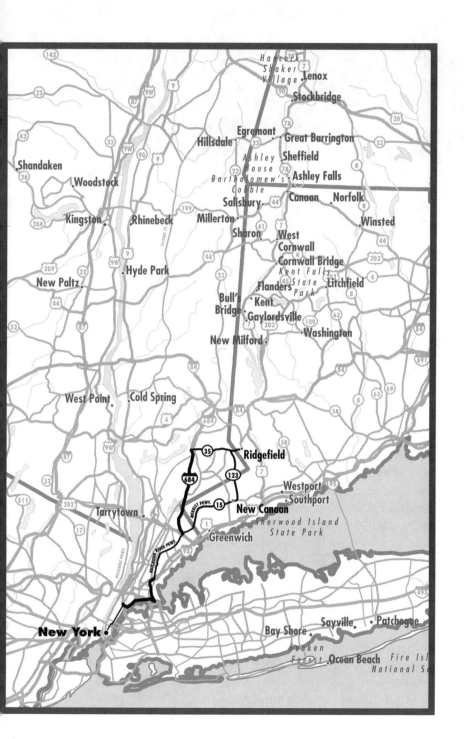

Ridgefield's Keeler Tavern Museum dates from 1715.

than an hour and a half. Though there are several ways to get there, we recommend taking I–684 north and getting off at the Katonah/Cross River exit. Turn right and follow NY 35, which becomes CT 35 and takes you right into Ridgefield. If you have more time, consider combining this trip with our Northern Westchester escape (New York Escape Four). The two fit together beautifully.

Once you get to Ridgefield, start by grabbing a parking spot (there's a lot behind the Ridgefield Bank and Town Hall) and then set out to explore by foot. The hub of town can best be seen by walking down one side of Main Street (starting at the corner of Market Street, opposite St. Stephen's Church) to Ballard Park, then returning on the opposite side. Though it's just a 2- or 3-block walk, allow yourself plenty of time to meander in and out of the shops. Some standout shops include **Hunter's Consignments,** 426 Main Street, Ridgefield, CT 06877; (203–438–9065;

the entrance is actually in an alleyway linking Main Street with the aforementioned parking area), and the **Silver Lining Consignment,** 470 Main Street, Ridgefield, CT 06877; (203 431–0132. Both are consignment shops crammed with everything from silver cigarette holders to monster armoires.

Though you'll be tempted to lunch at Gail's Station House, 378 Main Street, consider saving it for Sunday brunch. If it's a beautiful day, you may want to take a couple of Leonard's hot dogs into **Ballard Park,** which is a lovely green with lots of inviting benches. If you really want to go gourmet, gather picnic items at **Hay Day,** 21 Governor Street, Ridgefield, CT 06877 (203–431–4400; accessible from the aforementioned parking area). Don't be shocked, however, if your picnic ends up costing a bundle. Hay Day, which prides itself on its ultrafresh fruits and vegetables, home-baked breads and desserts, and astounding selection of wines, cheeses, and prepared dishes, is on the pricey side. Still, its foods and wines are nonpareil. The adjoining **Hay Day Cafe,** 21 Governor Street, Ridgefield, CT 06877 (203–431–4400), is a good alternative to a picnic lunch. There's a satiating selection of salads, pastas, and soups, as well as entrees of seafood, beef, lamb, and chicken—all made with the freshest ingredients imaginable. Beware of the desserts, however; they are not for the calorie-conscious.

Afternoon

After lunch wander up the street to the **Aldrich Museum of Contemporary Art,** 258 Main Street, Ridgefield, CT 06877 (203–438–4519), which has changing exhibits along with a sculpture garden that elicits all sorts of puzzled looks and "Is this really art?" kinds of comments.

From the museum it's a fifteen-minute walk (or couple-minute drive) to the **Keeler Tavern Museum,** 132 Main Street, at the junction of Routes 33 and 35, Ridgefield, CT 06877 (203–438–5485). Here you can learn all about the town's history, which has its roots in Colonial times, when it was a way station on the carriage road between New York and Boston. The Keeler Tavern (which dates from 1715) was an inn providing accommodations for the carriage passengers. Now it's a museum complete with guides dressed in period costumes. One of its most noticeable features, however, is a cannonball lodged in a wall. During the Battle of Ridgefield (1777) in the Revolutionary War, it was "sent" by the British.

To see a small but stop-in-your-tracks-and-stare collection of some of Ridgefield's most stunning homes, detour over to High Ridge Road (from the Keeler Tavern head west on Route 35, turn right onto Parley, and then right onto High Ridge). These magnificent mansions, surrounded by flawless lawns, are especially attractive during the year-end holidays, when each one vies for your attention with wreaths adorning every window.

DINNER: A popular choice for wedding receptions and other celebrations, **Stonehenge Inn,** Route 7, Ridgefield, CT 06877 (203–438–6511), combines both good looks (its photogenic pond and grounds are every bridal couple's dream backdrop) and quality French cuisine.

LODGING: Elms Inn, 500 Main Street, Ridgefield, CT 06877 (203–438–2541), is a historic inn, built in the 1760s. Guest rooms are furnished with some antiques and four-poster beds. The kitchen, which in recent years was taken over by chef Brendan Walsh, is one of the best in Fairfield County.

Day 2 / Morning

BRUNCH: If it's Sunday, make sure you beat the après-church crowds for brunch at **Gail's Station House,** 378 Main Street, Ridgefield, CT 06877 (203–438–9775), and if you can, grab one of the tables by the front windows so that you can watch the passersby or a table outside if it's a nice day. Also . . . go starved. This funky little restaurant serves huge portions (try the Texas Pink—scrambled eggs with jalapeños, sour cream, and salsa served in a skillet along with home fries and toast) and yummy home-baked goods.

Afternoon

After brunch you can take your time driving back to New York, stopping in **New Canaan** (and any antiques shops or tag sales) along the way.

To reach New Canaan, follow Route 35 west. Just after you cross the New York border, turn left onto Route 123. Several miles down you'll cross the border again, into New Canaan. This route takes you through serenely scenic landscapes, passing horse farms, a golf course, and quite a few megahomes.

New Canaan, the center of which you can reach by turning right onto Locust Avenue, is a spick-and-span residential community where most residents look as though they could model for a Ralph Lauren catalog. This is Connecticut just as you pictured it. The side streets are lined with large multichimneyed houses with wraparound porches, graceful columns, and the kind of gardens you see featured in glossy magazines.

New Canaan is home to the **Silvermine Guild Arts Center,** 1037 Silvermine Road, New Canaan, CT 06840 (203–966–5617), which is an art school with galleries showcasing the works of member artists and artisans. There is also the **New Canaan Historical Society,** 13 Oenoke Ridge Road, New Canaan, CT 06840 (203–966–1776), which oversees the original town hall, library, and drugstore among other buildings. Both of these facilities have limited visiting hours, so call ahead.

If it's a beautiful day, take time out to walk around the **New Canaan Nature Center,** 144 Oenoke Ridge Road, New Canaan, CT 06840 (203–966–9577). Here there are more than forty acres of woodland, meadows, and ponds plus gardens and hands-on exhibits.

Before heading back consider stopping at **Gates Restaurant,** 10 Forest Street, New Canaan, CT 06840 (203–966–8666), for a cup of cappuccino. Then return to Route 123, which will take you back to the Merritt Parkway for your return trip home.

There's More

Crafts. Brookfield Craft Center, 286 Whisconier Road, Brookfield; (203) 775–4526. About fifteen minutes away from Ridgefield, this craft center is worth a detour. Here you'll find a school for craftsmanship, an exhibition gallery, and a gift shop. It's located in a historic gristmill complex on Route 25, just east of the four corners intersection with Routes 7 and 202, a few miles north of I–84.

Mall shopping. The Danbury Mall, which used to be the Danbury Fair, is not far from Ridgefield (follow Route 7 north). It has all the big stores—Macy's, Lord & Taylor, Sears—as well as a variety of food vendors.

Sight-seeing flights. Scenic small-plane rides can be scheduled at the Danbury Municipal Airport. Trips generally start at about $52 each for a half-hour flight (based on two people). For information call (203) 743–3300.

Special Events

Mid-May through mid-June. Art of Northeast USA Exhibition, Silvermine Guild Arts Center, 1037 Silvermine Road, New Canaan, CT

06840; (203) 966–5617. A juried competition with paintings, drawings, and sculpture by participants from the Northeast states.

June–September. Chamber Music Festival, Silvermine Guild Arts Center, 1037 Silvermine Road, New Canaan, CT 06840; (203) 966–5618 (programs). Evening concerts.

September. Annual Fairfield County Region Antique Car Show, East Ridge Middle School, Ridgefield, CT 06877. An annual event, held the first Saturday after Labor Day from 10:00 A.M. to 3:00 P.M. The longest-running antique car show in America. It is the last pre–World War II antique car show in America, which means entries are restricted to unmodified 1942-and-older vehicles. The show usually draws more than 200 cars.

Other Recommended Restaurants and Lodgings

New Canaan

The Maples, 179 Oenoke Ridge, New Canaan, CT 06840; (203) 966–2927. A twenty-five-room inn with a grand wraparound porch.

Roger Sherman Inn, 195 Oenoke Ridge, New Canaan, CT 06840; (203) 966–4541. An antiques-furnished inn with just seven rooms, some with fireplaces.

Tequila Mockingbird, 6 Forest Street (between East Avenue and Locust), New Canaan, CT 06840; (203) 966–2222. A Mexican-style cafe with terra-cotta tiled floors, a gaily painted mural, and a good selection of Southwestern and Mexican dishes.

Ridgefield

Bernard's Inn at Ridgefield, 20 West Lane, Ridgefield, CT 06877; (203) 438–8282. A small inn known for its French cuisine and its Victorian patio gardens.

Patisserie des Anglaises, 408 Main Street, Ridgefield, CT 06877; (203) 894–8070. An adorable patisserie serving sandwiches and coffee in addition to pastries.

Stonehenge Inn, Route 7, Ridgefield, CT 06877; (203) 438–6511. In addition to being a wonderful restaurant (see description earlier in this chapter), Stonehenge is also a lovely country inn.

West Lane Inn, 22 West Lane, Ridgefield, CT 06877; (203) 438–7323. A sixteen-room early 1800s Colonial home restored with luxurious comforts.

For More Information

Coastal Fairfield County Convention and Visitors Bureau, 20 Marshall Street, South Norwalk, CT 06854; (203) 840–0770 or (800) 473–4868.

Connecticut Office of Tourism, Department of Economic Development, 505 Hudson Street, Hartford, CT 06067-3405; (860) 270–8080 or (800) 282–6863.

Ridgefield Chamber of Commerce, 9 Bailey Avenue, Ridgefield, CT 06877; (203) 438–5992.

Lower Connecticut River Valley

River Valley Towns

1 Night

With its roots back in the settlement of the New World, this little piece of south-central Connecticut is densely historic. Back in the early 1600s, many colonists settled along the banks of the Connecticut River, from which trading (with ports as far away as the West Indies and the Mediterranean) became a popular activity for centuries to follow.

- ☐ River views
- ☐ River history
- ☐ Antiques shops
- ☐ Art galleries
- ☐ Eighteenth- and nineteenth-century houses
- ☐ Traditional New England fare
- ☐ Vintage steam train
- ☐ Riverboat cruise

Today the area is punctuated with small scenic towns that were originally established as shipbuilding and merchant communities. Along the way there are several worthwhile restaurants specializing in New England cuisine, shops where you can buy crafts, antiques, and artwork, and truly warm and welcoming inns.

This two-day excursion takes you to the highlights of the area, including Essex, which is one of Connecticut's most visited towns. Be advised that during summer weekends it can be uncomfortably crowded.

Day 1 / Morning

The quickest and most direct route to the area from Manhattan is I–95, which roughly follows the Connecticut shoreline. Get off at Westbrook (exit 65) and turn right onto Route 153. Follow Route 153 until you come to Route 1, which is locally known as the Shore Route, a steadily scenic road that takes you past picturesque marinas and salt marshes and into **Old Saybrook,** your first stop of the day.

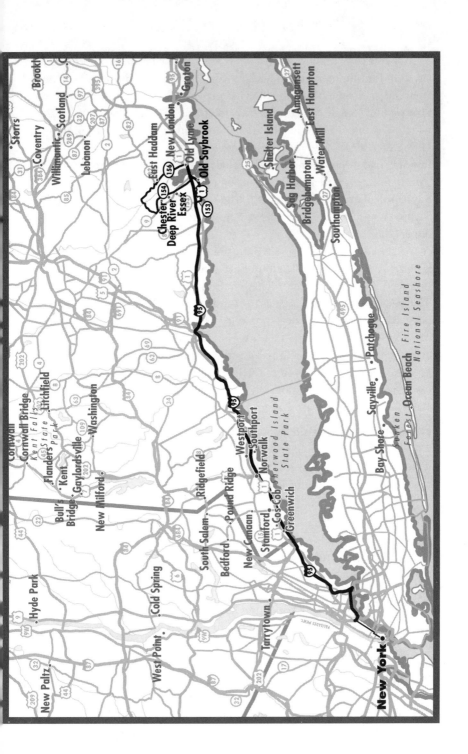

Once a shipbuilding and fishing town, Old Saybrook is now a popular spot for summer vacationers. If you're traveling during a summer weekend, take time out to see the Georgian-style **General William Hart House,** 350 Main Street, Old Saybrook, CT 06475 (860–388–2622), which was once the residence of a prosperous merchant and politician. Home of the Old Saybrook Historical Society, it is open from mid-June through mid-September, Friday through Sunday, from 1:00 to 4:00 P.M. Those in the market for antiques might want to check out **Essex Saybrook Antiques Village,** 985 Middlesex Turnpike (Route 154), Old Saybrook, CT 06475 (860–388–0689), where about 130 antiques dealers display their wares.

Afterward continue along Route 154 to head inland to **Essex,** which is home to a stunning collection of beautiful Colonial and Federal houses that were built during the town's eighteenth-century shipbuilding days. The best way to enjoy Essex is to wander about on foot. Main Street is lined with shops selling sweets, jewelry, antiques, artwork, clothing—you name it. To see some of the town's oldest houses, walk up Pratt Street. One of the landmark buildings in town is the **Griswold Inn,** 36 Main Street, Essex, CT 06426, where you can settle in for lunch. Dating from 1776, this Essex institution is affectionately referred to as the Gris (pronounced "Griz"). To reach it, walk down Main Street (from Essex Square).

LUNCH: The **Griswold Inn,** 36 Main Street, Essex, CT 06426 (860–767–1776), is well known and respected for both its accommodations and its food. At lunchtime you can try its own brand of sausages or order a sandwich or salad plate for less than $10.

Afternoon

From the Griswold Inn walk to the riverside end, which is known as the Foot of Main, and you'll come to the **Connecticut River Museum,** 67 Main Street, Steamboat Dock, Essex, CT 06426 (860–767–8269). It is housed in a restored 1878 warehouse where steamboats used to stop on their trips between New York and Hartford, unloading passengers and/or freight. A noteworthy attraction in the museum is a full-size reproduction of the *American Turtle,* the world's first submarine. Hours are 10:00 A.M. to 5:00 P.M. Tuesday through Sunday.

From downtown Essex follow Route 154 (Railroad Avenue) west toward Ivoryton, and you'll come to the **Valley Railroad Station,** One Railroad Avenue, Essex, CT 06426 (860–767–0103). There you can climb aboard a vintage steam train that hoots and whistles its way through the countryside to Chester and back. The trip takes about an hour and a half. You can also combine the train ride with a riverboat sightseeing cruise by getting off at the Deep River station. The combination train/boat ride adds up to about three hours of your time. The main season for the steam train and riverboat is May through October; call for information on their Christmas schedule.

Afterward you can continue upriver by following Route 154 (just keep bearing right when the road forks). It'll take you right to **Deep River,** your home for the night.

DINNER: In nearby Ivoryton you'll find the **Copper Beech Inn,** 46 Main Street, Ivoryton, CT 06442 (860–767–0330), for an elegant French meal. There are also thirteen rooms for staying overnight at this 1890 country home.

LODGING: **Riverwind Country Inn,** 209 Main Street, Deep River, CT 06417 (860–526–2014), has just eight rooms (all with private bath), each beautifully decorated with antiques and stenciling. There are also several common rooms with fireplaces.

Day 2 / Morning

BREAKFAST: A Southern buffet breakfast (ham, biscuits, hot casseroles, fresh fruit, coffee cake) is included in the room rate at the Riverwind.

Return to Route 154 and follow it to **Chester,** an attractive village most writers cannot resist calling picture-postcard perfect. Indeed it is. Turn left from Route 154 onto Main Street and you'll find a handful of shops, galleries, and restaurants in the buildings that line the street. Also in Chester is the **Connecticut River Artisans Cooperative,** 4 Water Street, Chester, CT 06412 (800–526–5575), which showcases one-of-a-kind works including paintings, photographs, furniture, pottery, folk art, jewelry, and clothing. Call for hours.

Just east of the town center, on Route 148, you can climb aboard a ferry that's been shuttling between the east and west banks of the Connecticut since 1769. The five-minute crossing operates throughout the day, from April through November, at a nominal charge.

Once on board, all eyes turn on **Gillette Castle State Park,** 67 River Road, East Haddam, CT 06439 (860–526–2336), which looms over the river on the east bank in East Haddam. It was built as a dreamhouse-come-

The Goodspeed Opera House overlooks the Connecticut River.

to-life by the actor/playwright William Gillette. When he died, the state of Connecticut purchased it and turned it and the surrounding land into a state park. There are picnic grounds, rest rooms, food concession stands, and canoe rentals. Call for more information. The castle is open from Memorial Day through Columbus Day, daily from 10:00 A.M. to 5:00 P.M. There are limited hours also in October and November (call ahead).

Nearby in **East Haddam,** you'll find the **Goodspeed Opera House,** Route 82, East Haddam, CT 06423 (860–873–8668), which has a statewide (and actually, even wider) reputation for reviving old American musicals. The opera house itself, a Victorian jewel, is exquisite both inside and out. Tours are given on Mondays and Saturdays in July, August, and September. The theater season runs from April to December.

East Haddam is an attraction in itself, with many impeccably pre-served buildings dating from the steamboat days. There's also a little red schoolhouse where Nathan Hale taught in 1773–74, before he was hanged as a spy by the British.

Head south on Route 156 to **Old Lyme,** which is right near the mouth of the river, across from Old Saybrook. Its popularity began in the days of clipper ships and the China trade but later, like all beautiful places, was discovered and colonized by quite a few artists, including Childe Hassam, Willard Metcalf, and Henry Ward Ranger, who called themselves American Impressionists. These artists stayed at "Miss Florence's" boarding-house, which is now the **Florence Griswold Museum,** 96 Lyme Street, Old Lyme, CT 06371 (860– 434–5542). Florence Griswold, an art lover, was the daughter of a ship captain. The house, which was built in 1817, is filled with period furnishings and showcases changing exhibitions including New England furnishings and decorative arts. The museum recently opened a new gallery to house an expansive collection of American art given to them by the Hartford Steam Boiler Inspection and Insurance Company. It's open from April through December, Tuesday through Saturday from 10:00 A.M. to 5:00 P.M. and Sunday from 1:00 to 5:00 P.M. The rest of the year it's open Wednesday through Sunday from 1:00 to 5:00 P.M.

LUNCH: Right next door to the Florence Griswold Museum is the **Bee and Thistle Inn,** 100 Lyme Street, Old Lyme, CT 06371 (860–434–1667), a very welcoming inn that dates from 1756. You can order a simple sandwich or perhaps a more elaborate seafood dish (there are usually daily specials).

Other worthwhile stops in town include the **First Congregational Church** on Lyme Street, Old Lyme, CT 06371, (860–434–0220) which is a 1910 copy of the original 1816 structure that was destroyed by fire, and the **Lyme Academy of Fine Arts,** 84 Lyme Street, Old Lyme, CT 06371 (860–434–5232), which has changing exhibits during the summer months. Hours are Tuesday through Saturday from 10:00 A.M. to 4:00 P.M. and Sunday from 1:00 to 4:00 P.M.

From Old Lyme you can easily hop back on I–95 south and return to New York City.

There's More

Cruises. Camelot Cruises, 1 Marine Park, Haddam, CT 06438 (860–345–8591), offers lunch, dinner, Sunday brunch, and special-theme cruises (mystery outings, fall foliage trips) aboard the 400-passenger cruise ship Camelot.

Parks. The Selden Neck State Park is a 528-acre park in the Connecticut River that you can reach only by water. It's located 2 miles south of Gillette Castle State Park in East Haddam, from which you can get additional information and permits (call 860–526–2336). Canoes and kayaks can be launched at the ferry slip below the castle. Hammonasset Beach State Park, Route 1, Madison, CT (860–245–2785) is the largest of Connecticut's shoreline parks.

Special Events

Mid-February. Annual Winter Carnivale and Ice Competition in Chester Center. This very popular event attracts ice carvers—both amateur and professional—and includes a variety of events, including a Chilly Chili Cook-Off.

Mid-July. Annual Ancient Muster, Deep River. Fifty to seventy fife-and-drum corps recall Revolutionary War days in this annual parade that has been taking place for more than 120 years.

Late July. Annual Arts and Crafts Show, Old Saybrook. Held on the Town Green and Main Street, this annual event attracts more than twenty-five thousand people.

December. Victorian Christmas at Gillette Castle in East Haddam. Every year the castle is decorated with evergreens and Victorian ornaments. Musical groups perform on weekend afternoons; (860) 526–2336.

Mid-December. Torchlight Parade, Old Saybrook. This parade is a tradition that dates from early colonial days. Fife-and-drum corps march down Main Street to meet townspeople on the Town Green to sing carols.

Other Recommended Restaurants and Lodgings

East Haddam

Bishopsgate Inn, 7 Norwich Road, East Haddam, CT 06423; (860) 873–

1677. Right across from the Goodspeed Opera House, this early-nineteenth-century shipbuilder's house has half a dozen tastefully decorated rooms, all with theatrical names.

Essex

Griswold Inn, 36 Main Street, Essex, CT 06426; (860) 767–1776. In addition to dining (described earlier in this chapter), "the Gris" is a fine choice for staying overnight. It's every inch New England, with exposed rough-hewn rafters, low ceilings, and hooked rugs. Its Sunday morning "Hunt Breakfasts" are legendary, with help-yourself, unlimited servings of all sorts of breakfast favorites, including kippers and grits.

Old Lyme

Old Lyme Inn, 85 Lyme Street, Old Lyme, CT 06371; (860) 434–2600. Dating from the 1850s, this clapboard farmhouse is beautifully furnished with canopy beds, marble-topped dressers, and antique pieces. The dining room is open for lunch and dinner.

Old Saybrook

Saybrook Point Inn and Spa, 2 Bridge Street, Old Saybrook, CT 06475; (800) 243–0212 or (860) 395–2000. An eighty-room contemporary hotel with eighteenth-century repro English decor. Ask for a room facing the marina.

For More Information

Connecticut Office of Tourism, Department of Economic Development, 505 Hudson Street, Hartford, CT 06067-3405; (860) 270–8080 or (800) 282–6863.

Connecticut River Valley and Shoreline Visitors Council, 393 Main Street, Middletown, CT 06457; (860) 347–0028 or (800) 486–3346.

Old Saybrook Chamber of Commerce, 146 Main Street, Old Saybrook, CT 06475; (860) 388–3266.

Southeastern Shoreline

Maritime Mystic and More

1 Night

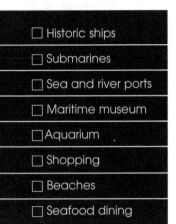

- ☐ Historic ships
- ☐ Submarines
- ☐ Sea and river ports
- ☐ Maritime museum
- ☐ Aquarium
- ☐ Shopping
- ☐ Beaches
- ☐ Seafood dining

Connecticut's maritime roots are most visible in this part of the state, especially in the towns of New London, Groton, Mystic, and Stonington.

You could easily spend a whole day at Mystic Seaport; however, there are many other attractions in the area. Consider combining this trip with the Southern New England Escape Three, which takes you to the nearby towns in the Lower Connecticut River Valley.

Day 1 / Morning

Like the rest of the Connecticut shoreline, this area can be easily reached by taking I–95 north. Set out as early as you can, as there is a lot to squeeze into two days.

Make your first stop **New London** (exit 83), a former whaling town. The number-one attraction here is the **United States Coast Guard Academy,** 15 Mohegan Avenue, New London, CT 06320 (860–444– 8270). Visitors can tour the grounds, the visitors center and museum, the chapel, and the tall ship Eagle when it's in port. The latter is used by cadets for training purposes.

Whale Oil Row, 105–119 Huntington Street, is another interesting attraction in New London. It's a collection of four 1832 temple-front mansions.

Also in town is the **Monte Cristo Cottage,** 325 Pequot Avenue, New London, CT 06320 (860–443–0051), which was the boyhood home of playwright Eugene O'Neill as well as the setting for two of his plays, *Ah! Wilderness* and *Long Day's Journey into Night.*

From New London it's a short drive east to **Groton,** which is known as "The Submarine Capital of the World." Indeed, this shore-hugging

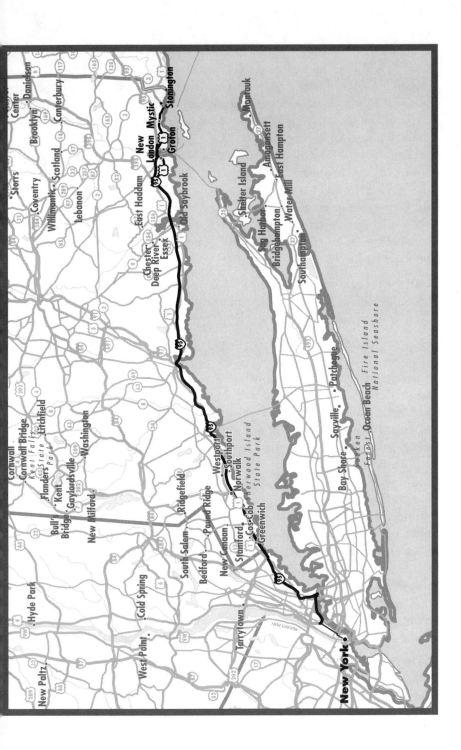

community is home to the **USS *Nautilus* Memorial,** U.S. Naval Base, One Crystal Lake Road, Groton, CT 06349 (800–343–0079). The USS *Nautilus* was the world's first nuclear-powered submarine and is now a National Historic Landmark, permanently berthed. There are meticulously assembled museum displays re-counting the history of the U.S. Submarine Force. It's open for touring year-round, but hours vary; call ahead.

From Groton drive east on Route 1 to **Mystic,** where you'll find the famed **Mystic Seaport,** 50 Greenmanville Avenue, Mystic, CT 06355 (860–572–5315 or 888–973–2767), a huge open-air museum. It's open daily, year-round, except Christmas Day. Admission prices vary. Shops and exhibits are open from 9:00 A.M. to 5:00 P.M. April through October, and 10:00 A.M. to 4:00 P.M. November through March. Start by taking time out for lunch.

LUNCH: The **Seamen's Inne,** 75 Greenmanville Avenue, Mystic, CT 06355 (860–572–5303), located right next to the seaport entrance, serves New England fare.

Afternoon

Once you've fortified yourself with a good lunch, head into the Mystic Seaport. Here you'll see more historic seagoing vessels, from a dugout canoe to America's sole surviving wooden whaling ship, than most people see in a lifetime. The star attraction for many is the 113-foot *Charles W. Morgan,* a whaling ship that was built in 1841. The height of America's shipbuilding and whaling prosperity is magnificently captured at this seventeen-acre living-history museum. On land there are dozens of nineteenth-century buildings that were brought to the seaport and restored. Highly skilled men and women, in period costume, demonstrate various maritime skills such as sail handling, oystering, and ropework. Allow at least a couple of hours (even three or four) to roam around.

Shoppers shouldn't miss the **Mystic Seaport Museum Store,** which is right at the main gate (South Gate). There are two floors where you can find all sorts of must-haves from simple old-fashioned candies to multi-thousand-dollar lightship baskets. It's open daily from 10:00 A.M. to 5:30 P.M. You'll find more shops inside the seaport, but this one gets first prize.

DINNER: Abbott's Lobster in the Rough, 117 Pearl Street, Noank, CT 06340 (860–536–7719), is a must if you love seafood. It's a huge, massively popular seaside restaurant with picnic tables upon which huge plat-

Built in 1841, the Charles W. Morgan is the last surviving wooden whaling ship.

ters of spanking-fresh seafood are devoured. Expect to wait in line. Noank is about ten minutes south of Mystic.

LODGING: The **Old Mystic Inn,** 52 Main Street, Old Mystic, CT 06372 (860–572–9422). Not to be confused with the Inn at Mystic, this eight-room inn is in nearby Old Mystic (1½ miles north of I–95 on Route 27), which makes it within easy reach of the seaport and all the other area attractions but sets it apart from the crowd. The building, which was built in the early 1800s, was originally the Old Mystic Book Shop.

Day 2 / Morning

BREAKFAST: A country breakfast (coffee, tea, or hot chocolate, plus juice and pancakes or French toast or eggs, any style) is included in the room rate at the Old Mystic Inn.

After breakfast take a look around the **Mystic Aquarium,** 55 Coogan Boulevard, Mystic, CT 06355 (860–572–5955), which is home to all sorts of amphibians and other marine habitants including sea lions, seals, and penguins. The aquarium is open daily from 9:00 A.M. to 6:00 P.M. from July through Labor Day. All other times the daily hours are 9:00 A.M. to 5:00 P.M.

If you feel like doing a little shopping, head for **Olde Mystick Village** (entrances are on Coogan Boulevard, Mystic, CT 06355; 860–536–4941). The village is a collection of Colonial-style buildings housing about sixty shops that sell an assortment of souvenirs, local food products, and other items.

From Olde Mystick Village drive east on Route 1 for about 5 miles, and you'll come to **Stonington,** a traditional New England seacoast village that deserves a walk around. To get the lay of the land, start by climbing the stone steps to the top of the tower at the **Old Lighthouse Museum,** 7 Water Street, Stonington, CT 06378 (860–535–1440). Inside the 1823 granite lighthouse, there are displays of maritime history and memorabilia of the Orient trade and whaling and fishing days. It's open from May through October, but hours vary, so call ahead. Then wander about admiring the eighteenth- and nineteenth-century architecture throughout the town. Water Street is the town's main street, where you'll find several boutiques, antiques shops, and restaurants.

LUNCH: Boom Restaurant, 194 Water Street, Stonington, CT (860–535–2588) is located at the edge of a working boatyard overlooking the harbor. It features fish and shellfish.

Afternoon

After lunch head back to New York on I–95.

There's More

Beach and amusement complex. Ocean Beach Park, near Harkness Memorial State Park south of New London, exit 75–76 from I–95; (860) 447–3031. This major recreation area has saltwater and pool swimming, nature trails, and amusement rides.

Casinos. Foxwoods Resort Casino on Route 2 in Mashantucket (800–752–9244) and the Mohegan Sun Casino in Uncasville (888–226–7711) attract thousands of visitors daily. Both are open daily, twenty-four hours a day.

Hiking. There are more than twenty parks with trails for all levels of hikers throughout the Mystic Coast and County region.

Museums. The Children's Museum of Southeastern Connecticut (409 Main Street, Niantic, CT 06357; 860–691–1111) is a hands-on interactive museum for children ages one through twelve. The Mashantucket Pequot Museum and Research Center (110 Pequot Trail, Mashantucket, CT 06339; 800–411–9671) has extensive permanent exhibits on the native and natural history of New England.

Spa. In nearby Norwich the Norwich Inn & Spa, 607 West Thames Street, Norwich, CT 06360; (860) 886–2401 or (800) 275–4772. Facilities include a full-service health spa.

Theater. Eugene O'Neill Theater Center, 305 Great Neck Road, Waterford, CT 06385; (860) 443–5378. An organization devoted to developing new stage works.

Special Events

Late May. Lobster Weekend, Mystic Seaport, Mystic. Lobster feasts, music, and other entertainment.

Early June. Yale-Harvard Regatta, New London. A rowing regatta with crews from both Yale and Harvard universities.

July 4th weekend. Independence Weekend, Mystic. A re-creation of an 1870s Fourth of July by costumed role-players. Also a parade and other activities.

October. Chowderfest Weekend. Every year Mystic Seaport hosts its annual battle of the chowderpots, where local community groups serve up their own version of the perfect chowder. The festival includes folk music, gallery exhibitions, and all sorts of activities.

Other Recommended Restaurants and Lodging

Mashantucket

Grand Pequot Tower at Foxwoods, Route 2, Mashantucket, CT 06339;

(800) 369–9663. A world-class hotel with 824 rooms and suites, gourmet restaurants, and casinos.

Mystic

Captain Daniel Packer Inne, 32 Water Street, Mystic, CT 06355; (860) 536–3555. A 230-year-old restaurant serving American fare, including rack of spring lamb, filet mignon, and some fish dishes.

Inn at Mystic, on US 1, at junction of CT 27 (2 miles south of I–95, exit 90), Mystic, CT 06355; (860) 536–9604. A sixty-seven-room inn ¼ mile from Long Island Sound. Some rooms have fireplaces; some have whirlpools.

Steamboat Inn, 73 Steamboat Wharf, Mystic, CT 06355; (860) 536–8300. Located in the heart of Mystic, right on the river. Six of the rooms have fireplaces; four have kitchenettes.

North Stonington

Randall's Ordinary, Route 2, North Stonington, CT 06359; (860) 599–2261. An eighteen-room Colonial wayside inn listed on the National Register of Historic Places and on the Connecticut Freedom Trail. Authentic Colonial cuisine prepared entirely in open-hearth fireplace.

For More Information

Connecticut's Mystic and More Convention and Visitors Bureau, 470 Bank Street, New London, CT 06320; (860) 444–2206 or (800) 863–6569.

Connecticut Office of Tourism, Department of Economic Development, 505 Hudson Street, Hartford, CT 06067-3405; (860) 270–3405 or (800) 282–6863.

Northeast Corner

A Quiet Getaway

1 Night

The nickname for the northeastern corner of Connecticut is "The Quiet Corner." Indeed it is quiet. It's also one of the Northeast's most unspoiled chunks of land, made up of fertile pastures, low-rising hills, rivers, forests, and historic villages.

☐ Historic homes

☐ Mill villages

☐ Hilltop vistas

☐ Vineyards

☐ Gardens and nurseries

☐ Hiking

☐ Cross-country skiing

Day 1 / Morning

To reach the area take I–684 north to I–84 east. Get off at exit 67 and go south on Route 31 to the junction of Route 44. Take 44 east to Route 31 again and follow that into **Coventry,** where you'll find **Caprilands Herb Farm,** 534 Silver Street, Coventry, CT 06238 (860–742–7244). The farm, which has an eighteenth-century farmhouse, was owned by author and herbalist Adelma Simmons who died in 1997. Spend some time walking through the herb gardens, check out the shops, and then sip a cup of herbal tea in the dining room. It's open daily from 10:00 A.M. to 5:00 P.M. Garden tours are conducted by request.

Coventry has a handful of other attractions including the **Nathan Hale Homestead,** 2299 South Street, Coventry, CT 06238 (860–247–8996), which was the family home of the state hero. It's open from May 15 through October 15, from 1:00 to 4:00 P.M. Wednesday through Sunday. Nearby is the **Strong-Porter House Museum,** 2382 South Street, Coventry, CT 06238 (860–742–9042), a farmhouse that was built around 1730 by a great-uncle of Nathan Hale. There are several outbuildings to tour including a carpenter's shop, a carriage shed, and a barn with exhibits. You can buy a combined ticket for admission to both this museum and the Nathan Hale Homestead. In Coventry there's also an old one-room schoolhouse called the **Brick School House,** Merrow Road,

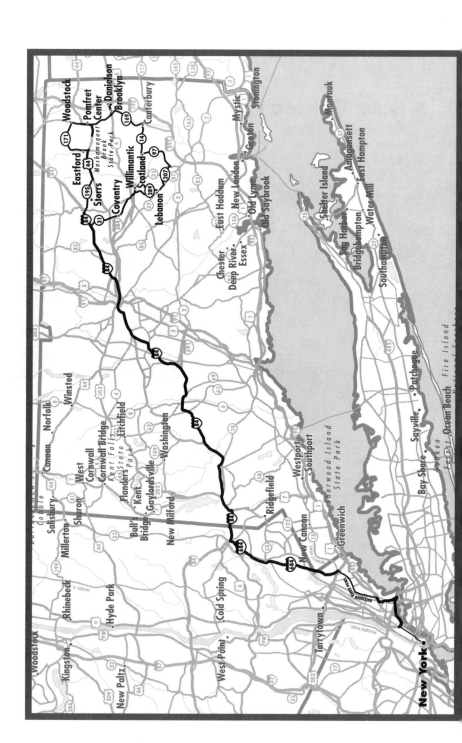

Coventry, CT 06238 (860–742–1419), which was built between 1823 and 1825. It's open by appointment only.

LUNCH: Bidwell Tavern, 1260 Main Street, Coventry, CT 06238 (860–742–6978), is located right in the heart of Coventry's antiquing district. It's a historic restaurant serving New England cuisine including a wonderful Yankee pot roast.

There's also a winery—the **Nutmeg Vineyards Farm Winery,** 800 Bunker Hill Road, Coventry, CT 06238 (860–742–8402)—where you can take a tour followed by a tasting. It's open year-round on Saturday and Sunday, from 11:00 A.M. to 5:00 P.M.

Afternoon

From Coventry drive a short distance south to **Willimantic,** where you can stop to see the **Windham Textile and History Museum,** 157 Union and Main Street, Willimantic, CT 06226 (860–456–2178). It's a fascinating museum, with exhibits devoted to textile production at the height of the Industrial Revolution. There's a re-created 1880s mill shop floor, a company store, a tenement home, a library dating from 1877, and a mill agent's mansion. Hours vary; call ahead.

Make your next stop in the town of **Lebanon** (follow Route 289 south). There are some very worthwhile attractions here including the **Jonathan Trumbull Jr. House,** 780 Trumbull Highway, on the Green, Lebanon, CT 06249 (860–642–6100), and the Trumbull family's store, which is known as the **Revolutionary War Office,** 149 West Town Street, Lebanon, CT 06249 (860–642–6579). Trumbull was the only Colonial governor who supported America's war for independence. The war office stocked war supplies and became a meeting place of the Council of Safety. Both have limited hours; call ahead. Also on West Town Street is the **Dr. William Beaumont House,** 169 West Town Street, on the Green, Lebanon, CT 06249 (860–642–6579). This eighteenth-century cottage was the birthplace of the "Father of Physiology of Digestion." Inside there are several displays of early surgical instruments. It's open on Saturdays only, from 1:00 to 5:00 P.M., from mid-May through mid-October.

From Lebanon head east on Route 207 and turn left onto Route 97. Then turn right on 14 East. That will take you right into **Canterbury,** where you'll find the **Prudence Crandall House Museum,** at the junction of Routes 14 and 169, Canterbury, CT 06331 (860–546–9916). This was New England's first school for black women. It's open Wednesday

The Jonathan Trumbull House on the Green in Lebanon

through Sunday from 10:00 A.M. to 4:30 P.M.; closed December 15 through January 31. Canterbury is also home to **Wright's Mill Tree Farm,** 63 Creasey Road, Canterbury, CT 06331 (860–774–1455), which has more than 250 acres of ponds, waterfalls, and mill sites to explore. It's open daily from 9:00 A.M. to 5:00 P.M. year-round.

Turn left onto Route 169 and you'll find yourself passing through a densely scenic landscape. This road has been designated by Scenic America as one of the ten most scenic highways in the United States.

Continue about 7 miles to **Brooklyn** and stop to have a look around the **Daniel Putnam Tyler Law Office,** on Route 169, Brooklyn, CT 06234 (860–774–7728), where Tyler practiced law from 1822 to 1875. Hours are very limited, however, so call ahead. Brooklyn is home to the **New England Center for Contemporary Art,** Route 169, Brooklyn, CT 06234 (860–774–8899), which showcases changing exhibits in its pre-

Revolutionary barn setting. It's open Wednesday through Sunday from 1:00 to 5:00 P.M. from April through November. Brooklyn also has two beautiful churches to see: the **Unitarian Church** on the Green and **Old Trinity Church** (take Route 6 east for a mile and turn left onto Church Street). Both date from 1771. In nearby **Danielson** (follow Route 6 east of town), you'll find **Logee's Greenhouses,** 141 North Street, Danielson, CT 06239 (860–774–8038), which has more than two thousand varieties of indoor plants, including 400 types of begonias. The greenhouses are open Monday through Saturday from 9:00 A.M. to 5:00 P.M. and Sunday from 11:00 A.M. to 5:00 P.M. (You'll be coming back to Brooklyn for dinner.)

Continue north to the picturesque town of **Pomfret Center,** which is home to the elite Pomfret Preparatory School. You can tour the village's last mill, which is now a museum listed on the National Register of Historic Places known as the **Brayton Grist Mill,** Route 44, Pomfret Center, CT 06259 (entrance is at Mashamoquet Brook State Park). Pomfret Center is also home to the **Connecticut Audubon Center at Pomfret,** 189 Pomfret Street, Pomfret Center, CT 06259; (860) 928–4948. You'll find some of the best birding in the state of Connecticut on its 667 acres.

Woodstock, about 5 miles from Pomfret Center, is next on your itinerary as well as your stopover for the night. Try to get there before 5:00 P.M. so that you can get in to see **Roseland Cottage–Bowen House,** 556 Route 169, Woodstock, CT 06281 (860–928–4074). Roseland is a Gothic Revival summerhouse that was built by merchant and publisher Henry Bowen. Be sure to take a look inside the barn; it contains what's possibly the oldest indoor bowling alley in the country. The cottage, which is filled with original family furnishings, is open from June 1 through October 15, Wednesday through Sunday. Tours given every hour from 11:00 A.M. to 4:00 P.M.

DINNER: The **Golden Lamb Buttery,** 499 Wolf Den Road, Brooklyn, CT 06259 (860–774–4423), is located in a converted barn well known among gourmets. The menu generally includes classic American dishes and whatever's ready to be plucked from the garden. There's usually a wonderful soup to start, followed by a choice of entrees (duck, lamb, various seafood) prepared a different way every day.

LODGING: The **Inn at Woodstock Hill,** 94 Plaine Hill Road, Woodstock, CT 06281 (off Route 169) (860–928–0528), is a twenty-two-room inn listed on the National Register of Historic Places. It's a restored country estate on nineteen rolling acres.

Day 2 / *Morning*

BREAKFAST: A continental breakfast (included in the room rate) is served at the inn.

If you're interested in antiquing, head east on Route 171 to **Putnam,** which has several antiques shops. Then head west on Route 44, which will take you to **Storrs,** the area's cultural center. You could stay busy for hours browsing through the collections at the **University of Connecticut** alone: the Atrium Gallery of Contemporary Art (860–486–3930); the William Benton Museum of Art, which features European and American works (860–486–4520); and the Connecticut State Museum of Natural History (860–486–4460). By the way, "UConn" has a dairy bar where the ice cream is nonpareil.

Nonuniversity attractions nearby include the **Gurleyville Grist Mill,** Stone Mill Road, Mansfield, CT 06268 (860–429–9023), which is the state's only remaining stone gristmill. Hours are limited; call ahead. The **Mansfield Historical Society Museum,** 954 Storrs Road, Storrs, CT 06268 (860–429–6575), has exhibits relating to local history. Hours are limited; call ahead.

LUNCH: The **Depot Restaurant,** 57 Middle Turnpike, Mansfield, CT 06251 (860–429–3663), has a good selection of soups, salads, and sandwiches plus daily specials such as pasta dishes and seafood crepes.

Afternoon

Return to New York City by heading north on Route 195 to I–84 west. Take I–84 right over the New York border and head south on I–684.

There's More

Auto racing. Due north of Storrs, in Stafford Springs, is the Stafford Motor Speedway, Route 140, Stafford Springs, CT 06076; (860) 684–2783.

Special Events

Mid-May. Springtime Festival, Danielson, CT 06239. A parade, a road race, arts and crafts, food booths, a petting zoo, and more.

Early September. Woodstock Fair, on the fairgrounds at Routes 169 and 171, South Woodstock, CT 06267. This is the state's best-attended family fair. There's a horse show, go-cart racing, vaudeville acts, arts and crafts—you name it.

Mid-September. Lions Outdoor Arts and Crafts Show, Davis Park, Danielson, CT 06239. More than 150 artists and artisans from all over the Northeast show their work here.

October. Oktoberfest, Wright's Mill Farm, 63 Creasey Road, Canterbury, CT 06331; (860) 774–1455. Includes full German buffet and yodeling contest.

Other Recommended Restaurants and Lodgings

Brooklyn

Friendship Valley Inn, 60 Pomfret Road, Brooklyn, CT 06234; (860) 779–9696. Historic 1795 inn with five beautifully furnished guest rooms, all with private baths.

Storrs

Altnaveigh Inn, Route 195, Storrs, CT 06268; (860) 429–4490. This is a bed and breakfast in a farmhouse that was built in 1734. It has five rooms very simply decorated in a New England country style. Downstairs the restaurant serves seafood, beef, and chicken dishes. A continental breakfast is included in the room rate.

Woodstock

Bed & Breakfast at Taylor's Corner, 880 Route 171, Woodstock, CT 06281; (860) 974–0490. Listed in the National Register of Historic Places, this eighteenth-century home features just three guest rooms, each with its own private bath and fireplace.

For More Information

Connecticut Office of Tourism, Department of Economic Development, 505 Hudson Street, Hartford, CT 06067-3405 (860) 270–8080 or (800) 282–6863.

Northeast Connecticut Visitors District, 13 Canterbury Road, Brooklyn, CT 06234 (860) 779–6383.

The Litchfield Hills

Traditional New England

2 Nights

For lots of wealthy New Yorkers and celebrities (Meryl Streep, Dustin Hoffman, and Henry Kissinger, to name just a few), this little northwestern corner of Connecticut is a "have your cake and eat it too" location. It has all the things that make New England New England, such as white steepled churches, stately old houses, covered bridges, stone walls, fields filled with large-eyed cows, and big old barns sagging with the contour of the land. At the same time the area is home to a surprising number of up-to-urban-standards restaurants (many with European- or Culinary Institute of America–trained chefs), dozens of art galleries and museums, and an impressive collection of inns and other buildings listed on the National Register of Historic Places.

☐ Antiques shops
☐ New England scenery
☐ Art galleries
☐ Country fairs
☐ Woodland walks
☐ Fine dining

There are more than three dozen towns scattered throughout the Litchfield Hills, most of them with fewer than five thousand inhabitants. This short trip takes you to the area's highlights, on a loop tour that roughly begins and ends in New Milford.

Day 1 / Morning

Less than two hours from Manhattan (about 100 miles), the Litchfield area can be reached by following the Henry Hudson Parkway to the Saw Mill River Parkway to I–684 to Route I–84 east, then following Route 7 north (exit 7) to New Milford. (An alternative route is to take Route 684 north to Route 22 and cross over the state line on Route 55, heading into Gaylordsville.)

Either way, as you proceed north, you can't help feeling as though you've left the city far behind. Once you pass New Milford, it's time for

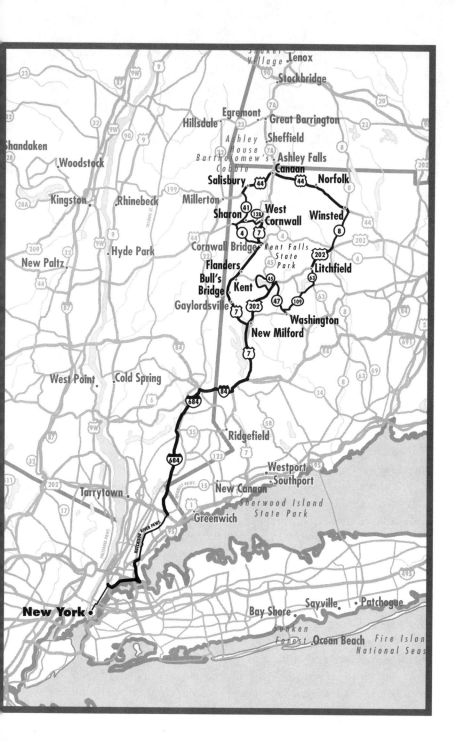

passengers to stop reading the map or catnapping and start looking at the scenery. From here on the landscape is steadily scenic—wooded hills, vintage farmhouses, lakes and rivers that really do sparkle, and small villages that inevitably elicit all sorts of cliché adjectives like "charming," "postcard-perfect," and "cute."

If you're a food lover, consider making a stop at the **Silo: the Store and the School,** 44 Upland Road, New Milford, CT 06776 (860–355–0300). This former farm is now a cooking school and retail store, with kitchenware from around the United States, Mexico, and Europe. Take a look around the adjoining silo, which usually has marked-down items for sale. Upstairs in the silo there's a gallery showcasing the work of local artists and artisans. On Sundays there are often recitals accompanied by wine and cheese receptions. Call ahead for a schedule of events and, if you're interested in taking a class (on bread baking, low-fat Chinese, even barbecue cuisine), class schedules. All classes, which start in early spring and go on every weekend up to Christmas, are three hours long and self-contained.

Make your next stop **Bull's Bridge,** one of the state's two covered bridges that you can drive through (the other one is in nearby West Cornwall). It's just before Kent and spans the Housatonic River. As well as being very picturesque, the bridge has a historical claim to fame in that Washington crossed it back in 1781. Supposedly one of his horses fell in the river (it was March) and had to be pulled out.

Plan to spend a chunk of time in **Kent** (Route 7 takes you right through the heart of it), especially if you enjoy browsing around galleries and antiques shops. Be forewarned, however: Kent can be a mob scene on fall weekends.

Kent is also home to the **Sloane-Stanley Museum,** Route 7, Kent, CT 06757, about 2 miles north of Kent Center (860–566–3005), which has a collection of early American farm and woodworking tools that were amassed by Eric Sloane, the artist and writer. The museum is open from mid-May through October, Wednesday through Sunday. Carry on and you'll come to **Flanders Historic District,** which is a preserved group of houses that were originally part of the center of Kent. One of them, the Seven Hearths, is now a museum filled with artwork by the American portrait painter George Lawrence Nelson.

A bit farther north on Route 7 is **Kent Falls State Park** (860–927–3238), a 295-acre park with a beautiful waterfall that's been featured in many ads. With its webwork of trails and picnic facilities, this is a lovely park in which to while away a couple of hours. You can climb up to the head of the falls (something like 25 feet) on a wide, stepped pathway.

Before leaving the area stop by to pick up a picnic lunch in town. Check out the deli at the Davis IGA on the Kent Green (860–927–1343).

LUNCH: Picnic in Kent Falls State Park.

Afternoon

Continue north on Route 7 to **West Cornwall,** which many people consider Connecticut's prettiest town, where, on Route 128, you'll find the state's other passable **covered bridge.** It has been in continuous service since 1837. Detour a bit to **Sharon,** west on Route 4 or Route 128, if you'd like to see more beautiful New England scenery and pick your own fruit (strawberries in June and July, raspberries in July and August, and apples in September and October) at **Ellsworth Hill Farm** on Route 4, Sharon, CT 06069 (860–364–0025). Then stop at the **Audubon Center at Sharon,** 325 Route 4, Sharon, CT 06069 (860–364–0520), a 2,000-acre sanctuary with self-guiding trails, wildflower and herb gardens, a farm area, an interpretive center, and a gift shop. It's open year-round, Monday through Saturday from 9:00 A.M. to 5:00 P.M. and Sunday from 1:00 to 5:00 P.M.

From Sharon head north on Route 41 to get to **Salisbury,** which is home to a handful of shops and a welcoming little tearoom called **Chaiwalla,** One Main Street, Salisbury, CT 06068 (860–435–9758). There are more than a dozen teas imported from around the world, and each one is freshly brewed from Salisbury spring water. Of course, a cup of tea would not be complete on its own, so there is an equally impressive selection of edibles, including traditional scones, sausage pies, onion tarts, and a variety of desserts. Chaiwalla is open from 10:00 A.M. to 6:00 P.M. daily, year-round. Chaiwalla is also a center for tea tastings, lectures on tea, and poetry and short-story readings over tea.

In nearby **Lakeville** on Route 112 you'll find **Lime Rock Park,** where sports-car races take place from April through November. For ticket information call (860) 435–5000 or (800) 722–3577.

From Salisbury it's a short drive up to **Canaan,** which is home to the **Housatonic Railroad,** one of the nation's oldest railroads. There are scenic rides throughout the summer and autumn months. For details call (860) 824–0850.

Carry on east on Route 44 to **Norfolk.** In the late 1800s, Norfolk was a scheduled stop on the railroad between New York City and Pittsfield, Massachusetts. At that time it became a popular resort for the

The covered bridge in West Cornwall has been in continuous service since 1837.

affluent, who built many of the large houses you see there today. The village green is surrounded by buildings listed on the National Register of Historic Places. There's a small **historical museum** at the Norfolk Historical Society here on the green, Norfolk, CT 06058 (860–542–5761), that houses local artifacts and some old Connecticut-made clocks. It's open from mid-June through mid-October on Saturday and Sunday only. One of the most enjoyable ways to see the town is to take a **horse-drawn carriage** (or sleigh, in winter). For schedules stop by or call **Loon Meadow Farm,** 41 Loon Meadow Drive, Norfolk, CT 06058; (860) 542–6085.

Nearby there are a couple of hiking opportunities including **Haystack Mountain,** 1 mile north on Route 272. From the top there are stunning views of the Berkshires and **Campbell Falls,** 6 miles north of Norfolk on Route 272. Two miles south of Norfolk, on Route 272, is **Dennis Hill,** which is topped by a summit pavilion (it used to be a summer residence) where you can get a far-reaching view of the Litchfield Hills.

DINNER: The **Cannery Cafe,** 85 Main Street, Canaan, CT 06018 (860–824–7333), serves imaginatively prepared American cuisine along with a very good selection of wines.

LODGING: In Norfolk there are two truly top-notch bed and breakfasts. **Greenwood's Gate,** 105 Greenwoods Road East, Norfolk, CT 06058 (860–542–5439), is a beautifully restored 1797 Colonial home furnished with antiques. The **Manor House,** 69 Maple Avenue, Norfolk, CT 06058 (860–542–5690), is an English Tudor mansion, with Tiffany stained-glass windows, also filled with antiques.

Day 2 / Morning

BREAKFAST: At your bed and breakfast.

From Norfolk follow Route 44 east to **Winsted,** the self-proclaimed mountain-laurel capital, and then head north on Route 20 to **Riverton,** which has long been known as the Laurel City because of the abundance of laurel in the area. In fact, each year in June the town hosts the Laurel Festival, complete with a parade, the Laurel Ball, and the crowning of a Laurel Queen. In Winsted you can get on Route 8 and head south to Route 202 west, which will take you right to the town of **Litchfield.**

Litchfield is about as New England as a town can be, complete with a village green, a spick-and-span white church, and stately eighteenth-century houses lined up along wide maple-tree-lined streets as if contestants in a beauty pageant. The town, which sits on a plateau above the Naugatuck Valley, was spared early industrialization because the railroads laid their main lines down in the valley. Its most famous early resident was Harriet Beecher Stowe, author of *Uncle Tom's Cabin.* She grew up here.

One of Litchfield's most celebrated, and photographed, attractions is the **Congregational Church,** at the junction of Routes 202 and 118, Litchfield, CT 06759. Built in 1828, it's the perfect New England church. Also perfect is **Litchfield's green,** which was laid out in the 1770s. If time permits, have a look around the **Litchfield Historical Society Museum,** on the green, Litchfield, CT 06759 (860–567–4501), a good source of local history. It's open from mid-April through mid-November, Tuesday through Saturday, from 11:00 A.M. to 5:00 P.M. and Sunday from 1:00 to 5:00 P.M. The **Tapping Reeve House and Law School** on South Street, Litchfield,

CT 06759 (860–567–4501) are worth visiting. Both date from the 1700s. The law school was America's first and included graduates Aaron Burr and John C. Calhoun. They're open from mid-April through mid-October, Tuesday through Saturday from 11:00 A.M. to 5:00 P.M., and Sunday from 1:00 to 5:00 P.M.

Also in Litchfield, just off Route 118 on Chestnut Hill Road, Litchfield, CT 06759, is the **Haight Vineyard and Winery** (860–567–4045), where tours and tastings take place year-round except on major holidays.

For those wanting to get a little fresh air, the **White Memorial Foundation** is a 4,000-acre conservation area 2½ miles west of town on Route 202, Litchfield, CT 06759 (860–567–0857). There are more than 35 miles of trails threaded through the woodlands.

Just south of town is **White Flower Farm,** Route 63, Litchfield, CT 06759 (860–567–8789), a sprawling retail and mail-order nursery with ten acres of display gardens and thirty acres of growing fields. The farm is open from 9:00 A.M. to 6:00 P.M. daily from April through September and 10:00 A.M. to 5:00 P.M. daily from October through March.

LUNCH: The **West Street Grill,** 43 West Street, Litchfield, CT 06759 (860–567–3885). The cuisine is contemporary American that's unfailingly fabulous.

Afternoon

From Litchfield head south on Route 63, then turn right onto Route 109, and follow that to **Washington,** a little village built around a church. There are a handful of sights to check out in the area including the **Gunn Memorial Library and Museum,** on the green in Washington, CT 06793 (860–868–7756), a house built in 1781 containing local-history collections and exhibits, antique furniture, old dolls and doll houses (open Thursday through Sunday from noon to 4:00 P.M.), and the **Institute for American Indian Studies,** 38 Curtis Road, Washington, CT 06793 (860–868–0518), which houses an impressive collection of Indian artifacts as well as a complete outdoor Indian village. The latter is open from 10:00 A.M. to 5:00 P.M. Monday through Saturday and noon to 5:00 P.M. Sunday.

DINNER: The restaurant at the **Mayflower Inn,** 118 Woodbury Road (Route 47), Washington, CT 06793 (860–868–9466), overseen by chef John Farnsworth, is not only beautifully situated at one of the state's best inns but has wonderful food and wines to match.

LODGING: The **Mayflower Inn,** 118 Woodbury Road (Route 47), Washington, CT 06793 (860–868–9466), has twenty-five rooms, all over-looking gardens filled with rare flora.

Day 3 / Morning

BREAKFAST: Breakfast is delicious at the Mayflower Inn, although it is not included in the room rate. Menu items include farm–fresh eggs prepared in a variety of ways, French toast, waffles, pastries, and lots of fresh fruit.

From Washington take Route 47 north to Route 202, turn left, and then turn right onto Route 45. About 2 miles up on the left, you'll come to North Shore Road. Turn onto it and take the second right onto Hopkins Road, which is home to **Hopkins Vineyard,** 25 Hopkins Road, New Preston, CT 06777 (860–868–7954). There are tours of the winery as well as tastings.

LUNCH: The **Boulders Inn,** East Shore Road, New Preston, CT 06777 (860–868–0541), starts serving "dinner" at noon on Sunday. The fare is contemporary New England cuisine.

After lunch (or an early dinner) take a leisurely drive around the lake before heading back to New York City.

There's More

Bird-watching. There are plenty of opportunities to pull out the binoculars in the Litchfield area. Here are some of the best spots:

H. C. Barnes Memorial Nature Center, 175 Shrub Road, Bristol, CT 06010; (860) 589–6082.

Flanders Nature Center, office at Flanders Road, off Route 6, Woodbury, CT 06798; (860) 263–3711.

Audubon Center at Sharon, 325 Route 4, Sharon, CT 06069; (860) 364–0520.

White Memorial Foundation, Route 202, Litchfield, CT 06759; (860) 567–0857.

Horseback riding. Lee's Riding Stable, Inc., East Litchfield Road (off Route 118), Litchfield, CT 06759; (860) 567–0785.

Skiing. Mohawk Mountain Ski Area, Great Hollow Road, Cornwall, CT 06753; (860) 672–6100. Connecticut's largest ski resort, with 23 trails.

Special Events

Mid-June. Laurel Festival, Winsted. Driving routes for viewing mountain laurels in bloom; laurel queen; parade. For more information call (860) 379–2713.

Mid-June through mid-August. Norfolk Chamber Music Festival, Norfolk. This annual festival takes place on the grounds of a charming nineteenth-century estate. For program and ticket information, call (203) 432–1966 between September and May or (860) 542–3000 during June, July, and August.

Mid-July. Annual Litchfield Open House Tour, Litchfield. Tour includes Litchfield homes of historic and architectural interest. Call (860) 567–9423 for more information.

Late September. Fall Festival, Kent. An annual festival on the grounds of the Connecticut Antique Machinery Museum.

Other Recommended Restaurants and Lodgings

Litchfield

Tollgate Hill Inn and Restaurant, Route 202 (Tollgate Road), Litchfield, CT 06759; (860) 567–4545. This is both a delightful inn and an award-winning restaurant specializing in contemporary American cuisine.

New Preston

Boulders Inn, East Shore Road, New Preston, CT 06777; (860) 868–0541. This country inn on Lake Waramaug has a selection of accommodations in the main house (built in 1895), the carriage house, and guest houses.

Salisbury

White Hart Inn, Village Green (Routes 41 and 44), Salisbury, CT 06068; (860) 435–0030. Both a welcoming inn and fine choice for meals, the White Hart Inn is a meticulously renovated inn that began operating in the early nineteenth century. Informal meals are served in the Tap Room (be sure to try the house pâté), whereas more elegant meals (dinner only) are served in the Sea Grill Restaurant.

Under Mountain Inn, 482 Under Mountain Road, Salisbury, CT 06068; (860) 435–0242. This is a gracious little B&B in an eighteenth-century farmhouse.

For More Information

Connecticut Office of Tourism, Department of Economic Development, 505 Hudson Street, Hartford, CT 06067-3405; (860) 270–8080 or (800) 282–6863.

Litchfield Hills Visitors Bureau, P.O. Box 968, Litchfield, CT 06759; (860) 567–4506.

Newport

Masts and Mansions

2 Nights

Gleaming yachts, palatial mansions, Newport Jazz Festival, tennis tournaments—these are the things that come to most people's minds at the mere mention of Newport. This sensationally situated Rhode Island city (poised on the southern tip of Aquidneck Island and bounded by water on three sides) does offer a slice of the good life.

☐ Opulent summer cottages

☐ Historic waterfront

☐ Oldest standing synagogue in the United States

☐ Renowned restaurants

☐ Sailing

☐ Tennis

☐ Beaches

Newport had two periods of history during which it enjoyed prominence. During colonial days it was a very important trade center. Later on, in the nineteenth-century "Gilded Age," it became a popular resort for old-money families (including the Vanderbilts, Astors, and Belmonts) who built opulent summer "cottages."

Thanks to the Preservation Society of Newport County and the Newport Restoration Foundation, the history of Newport has been beautifully restored and preserved. During a short visit you can combine a walking tour of its colonial section in the northwest with a driving tour of its enormous mansions in the southern end.

Newport is a place you can go back to year after year, discovering new places or revisiting old ones. Squeezing everything into one weekend is a tall order, especially if you want to spend some time relaxing on a veranda or a breezy beach.

Day 1 / Morning

The fastest way to reach Newport from New York is to take I–95 north

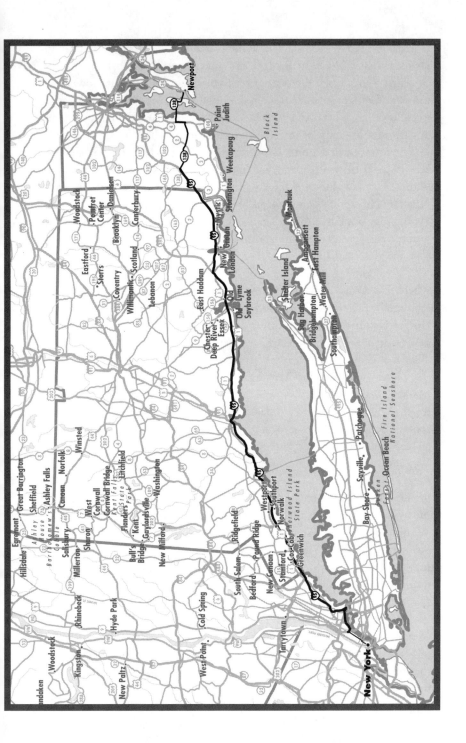

to exit 3A, Route 138 east, in Rhode Island. Follow 138 east over the Jamestown and Newport Bridges and directly into Newport. First things first: Ditch your car. If you're staying at the Inntowne, you can park for a nominal fee (free in the off-season). You'll spend today touring **Colonial Newport,** which can best be explored on foot. It's the northwestern section of the city, clustered around the harbor.

A good starting point is Washington Street, which runs from Long Wharf to Battery Park and is lined with old gas lamps and Colonial houses. From Washington Square walk north and make your first stop **Hunter House,** 54 Washington Street, Newport, RI 02840 (401–847–1000). This Colonial home dates from 1748 and has been faithfully restored inside and out. It's open from May through October from 10:00 A.M. to 5:00 P.M. daily.

From Hunter House walk north up Washington to Popular Street, where you'll turn right and follow to Farewell Street. Here there are several ancient cemeteries including an eighteenth-century **Common Burial Ground** on Warner Street (a continuation of Popular Street on the other side of Farewell Street). From there walk south on Farewell Street to Thaymes Street until you reach Washington Square.

Here you'll find the **Museum of Newport History** at the Brick Market (Washington and Touro Streets, Newport, RI 02840; 401–841–8770), which was built in 1760 and has been used in a variety of ways. For some time it was used as a theater, later on it was a town hall, and now it's an exhibit hall devoted to Newport history. It's open Monday and Wednesday through Saturday from 10:00 A.M. to 5:00 P.M. and Sunday from 1:00 to 5:00 P.M. from April through October. Hours are 10:00 A.M. to 4:00 P.M. Friday and Saturday and 1:00 to 4:00 P.M. Sunday from November through March. Nearby you'll see the **Old Colony House** on Washington Square, (Newport, RI 02840; 401–846–2980) which was the headquarters of the Colonial and state governments. The Declaration of Independence was read from the balcony of this building. In summer months there are tours Monday through Saturday from 9:00 A.M. to 4:00 P.M. Tours are conducted by appointment only; call ahead.

Newport's oldest house, the **Wanton–Lyman Hazard House,** is a couple of blocks away at 17 Broadway, Newport, RI 02840 (401–846–0813). Here you'll find a museum, eighteenth-century cooking demonstrations, and a Colonial garden. Hours are Thursday through Saturday, from 10:00 A.M. to 4:00 P.M. in summer; other times by appointment.

The **White Horse Tavern** can be your next stop. Walk west on Broadway and north on Farewell to Marlborough Street; it's on the corner. This Newport landmark has been in operation since 1687.

LUNCH: The **White Horse Tavern**, 26 Marlborough Street, Newport, RI 02840 (401–849–3600), combines both historical charm (fireplaces, dark-beamed ceilings, slanting wood floors) and decent food (salads, seafood, some pasta dishes). If it's a beautiful day and you'd rather picnic, stop by the **Market-Newport Cafe,** 43 Memorial Boulevard, Newport, RI 02840 (401–848–2600), where you can pick up picnic fixings.

Afternoon

On the same corner you'll find the **Great Friends Meeting House,** 29 Farewell Street, Newport, RI 02840 (401–846–0813), which dates from 1699. It's the oldest Quaker meetinghouse in America. It's open Thursday through Saturday in summer; other times by appointment.

From there walk back through Washington Square and turn left onto Touro Street, where you'll find the **Touro Synagogue,** 85 Touro Street, Newport, RI 02840 (401–847–4794), the oldest standing temple in the United States. Call ahead for the current tour schedule. Open Thursday through Saturday during the summer, 10:00 A.M. to 4:00 P.M. The **Newport Historical Society** (401–846–0813) is a couple of doors down at 82 Touro Street, Newport, RI 02840. Many of the guided walking tours begin here. Inside there's a museum devoted to local history. Hours are Tuesday through Friday from 9:30 A.M. to 4:30 P.M. and Saturday from 9:30 A.M. to noon.

Walk south down Division Street to the corner of Spring and Church Streets and you'll spot **Trinity Church** on Queen Anne Square, Newport, RI 02840 (401–846–0660), a beautiful example of Colonial architecture. When it was built in 1726, it was hailed as "the most beautiful timber structure in America." It's open daily from 10:00 A.M. to 4:00 P.M.

Carry on east along Church Street to the **Redwood Library,** 50 Bellevue Avenue, Newport, RI 02840 (401–847–0292) at the beginning of Bellevue Avenue. Not only is this the country's oldest library in continuous use, but it has a wonderful collection of Early American paintings inside. Guided tours are available Monday through Friday at 10:30 A.M. The library is otherwise open Tuesday through Thursday from 9:30 A.M. to 8:00 P.M., Monday, Friday, and Saturday from 9:30 A.M. to 5:30 P.M., and Sunday from 1:00 to 5:00 P.M.

The **Newport Art Museum and Art Association,** 76 Bellevue Avenue, Newport, RI 02840 (401–848–8200), is on the next block. It showcases changing exhibits by contemporary New England artists. It's open Tuesday through Saturday from 10:00 A.M. to 5:00 P.M. and Sunday from 1:00 to 5:00 P.M.

Turn left onto Memorial Boulevard and follow it to the end where the 3-mile **Cliff Walk** begins. The walk, which is a little challenging (don't attempt it if you're traveling with young children or a handicapped person), takes you along Newport's cliffs, offering fabulous views of many of its mansions.

DINNER: **La Petite Auberge,** 19 Charles Street, Newport, RI 02840 (401–849–6669), is a well-established restaurant in town, serving celestial French cuisine.

LODGING: **Inntowne Inn,** 6 Mary Street, Newport, RI 02840 (401–846–9200 or 800–457–7803) is located within easy walking distance of many Newport sights. Each of the seventeen rooms in this bed and breakfast is attractively and individually decorated. Because time is limited, it's a good idea to book two nights' lodging rather than changing hotels for your second night.

Day 2 / Morning

BREAKFAST: A continental breakfast is included in the price at the Inntowne Inn.

You'll spend most of today exploring the mansions for which Newport is so famous. Because distances between them can be long, your best bet is to drive. Several of them have guided tours that last about an hour. Most of the mansions are open daily between 10:00 A.M. and 5:00 P.M. in summer; winter hours vary. The Breakers opens at 9:00 A.M. For information on the mansions, call The Preservation Society of Newport County at (401) 847–1000.

Start by visiting **Kingscote,** Bowery Street off Bellevue Avenue, which is relatively modest compared with some of the others. It was built in 1840 for a plantation owner. The **Elms,** which is a little farther south on Bellevue, is a classical building surrounded by formal gardens, fountains, and a sweeping lawn. It was built for a coal baron at the turn of the century. Continue south on Bellevue and you'll come to **Château-sur-Mer,** which was the residence of William Shepard Wetmore, who made his fortune in the China trade. The most famous of the Newport mansions, the **Breakers,** is on Ochre Point Avenue (turn left on Victoria and continue to Ochre Point Avenue). This stunning property has seventy rooms. It was built in 1893 for Cornelius Vanderbilt II and his family. Return to Bellevue and continue south to **Rosecliff,** which has been used as a set for several movies, including *The Great Gatsby.* Farther south on Bellevue is the **Astor's Beechwood.** Here you can watch costumed actors and actresses re-create the lives of the Astor family, their guests, and staff. **Marble House** is the next stop continuing down Bellevue. This house, which must be seen to be believed, was designed by Beaux Arts–trained Richard Morris Hunt, whom William K. Vanderbilt asked to create "the very best living accommodations that money could buy." The last mansion to visit on Bellevue Avenue is **Belcourt Castle,** which is filled with European and oriental treasures.

LUNCH: During the summer months the **Inn at Castle Hill** at 590 Ocean Drive, Newport, RI 02840 (401–849–3800) serves a great brunch (reservations are a must). Other times of the year, your best bet is to head back into town and take your pick of great lunch spots.

Afternoon

Ocean Drive follows the coast past **Hammersmith Farm.** The childhood home of Jacqueline Bouvier Kennedy Onassis is now privately owned and no longer open to the public but sits up on a hill and can be seen from the road.

Nearby is the **Museum of Yachting,** Fort Adams State Park, Ocean Drive, Newport, RI 02840 (401–847–1018), which showcases highlights of the America's Cup and other sailing events. It's open from mid-May through October, daily from 10:00 A.M. to 5:00 P.M.; the rest of the year by appointment.

DINNER: There are several good restaurants on the wharves along Newport Harbor including the **Black Pearl,** Bannister's Wharf, Newport, RI 02840 (401–846–5264), which serves mostly American fare and seafood.

LODGING: Return to the Inntowne Inn (or whatever other hotel you stayed in the first night).

Day 3 / *Morning*

BREAKFAST: The Inntowne Inn serves a continental breakfast to its guests, the cost of which is included in the room rate.

After breakfast make your way over to the **International Tennis Hall of Fame** and the **Tennis Museum** located in the Newport Casino which was designed by McKim, Mead and White (194 Bellevue Avenue, Newport, RI 02840; 401–849–3990). The first National Tennis Championships were held here in 1881. The hall of fame and museum are open from 9:30 A.M. to 5:00 P.M. daily.

Then return to the wharves for a look around the shops before heading back to New York City (take Route 138 west back to I–95 and follow that south to the metropolitan area).

There's More

Beaches. Newport Beach, on Memorial Boulevard, and King Park and Beach, on Wellington Avenue, are open to the public. There's also a small beach at Fort Adams State Park.

Bikes. Bikes can be rented at Ten-Speed Spokes, 18 Elm Street, Newport, RI 02840; (401) 847–5609.

Harbor Cruises. The Spirit of Newport (401–849–3575) gives one-hour cruises of Newport Harbor and Narragansett Bay. They depart daily from the Newport Harbour Inn on America's Cup Avenue from early May through late October every hour and a half.

State Park. Fort Adams State Park on Ocean Drive surrounds Fort Adams. Here you can enjoy beach swimming, fishing, boating, and picnicking.

Vintage Dinner Train. The Newport Dinner Train leaves the depot at 19 America's Cup Avenue, Newport, RI 02840; (401) 841–8700 or (800) 398–7427. This is a vintage train designed to take passengers back to an era of grace and romance. As you cruise along enjoying the scenery out a picture window, you'll feast on a gourmet meal replete with crystal, china, and linen.

Newport's harbor is always filled with yachts and sailboats.

Special Events

March. Newport Irish Heritage Month. Throughout the town there are a variety of events including concerts, plays, arts and crafts, a parade, and more.

Mid-August. JVC Jazz Festival, Newport. Outdoor concerts by some of the world's best jazz musicians.

December (month long). Christmas in Newport. Citywide celebration. Concerts, candlelight tours, Festival of Trees, Holly Ball, and visits by St. Nicholas.

Other Recommended Restaurants and Lodgings

Middletown

Flo's Clam Shack, 4 Wave Avenue, Middletown, RI 02841; (401) 847–8141. The place to go if you're in the mood for fried clams and oysters, lobster rolls, or raw shellfish.

Newport

Elm Tree Cottage, 336 Gibbs Avenue, Newport, RI 02840; (401) 849–1610. A beautiful, historic mansion, now a B&B, within easy walking distance of the beach.

Francis Malbone House, 392 Thames Street, Newport, RI 02840; (800) 846–0392. An inn with eighteen antiques-filled rooms situated around a central garden. The building itself was designed in 1760.

Inn at Castle Hill, Ocean Drive, Newport, RI 02840; (401) 849–3800. A classic New England inn with views of Newport Harbor.

Ivy Lodge, 12 Clay Street, Newport, RI 02840; (401) 849–6865. This is a small bed and breakfast close to many of the cottages along Bellevue.

Mama Luisa, 673 Thames Street, Newport, RI 02840; (401) 848–5257. This restaurant prides itself on its superb Italian food. Try the pumpkin-filled ravioli.

Mill Street Inn, 75 Mill Street, Newport, RI 02840; (401) 849–9500 or (800) 392–1316. Located close to the harbor and restaurants, this hotel offers contemporary suites.

Newport Harbor Hotel & Marina, 49 America's Cup Avenue, Newport, RI 02840; (401) 849–9000 or (800) 955–2558. Located in the heart of town, this hotel has wonderful harbor views as well as a full-service marina.

Weekapaug

Weekapaug Inn, 25 Spray Rock Road, Weekapaug, RI 02891; (401) 322–0301. If you want to consider extending your trip to combine a city visit with a night or two by the shore, book a room at the Weekapaug Inn. The inn is located only 12 miles from I–95, shortly after you cross the border from Connecticut into Rhode Island. Open during the summer only, it provides a wonderful retreat with easy access to a 2-mile-long glorious ocean beach. The inn is family-friendly and features all sorts of water sports, plus tennis, golf, croquet, and shuffleboard, and the food is outstanding. It makes for a wonderful weekend escape on its own, but reserve early. Loyal guests return year after year.

For More Information

Preservation Society of Newport County, 118 Mill Street, Newport, RI 02840; (401) 847–1000.

Newport County Convention and Visitor's Bureau, 23 America's Cup Avenue, Newport, RI 02840; (401) 849–8048 or (800) 326–6030.

Rhode Island Tourism Division Information Center, Route 95N, Hope Valley, Hopkinton, RI 02832; (401) 539–3031 or (800) 556–2484.

Block Island—
With or Without a Car

Offshore Touring

2 Nights

Anchored 12 miles off the coast of mainland Rhode Island, this bite-size island (a mere 11 square miles) is strewn with wildflowers, dotted with shingled cottages and placid pools, crisscrossed by hundreds of miles of stone walls, surrounded by white, duney beaches, and, on one coast, edged by cliffs that rise 200 feet above the sea.

- ☐ Beaches
- ☐ Bicycling
- ☐ Bird-watching
- ☐ Seafood
- ☐ Fishing
- ☐ Horseback Riding
- ☐ Sailing
- ☐ Tennis
- ☐ Water Sports

During summer months the island is its liveliest, with at least half a dozen ferries a day shuttling day-trippers over from the mainland. Most of them don't get much farther than Water Street and the nearby beaches, however, which leaves the rest of the island blissfully peaceful. Unlike some northeastern islands, Block Island has not fallen prey to the customary tourist trappings such as fast-food chains and tacky souvenir shops. In fact, there are not even any traffic lights on the island.

If you want to experience the island as the locals do, consider visiting during a weekend in October, when there's a slight nip in the air and not another tourist in sight.

Whatever time of year you go, for a short visit, your best bet is to leave your car on the mainland, ferry over, and rent bikes to get around. You can take a ferry from the Galilee State Pier in Point Judith, year-round, or from New London (Connecticut), Providence, and Newport during the summer months. There are also ferries from Montauk, Long Island, New York.

By the way, many places close on Block Island during winter months. Call the Block Island Tourism Council to check (800–383–2474 or 401–466–5200).

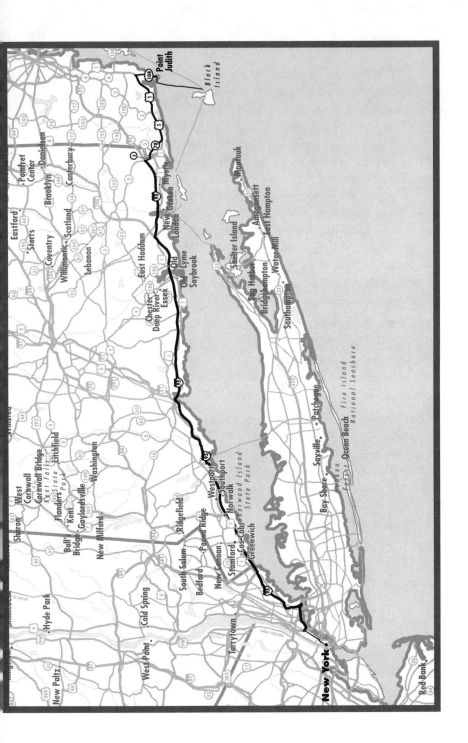

Day 1 / *Morning and Afternoon*

If you're traveling without a car, you'll probably spend a good chunk of the day traveling to the island. During summer months only, you can take Amtrak to New London, Connecticut, and then take a two-hour ferry ride over. On Friday the ferry leaves at 7:15 P.M. You can also take Amtrak to Westerly, Rhode Island, and then grab a cab over to the airport and fly to the island (it's a twelve-minute flight). For phone numbers, see "For More Information."

If you're driving your own car, take exit 92 off I–95N. Bear right onto North Stonington Road (Route 2E). Take a right onto Route 78. At the end of Route 78, turn left onto Route 1S. Follow that to the Galilee/Point Judith exit. Turn right onto Route 108 off the exit and then bear right onto Route 108S. Continue on Route 108S to the Block Island Ferry exit. If you want to take your car over to the island, be sure to have reservations well in advance.

DINNER: The **Oar,** at the Boat Basin in New Harbor, Block Island, RI 02807; (401) 466–8820. This casual restaurant is owned by the same family that owns and runs the island's successful Hotel Manisses and the 1661 Inn. Specialties include johnnycakes, fresh fish, burgers, New England clam chowder, and a raw bar serving raw shellfish.

LODGING: An elegant choice is the **Hotel Manisses,** Spring Street, Block Island, RI 02807(401–466–2421 or 800–MANISSES), a Victorian hotel (built in 1882, but renovated in the 1970s) within walking distance of the ferry landing in Old Harbor. Plan to stay there both nights so that you don't have to waste time moving.

Day 2 / *Morning*

BREAKFAST: When you stay at the **Hotel Manisses,** Spring Street (401–466–2421), breakfast—which is actually served in the **1661 Inn,** its sister inn—is included in the room price. It's a buffet breakfast with a selection of fish, waffles, French toast, roasted potatoes, corned beef hash, scrambled eggs, fruit juices, and fresh muffins. The setting, on a hill overlooking the water, is a wonderful place to start the day.

Lounging around on a white sandy beach is usually the top priority for most Block Island–bound weekenders. Nevertheless there are a handful of attractions to see as well as sensationally scenic roads to bike along. You'll find shops on Water Street, Dodge Street, and Weldon's Way that rent bikes.

Block Island's Southeast Lighthouse was originally built in 1874.

Though mopeds can also be rented, you'll find that the locals are not terribly fond of them because of the noise and the danger (there are several dozen accidents reported annually). Bicycles generally can be rented for between $6.00 (for a three-speed) and $12.00 (for a ten-speed) a day.

Make your first cycling destination **Mohegan Bluffs** and the nearby **Southeast Lighthouse.** You can do the trip in about an hour and get back to town for lunch and a browse around the shops. Start by heading out of town south on High Street. Though the road starts off hilly, it flattens out after a short distance, so don't panic. En route you'll pass the Block Island School, where all students on the island, from kindergarten to twelfth grade, go. The total enrollment hovers around a little more than one hundred students! Shortly after passing the school, the pavement ends and the road changes its name to Pilot Hill Road. Carry on and you'll eventually come to Mohegan Trail. Turn left and follow it until you come to a dirt road on the right. There's a rack where you can lock up your bike and then follow the path out to see the beautiful clay cliffs that drop dramatically into the water. Supposedly, in 1590, local island Indians (the Manisseans) fought off Mohegan Indians by forcing them to plunge over the cliffs to their deaths. The Southeast Lighthouse, which was recently moved 245 feet inland to save it from erosion, was originally built in 1874. It has one of the most powerful electric beacons on the East Coast, capable of being seen from as far away as 30 miles out to sea.

The return trip to town is largely downhill and takes you past many Victorian houses as well as along a piece of the island's shore.

Take time out to look around inside the **Spring Street Gallery** (across from the Hotel Manisses), where many local artists display their work. There are more galleries in town and several gift shops where you can buy local pottery, watercolors, and other Block Island originals.

LUNCH: Expect to wait for a table at the **Harborside Inn,** Water Street, Block Island, RI 02807 (401–466–5504). It's one of the island's most popular lunch spots, with a terrace cafe where you can get anything from a burger to a local seafood dish (such as broiled scallops or baked stuffed clams). It's right across the street from the ferry dock.

Afternoon

After lunch grab your towel, sunblock, and visor and plant yourself on the beach. **Crescent Beach,** which you'll spot as you come in on the ferry, is a popular choice. It stretches from Old Harbor for 3 miles north to the cliffs of Clay Head. For your own isolated piece of beach, simply wander north until the footprints thin out.

Later on if you feel like doing a little more pedaling, head to the southwest part of the island. All said and done, it'll take you about two hours. From Old Harbor take Chapel Street to Old Town Road to Center Road. Turn left and then right onto **Beacon Hill Road,** a rough dirt road leading to the island's highest point, a dizzying height of 210 feet above sea level. Don't laugh; there's a great view of the island from up there.

Turn left when you get back to Center Road and follow it up to West Side Road, where you'll turn left (by the Island Cemetery). This route takes you through some of the island's most densely scenic landscapes. Along the way pull over to see the view at the **West Side Baptist Church.** Carry on to Cooneymus Road where you'll take a left. This takes you to **Rodman's Hollow,** a glacial ravine. If you continue east on Cooneymus, you'll come to Old Mill Road and then **Smilin' Through,** a farmhouse once owned by director Arthur Penn. At the intersection that follows, you'll find the island's **Indian Cemetery,** which dates from some 300 years ago to the original settlers. Turn south onto Lakeside Drive. When the road turns sharply, consider continuing straight on Snake Hole Road, a dirt road; it leads to a beach area and wilderness preserve. Afterward follow the Mohegan Trail to Southeast Road and Spring Street back into town.

A beautiful way to top off the day is to sip drinks on the veranda of the **Spring House Hotel** (401–466–5844), looking out over the ocean at sunset.

DINNER: For the best food and setting on the island, choose the **Hotel Manisses,** Spring Street, Block Island, RI 02807 (401–466–2836), which is also a beautiful place to stay. The menu changes but almost always includes a good choice of local fish as well as roast duck and chicken dishes.

After dinner don't miss a Saturday night visit to the **Yellow Kittens,** Corn Neck Road, Block Island, RI 02807 (401–466–5855), which has live bands (rock and roll, country, rhythm and blues—you name it) during summer months.

LODGING: Return to the Hotel Manisses (or wherever else you stayed the first night).

Day 3 / Morning

BREAKFAST: Your best bet is to leisurely greet the day with breakfast in the hotel's dining room again. Once you feel revived and ready to roll, hop back on your bike for a trip to the northern part of the island. It's about a three-hour trip, starting and finishing in town near the Old Harbor.

Start by following Water Street and then turn onto Dodge. At the four-way intersection, turn right onto Corn Neck Road. Though it runs alongside Crescent Beach for about a mile, the view is often obstructed by dunes covered with sea grass. It's easy enough, however, to climb over and feast your eyes on the view. On the left is the **Great Salt Pond,** which is very good for shellfishing and shell collecting.

For a beach break, turn right onto Mansion Road, a dirt road leading to **Mansion Beach,** so named because it used to offer a view of the Edward Searles Mansion, which, unfortunately, burned down in the early 1960s.

Turn right once you get back to Corn Neck Road. You'll pass West Beach Road on the left and then come to **Clay Head Trail** on the right.

Follow it and you'll reach what is popularly known as the **Maze,** a webwork of trails winding through a wildlife preserve.

Once again get back on Corn Neck. After you pass **Sachem Pond** (a favorite swimming area), you'll reach the end of Corn Neck Road and **Settlers' Rock,** which was where Block Island's sixteen original white settlers landed on the island. This area is known as **Cow Cove.** Off in the distance you'll see the **North Light House** on Sandy Point, which has been standing since 1867. Take time to walk out to it, but avoid swimming as the currents are very strong; in fact, this area is also known as the **Palatine Graves,** where a ship sank in the 1700s.

LUNCH: For deliriously good and spanking-fresh seafood and fish dishes, choose **Finn's Seafood Restaurant,** Water Street, Block Island, RI 02807 (401–466–2473), in Old Harbor. They have their own fish market plus indoor and outdoor dining—and takeout, too.

Afternoon

If you didn't get enough time on the beach yesterday, spend the afternoon lolling about before catching the ferry back to the mainland. Retrace your route back to New York City.

There's More

Fishing. Several marinas on the island have boats for hire. Stop by any of the boat-rental and sportfishing businesses in New Harbor.

Horseback riding. Rustic Rides Farm, West Side Road; (401) 466–5060. There are guided rides, carriage rides, and pony rides for children.

Tennis. There are tennis courts at the Block Island Club on Corn Neck Road, Champlain's Marina in New Harbor, and the Neptune House on Connecticut Avenue.

Water Sports. You can go sailing and parasailing at Block Island Parasail (Old Harbor Dock; 401–864–2474) and take out kayaks and canoes or go sportfishing at Oceans and Ponds at the Orvis Store (Ocean and Center Avenues; 401–466–5131).

Special Events

Mid-June. Taste of Block Island Seafood Festival and Chowder Cook-Off. This is a great chance to sample all sorts of local seafood dishes.

June. Race Week on Block Island. An around-the-island race, this annual event is one of the largest sailing events on the East Coast.

July 4th weekend. To celebrate the Fourth, Block Island has fireworks, a parade, and a big barbecue.

Mid-August. Annual Block Island House & Garden Tour. Houses around Great Salt Pond open their doors and garden gates to the public.

Mid-September. Annual "Run Around the Block." This is a 15K road race around the island.

Early October. Block Island Birding Weekend. An ideal bird-watching island, especially during spring and fall. The Audubon Society of Rhode Island organizes a weekend of guided walks.

Other Recommended Restaurants and Lodgings

Atlantic Inn, High Street, Block Island, RI 02807; (401) 466–5883. A mansard-roofed Victorian dating from 1890, this is a delightful hotel with views of the old harbor.

1661 Inn and Guest House, Spring Street, Block Island, RI 02807; (401) 466–2421 or (800) 626–4773. Owned by the same family as the Manisses, the 1661 is a large white island house with twenty-eight thoughtfully and tastefully decorated guest rooms.

For More Information

Block Island Tourism Council, 23 Water Street, Block Island, RI 02807; (401) 466–5200 or (800) 383–2474.

Rhode Island Tourism Division Information Center, Route 95N, Hope Valley, Hopkinton, RI 02832; (401) 539–3031 or (800) 556–2484.

Getting There

By train: Amtrak (800) 872–7245

By bus: Greyhound (800) 231–2222

Bonanza (888) 331–7500

Rhode Island Public Transit Authority (401) 781–9400

By air: New England Airlines (800) 243–2460

By ferry: Interstate Navigation operates ferries from Point Judith, New London, Providence, and Newport. Call (401) 783–4613 for schedules and prices. For ferry information from Montauk, call Viking Ferry Lines at (631) 668–5700.

MASSACHUSETTS
ESCAPES

The Berkshires

Music, Mansions, and More

2 Nights

The Berkshire Hills are known for both their rural beauty (sprawling farms, tidy little villages, dozen of lakes and ponds, thousands of acres of forest) and their cultural assets (they're home to the Tanglewood Music Festival and Jacob's Pillow Dance Festival). Located in the western quarter of the state, they stretch all the way from Connecticut to Vermont (just south of the Green Mountains). The area, which is now massively popular for weekenders, especially during the summer months, first became famous when Nathaniel Hawthorne wrote *Tanglewood Tales*. Route 7 takes you right through the heart of them, passing through a series of wonderful little towns including Stockbridge, Lenox, Pittsfield, and Williamstown.

☐ Performing arts

☐ Fine dining

☐ Country inns

☐ Antiques and crafts shops

☐ Galleries

☐ Historical homes

☐ Rural scenery

☐ Hiking

During July and August, when the Tanglewood Music Festival and the area's other performing arts are in full bloom, the Berkshires can be very crowded. Many inns require a three-night minimum stay, and there are long waits at restaurants and cultural attractions. Your best bet is to visit midweek.

Day 1 / Morning

Head north on Route 684, then east on Route 84 to Route 7 north. Route 7 takes you right to the southern Berkshires.

Shortly after you cross over the Connecticut border into Massachusetts, turn onto Route 7A to reach **Ashley Falls.** Follow the signs from the center of Ashley Falls to your first stop, **Bartholomew's Cobble** (413–229–8600), a 294–acre preserve of 500-million-year-old

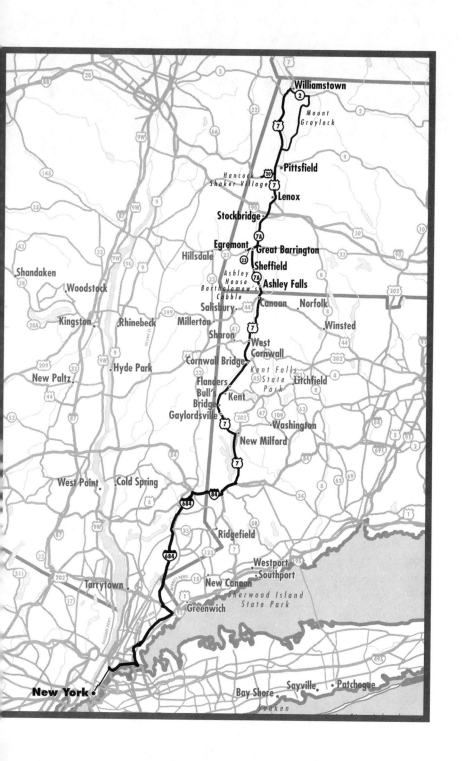

marble outcroppings above the Housatonic River. You can stretch your legs a bit by following the Ledges Interpretive Trail, which introduces you to some of the preserve's amazing variety of plants and flowers. Trails are open daily, year-round, from sunrise to sunset. Just across a field (you'll see signs) is the **Colonel John Ashley House** (also 413–229–8600), which dates from 1735, making it one of the oldest houses in the county. It's open from Memorial Day weekend through Columbus Day, Saturday and Sunday only plus those two Mondays, from 1:00 to 5:00 P.M.

Continue north on Route 7A to get back on Route 7 and **Sheffield,** your next stop. This town is crammed with antiques shops (a directory of who sells what is available in each one). Sheffield is also home to the state's oldest covered bridge (look for the red sign on the right).

Once you've done the shops of Sheffield, keep heading north on Route 7 until you reach Route 23 west. Turn left and follow it into **South Egremont,** where you can pause for lunch and have a look around more antiques shops and galleries.

LUNCH: **Gaslight Cafe,** Main Street, South Egremont, MA 01258; (413) 528–0870. Here you can grab a big club sandwich, a burger, or the cafe's special asparagus melt. The cafe is open every day (except Tuesday) for breakfast and lunch.

Afternoon

Backtrack to Route 7 and carry on to **Great Barrington,** where you'll find more shops, and then press on for about another 4 miles until you see **Monument Mountain** looming before you. If you're feeling up for it, take time out to hike to the summit. Be prepared, however; it could take about two or three hours.

The next stop is **Stockbridge,** which many people know from Norman Rockwell's famous illustrations that first appeared on the covers of the *Saturday Evening Post* and *McCall's.* You can see some of the original covers as well as the world's largest collection of the illustrator's works in the **Norman Rockwell Museum,** Route 183, Stockbridge, MA 01262 (413–298–4100). Hours are 10:00 A.M. to 5:00 P.M. daily from May through October and 10:00 A.M. to 4:00 P.M. Monday through Friday and 10:00 A.M. to 5:00 P.M. Saturday and Sunday from November through April. Just up the road from the museum is **Chesterwood,** Route 183, Stockbridge, MA 01262 (413–298–3579), the summer home of Daniel Chester French, who sculpted the *Seated Lincoln* in the Lincoln Memorial.

Antiques shops abound in the Berkshires.

The museum is open daily from 10:00 A.M. to 5:00 P.M. from May through October. There are house and studio tours as well as gardens and a museum of the artist's works. Two other top Stockbridge attractions are the **Mission House,** Main Street, Stockbridge, MA 01262 (413–298–3239), which houses a fine collection of Early American furnishings, and **Naumkeag,** Prospect Hill Road, Stockbridge, MA 01262 (414–298–3239), a summer "cottage" that was used during the nineteenth-century "gilded era" when families such as the Vanderbilts and Westinghouses vacationed in these hills. Both the Mission House and Naumkeag are open daily from 10:00 A.M. to 5:00 P.M. from Memorial Day to Columbus Day.

The **Red Lion Inn** on Main Street has been a major Stockbridge landmark for more than 200 years. Consider stopping in for a drink in the courtyard or on one of the rockers on the front porch. Then wander around the shops that crowd around Main Street.

DINNER: Choose the **Old Mill,** Route 23, South Egremont, MA 01258 (413–528–1421), which was once a blacksmith's shop as well as a mill. It's one of the most highly regarded restaurants in the Berkshires, with a good selection of fish, chicken, and steak dishes. An alternative is the **Castle Street Cafe,** 10 Castle Street, Great Barrington, MA 01230 (413–528–5244), a popular bistro (reservations are a must) known for its deliriously good pasta and grilled fish dishes.

LODGING: Year-round it's important to make reservations at Berkshire inns. During the busy months expect to find many places full. Though pricey, the **Red Lion Inn,** 30 Main Street, Stockbridge, MA 01262 (413–298–5545), which was originally built in 1773 as a stagecoach stop, is a New England classic.

Evening

In addition to Tanglewood (just north of Stockbridge in Lenox) and Jacob's Pillow (east of Stockbridge in Becket), the southern Berkshires have an abundance of other shows and cultural events. For program information and tickets, call ahead: Berkshire Choral Institute (413–229–8526); Aston Magna Festival (413–528–3595); Berkshire Opera Company (413–644–9000); Stockbridge Summer Music Series (413–443–1138); and DeSisto Estate Dinner Theatre and Cabaret (413–298–4032).

Day 2 / Morning

BREAKFAST: Enjoy a continental breakfast of oatmeal, granola, bagels, and fruit at the Red Lion Inn.

Afterward head north out of Stockbridge on Route 7. About 5 miles up, at the junction of Routes 7 and 7A, you'll find the **Mount,** Two Plunkett Street at the south junction of Routes 7 and 7A, Lenox, MA 01240 (413–637–1899), which was the summer residence of novelist Edith Wharton. The house, a Classical Revival, is sensationally situated on forty-nine acres. It's open daily between early June and early November, 9:00 A.M. to 5:00 P.M. (house) or 9:00 A.M. to 6:00 P.M (grounds).

Follow Route 7A to **Lenox,** which is home to **Tanglewood,** on West Street, Lenox, MA 01240 (413–637–1600), where legendary music can be heard under the stars throughout the summer months. Tanglewood is the summer home for the Boston Symphony Orchestra. If you're not planning to attend a performance, do take time to stroll around the grounds (there are 210 acres including formal gardens), which are open daily.

LUNCH: Church Street Cafe, 65 Church Street, Lenox, MA 01240 (413–637–2745), is a very successful bistro with all sorts of eclectic and ethnic dishes. Try to get a table outside if the weather's nice (closed Sunday and Monday from October through May).

Afternoon

From Lenox drive north on Route 7, making a stop at the **Berkshire Museum** in **Pittsfield,** right on Route 7 (locally known as South Street) at 39 South Street, Pittsfield, MA 01201 (413–443–7171). It has a good collection of nineteenth- and twentieth-century paintings as well as some local exhibits. It's open Monday through Saturday from 10:00 A.M. to 5:00 P.M. and Sunday from noon to 5:00 P.M. Also in Pittsfield is **Arrowhead,** 780 Holmes Road, Pittsfield, MA 01201 (413–442–1793), the house where Herman Melville wrote *Moby-Dick* along with three other novels. It's open from Memorial Day through October 31, daily from 9:30 A.M. to 5:00 P.M., and by appointment only the rest of the year.

About 5 miles west of Pittsfield (at the junction of Routes 20 and 41) is **Hancock Shaker Village,** Pittsfield, MA 01201 (413–443–0188), a living-history museum devoted to the Shakers. For about 200 years (1781–1960), the site was a Shaker community. It's open daily year-round. Late October through the Sunday of Memorial Day weekend hours are 10:00 A.M. to 3:00 P.M. From Memorial Day to late October, hours are 9:30 A.M. to 5:00 P.M.

The final stop for the day and your home for the night is **Williamstown,** which is not far from the Vermont border. Among the town's most notable attractions are the **Sterling and Francine Clark Art Institute,** 225 South Street, Williamstown, MA 01267 (413–458–2302), an outstanding collection of French Impressionists (including Renoirs) and Old Masters (open daily from 10:00 A.M. to 5:00 P.M.); and **Williams College,** 1 block east of the central green (413–597–3131), which has a fine collection of paintings as well as one of the nation's best collections of rare books.

DINNER: The **Orchards,** 222 Adams Road, Williamstown, MA 01267 (413–458–9611), at the inn of the same name, is cloud nine. Anything you order, whether it's poached salmon, grilled sirloin, or braised pheasant and polenta with shiitake-rosemary demiglace, will be flawlessly prepared.

LODGING: The **Orchards,** 222 Adams Road, Williamstown, MA 01267 (413–458–9611), is a top-of-the-line choice with the special touches of an inn (antique furnishings, cordials served in the living room) combined with the amenities of a fine-quality hotel (concierge, in-room movies, exercise room plus golf and tennis privileges).

Evening

During summer months the **Williamstown Theatre Festival** brings professionals and apprentices together for traditional and experimental theater. For program and ticket information, call (413) 597–3400.

Day 3 / Morning

BREAKFAST: The best bet for breakfast is to head over to **Spring Street,** which is 1 block west of Water Street in the midst of Williams College campus. The street is lined with small delis and eateries.

Spend a little time after breakfast browsing around Williamstown shops and then head back south, this time taking Route 2 east. Between Williams-town and North Adams on Route 2, you'll find an access road on the right (Notch Road) to **Mount Greylock.** The ride to the top of the state's highest peak (3,491 feet) takes about half an hour and offers a five-state view. At the summit there's an old lodge called **Bascom Lodge,** Adams, MA (413–743–1591), that's run by the Appalachian Mountain Club. Follow the road back down and you'll wind up in Lanesborough on Route 7, just north of Pittsfield.

Continue south on Route 7, stopping at farm stands along the way to stock up on fresh produce and dairy. Chances are that you'll also see signs for tag sales, at which you may or may not unearth some worthwhile finds. Trace your steps back to Manhattan, taking Route 7 to Route 84 west to 684 south.

There's More

Historic railroad. Berkshire Scenic Railway Museum, Willow Creek Road, Lenox, MA 01240; (413) 637–2210. Railroad museum and vintage train rides. Museum open from 10:00 A.M. to 4:00 P.M. Memorial Day weekend through October.

Nature trails. Northwest of Lenox is the Pleasant Valley Sanctuary, which offers several miles of trails to explore. It's open Tuesday through Sunday from dawn to dusk.

Skiing. There's downhill skiing at Butternut Basin, which is about 2 miles east of Great Barrington; Jiminy Peak in Hancock; Brodie Mountain in New Ashford; and other locations throughout the Berkshires.

Waterfalls. Bash Bish Falls, 12 miles southwest of South Egremont (just over the New York line), is a spectacularly scenic valley pierced by 50-foot Bash Bish Falls. A hiker's must at any time of year.

Special Events

Late January. Lenox Winter Event. A 10K cross-country ski race in Kennedy Park in Lenox.

Late June through late August. Williamstown Theatre Festival. Modern classics, contemporary plays, cabarets, and other performances. Call (413) 597–3400 for program and ticket information.

Late June through late August. Berkshire Theatre Festival, at the Berkshire Playhouse, East Main Street in Stockbridge. New and experimental theater. Call (413) 298–5576 for details.

Mid-July. Berkshire Charity Auto Show, Pittsfield. More than 500 antique and special-interest autos are displayed on the grounds of Hillcrest Hospital on West Street.

Berkshire Antiquarian Book Fair. Dozens of dealers display rare books at Stockbridge Plain School on Main Street.

July and August. Tanglewood Music Festival, Lenox. Summer home of the Boston Symphony Orchestra. Outdoor concerts. Write for a program: Symphony Hall, 301 Massachusetts Avenue, Boston, MA 02115; (617) 266–1492. During July and August only, you can call Tanglewood directly at (413) 637–1940.

July and August. Jacob's Pillow Dance Festival, Becket. A summer dance festival featuring ballet, modern dance, jazz, and mime. Contact Jacob's Pillow Dance Festival, (413) 243–0745.

Mid-July through early August. Aston Magna Festival, Great Barrington; (413) 528–3595. This summer festival takes place at St. James Church on Main Street.

The Berkshire Choral Festival (413–229–8526) offers five weeks of classical music at the Berkshire School concert shed.

Early August. Berkshire Craft Fair, Monument Mountain Regional High School, Great Barrington. A juried fair with more than one hundred artisans.

Mid-August. Sheffield Antiques Show, Sheffield. More than two dozen dealers from around the Northeast display their prize pieces at this annual event at the Mount Everett Regional High School on Berkshire School Road.

Mid-September. Barrington Fair, Great Barrington. An annual fair with exhibits, agricultural displays, livestock, and entertainment.

Late September. Apple Squeeze Festival, Lenox. Celebration of apples festival.

Early October. Autumn Weekend, Hancock Shaker Village, Pittsfield. Demonstrations of Shaker fall harvest activities.

Late December. House tours of Lenox. Usually the last Saturday of December.

Other Recommended Restaurants and Lodgings

Lenox

Apple Tree Inn, 10 Richmond Mt. Road, Lenox, MA 01240; (413) 637–1477. A wonderful inn, close to Tanglewood.

Blantyre, 16 Blantyre Road, Lenox, MA 01240; (413) 637–3556. A 1905 replica of a Scottish castle, this is a magnificently scenic setting for both staying and dining.

Canyon Ranch in the Berkshires, 165 Kemble Street, Lenox, MA 01240; (413) 637–4100 or (800) 742–9000. One of the best spas in the country. Consider spending a couple of nights here, dipping into its various spa treatments.

Gables Inn, 81 Walker Street, Lenox, MA 01240; (413) 637–3416 or (800) 382–9401. Conveniently located, Gateways is close to Tanglewood, the Berkshire Theatre Festival, and Jacob's Pillow Dance Festival.

Wheatleigh, West Hawthorne Road, Lenox, MA 01240; (413) 637–0610 or (800) 321–0610. This villa, built in sixteenth-century Florentine style, once belonged to a contessa. Today it's one of the Berkshires' most luxurious places to stay.

Williamstown

Field Farm Guest House, 554 Sloan Road, Williamstown, MA 01267; (413) 458–3135. A country guest house set on 296 acres with five rooms.

For More Information

Berkshire Visitors Bureau, Berkshire Common Plaza, Pittsfield, MA 01201; (800) 237–5747 or (413) 443–9186.

Massachusetts Office of Travel and Tourism, 10 Park Plaza, Suite 4510, Boston, MA 02116; (617) 973–8500 or (800) 227–6277.

The North Shore

Beauty and the Beach

2 Nights

For Bostonians the North Shore, which is roughly the area between Salem (immediately north of Boston) and Newburyport near the New Hampshire border, has long been a favorite quick escape. For New Yorkers it's a slightly longer haul (figure about four hours to Boston and another half hour or so to Salem), but well worth it.

☐ Gracious homes and public buildings

☐ Beaches

☐ Boats

☐ Seafood

☐ Antiques

☐ Witches

Back in the eighteenth and nineteenth centuries, magnificent ships were built in the North Shore towns, and they would set sail for ports in Africa and Asia, bringing great wealth to the area. Today many of the buildings, including majestic sea-captains' homes, still stand surveying strikingly beautiful stretches of coastline.

As you explore, you'll see sailboats gliding majestically in the wind, Victorian houses poised on the shores, and old salts puttering around seaside towns. You could easily spend a week exploring the attractions in this area. This short trip takes you to some of the highlights.

Day 1 / Morning

Unless you hit traffic, you should be able to whiz up to the Boston area on I–95 (which becomes Route 128) in about four hours. Just north of Boston you'll see signs for Route 114 and **Salem,** a great place to begin your explorations as well as have lunch.

LUNCH: You can take your pick of restaurants in Salem. If you want to just grab something simple before setting about your sightseeing, consider heading for **Red's Sandwich,** 15 Central Street, Salem, MA 01970 (978–745–3527), a diner always crowded with locals. You'll find all the mainstream

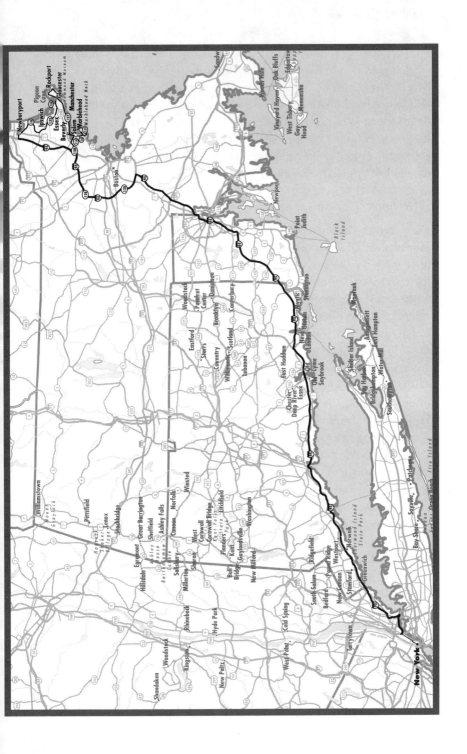

favorites, including burgers, BLTs, and club sandwiches. For a more formal meal, wander over to the **Grapevine Restaurant,** 26 Congress Street, Salem, MA 01970 (978–745–9335), and, weather permitting, get a table outside in the courtyard out back. Both the lunch and dinner menus include a wonderful selection of northern Italian dishes. If you're eager to get out to see the town and don't want to settle in for a long-drawn-out meal, you can always sit at the bar and order a bowl of linguine tossed with pesto and topped with sautéed vegetables.

Afternoon

Most people automatically think "witches" when they hear "Salem." Indeed this little seafront town was where the famous witch trials took place back in 1692. Ultimately, however, it has never been proven that there were witches in Salem, yet the belief lives on, and there are currently 5,000 practicing witches in town. Those interested in witches will find plenty of opportunities to indulge their fascination. Perhaps the best place of all is the **Salem Witch Museum,** Washington Square, Salem, MA 01970 (978–744–1692); there's an audiovisual re-creation of the witchcraft trials every half hour whenever it's open. The museum is located in a Gothic, churchlike building at the intersection of Brown and Hawthorne Boulevard. It's open year-round from 10:00 A.M. to 5:00 P.M. The **Witch House,** 310 Essex Street, Salem, MA 01970 (978–744–0180), was the home of Magistrate Jonathan Corwin, one of the judges in the witch trials. Those accused of witchcraft were held in the house before the trials. It's open from mid-March to June, daily from 10:00 A.M. to 4:30 P.M.; between July and Labor Day, daily from 10:00 A.M. to 6:00 P.M.; and between Labor Day and December 1, daily from 10:00 A.M. to 4:30 P.M. **Crow Haven Corner,** 125 Essex Street, Salem, MA 01970 (978–745–8763), is another must-see witch attraction in Salem. This tiny shop is owned by Laurie Cabot, Salem's most illustrious witch. Here you can buy all sorts of herbs, powders, and seeds to ward off evil or attract love, luck, and money. Also for sale are gargoyles and unicorns, witch books, crystals, moonstones, black cat candles, crystal balls, and magic wands. You can also make an appointment to have a tarot card reading with Laurie Cabot.

Aside from witches, however, Salem has a multitude of other attractions, which makes deciding exactly what to do a bit of a challenge (see "There's More"). In addition to the aforementioned witch sights, be sure to see the **House of the Seven Gables,** 54 Turner Street, Salem, MA 01970

(978–744–0991), which served as the setting of Nathaniel Hawthorne's novel of the same name (open from July through October 31, daily from 10:00 A.M. to 7:00 P.M. and from November through June, daily from 10:00 A.M. to 5:00 P.M. except Sunday, when it opens at noon), and the **Salem Maritime National Historic Site,** 174 Derby Street, Salem, MA 01970 (978–740–1660), which is a collection of historical buildings, including the Customs House and West Indies Goods Store, and Derby Wharf, overseen by the National Park Service. Start by picking up a copy of their walking map or join in on one of their guided tours. The site is open daily from 9:00 A.M. to 6:00 P.M. during the summer and from 9:00 A.M. to 5:00 P.M. the rest of the year.

Also extremely worthwhile is the **Peabody Essex Museum,** East India Square, Salem, MA 01970 (978–745–9500), which has impressive collections of the art, historical documents, and artifacts from the area's prosperous shipping days. It's open year-round from 10:00 A.M. to 5:00 P.M. Monday through Saturday and noon to 5:00 P.M. Sunday.

Be sure to take a walk around the waterfront area, **Pickering Wharf,** which has been restored and colonized by several restaurants, gift shops, antiques shops, crystal shops, a New Age bookstore, and the like. And don't miss **Harbor Sweets,** 85 Leavitt Street, Salem, MA 01970 (978–745–7648), where you can buy sailboat-shaped almond butter crunch chocolates right where they are made (you get to sample the selections beforehand).

From Salem it's an easy drive over to **Marblehead,** your home for the night.

DINNER: Flynnies on the Avenue, 28 Atlantic Avenue, Marblehead, MA 01945; (781) 639–2100. Located right in the historic town of Marblehead, Flynnies is a small eatery where you can get lots of seafood dishes as well as burgers, rollups, and salads.

LODGING: Located between Pearl and Pickett Streets, the **Harbor Light Inn,** 58 Washington Street, Marblehead, MA 01945 (781–631–2186), is beautifully situated in the center of Marblehead's historic district. There are twenty-three guest rooms, each one with either a four-poster or canopy bed, some with views of the harbor.

Day 2 / *Morning*

BREAKFAST: Roll out of bed and head right for **Driftwood Restaurant,** 63 Front Street, Marblehead, MA 01945 (781–631–1145). This full-of-character and full of characters restaurant attracts a crowd of local fishermen and boatbuilders. It's the kind of restaurant where you can order a heaping pile of pancakes and justify it by saying, "Oh well, we're on vacation."

After breakfast wander around Marblehead's cobbled Old Town, which dates from before the Revolution. It's a wonderful little village, well known among yacht and sailboat owners who come from around the world to race during summer months. Tour three of Marblehead's landmark buildings. **Abbot Hall,** Washington Street, Marblehead, MA 01945 (781–631–0000), is the town's government meeting place and home to one of America's most recognized paintings, *The Spirit of 1776.* Abbot Hall is open year-round, Monday, Tuesday, Thursday, and Friday from 8:00 A.M. to 5:00 P.M., Wednesday from 7:30 A.M. to 7:00 P.M., Saturday from 9:00 A.M. to 6:00 P.M., and Sunday from 11:00 A.M. to 6:00 P.M. **Jeremiah Lee Mansion,** near the intersection of Hooper and Washington Streets, Marblehead, MA 01945 (781–631–1069), is open from early June through October 15. Hours are 10:00 A.M. to 4:00 P.M. Monday through Saturday and 1:00 to 4:00 P.M. Sunday. **King Hooper Mansion,** 8 Hooper Street, Marblehead, MA 01945 (781–631–2608) is open from 10:00 A.M. to 4:00 P.M. Tuesday through Saturday and 1:00 to 5:00 P.M. Sunday.

Then drive the loop around **Marblehead Neck.** This quiet residential community is made up of several grand ocean- and harbor-front homes surrounded by handsome lawns and gardens. Along the way there's an **Audubon Bird Sanctuary** on Ocean Avenue, **Castle Rock** (from which the ocean views are staggeringly beautiful), and, at the tip, **Chandler Hovey Park,** which is home to the Marblehead Light and several benches on which you can sit and look out at the boat-filled harbor with the village as a backdrop.

Carry on up the coast, following Route 1A to Beverly, and then Route 127 to **Manchester,** which is poised on the shores of Cape Ann. Even if you're not a "beach type," don't deny yourself the experience of walking on **Singing Beach** along Beach Street. Not only does the sand "sing," but the coastal scene is arrestingly beautiful. Consider stopping in town first and picking up a couple of sandwiches for a picnic lunch.

Afternoon

North of Magnolia on Route 127, you'll see signs for the **Hammond Castle Museum,** 80 Hesperus Avenue, Gloucester, MA 01930 (978–283–7673), a castle that was built by inventor, electrical engineer, and collector Dr. John Hays Hammond Jr. The house is filled with his creations, which are all explained during a forty-five-minute tour. It's open daily from 10:00 A.M. to 5:00 P.M. during summer; hours vary the rest of the year.

Continue north to **Gloucester,** a major fishing port. Once in town you'll see signs directing motorists along the city's **Scenic Tour,** which takes you by the Harbor Cove, the Inner Harbor, the Fish Pier, and to the city's celebrated statue of a Gloucester fisherman.

Take time out on your own to see **Beauport,** the Sleeper-McCann House, 75 Eastern Point Boulevard, Gloucester, MA 01930 (978–283–0800), on Eastern Point (across the bay from downtown Gloucester). The house was built by Henry Davis Sleeper, an interior decorator and antiquarian of the 1920s. There are hour-long tours weekdays, from May 15 through September 15 from 10:00 A.M. to 4:00 P.M., and on weekends, from mid-September through mid-October from 10:00 A.M. to 4:00 P.M. Monday through Friday and 1:00 to 4:00 P.M. Saturday and Sunday. Another absolutely worthwhile stop in Gloucester is the **Rocky Neck Art Colony,** a huddle of artists' studios on the water and crammed together on narrow streets.

From Gloucester continue heading north up the coast to **Rockport,** which started off as a quiet fishing village, was discovered by artists, and has since sprouted into a resort. Rockport got its name because of the local granite—you'll find the durable stone in buildings and markers all over town.

During the summer the **Bearskin Neck,** a narrow peninsula jutting into the water off Dock Square, is practically sagging with tourists. Here you'll find one souvenir shop after another interspersed with art galleries and restaurants. The town's most photographed attraction is called "Motif No. 1," a red fisherman's shack that was named by the first painters who moved to Rockport. Actually the original shack was blown out to sea, so many people jokingly call this "Motif No. 2." If you're interested in seeing paintings, sculpture, and graphics by local artists, stop by the **Rockport Art Association,** 12 Main Street, Rockport, MA 01966 (978–546–6604). The RAA also has free lectures, artist demonstrations, and concerts.

You might want to note that Rockport is a "dry" town. This means that no liquor, wine, or beer is served in its restaurants or sold in its inns

Rockport's most photographed attraction, "Motif No. 1."

or shops. You can bring your own, but make sure you pick it up in Gloucester or elsewhere on your way up.

DINNER: You'll find seafood abundant in Rockport. If you want to keep the price down, head for **Ellen's Harborside,** just off Dock Square on T-Wharf, Rockport, MA 01966 (978–546–2512). It's always packed with fanatical regulars who pile in for the fresh seafood and homemade desserts (open mid-April through December).

LODGING: Addison Choate Inn, 49 Broadway, Rockport, MA 01966; (978) 546–7543. A sweet little inn in a building that dates from 1851. It's within easy walking distance of the town's attractions.

Day 3 / Morning

BREAKFAST: Ellen's Harborside, just off Dock Square on T-Wharf,

Rockport, MA 01966 (978–546–2512), is the place to go for a big American breakfast or just a corn muffin and coffee.

After breakfast take a drive around the Cape. Head north out of town on Route 127A, making your first stop at Pigeon Cove. If you have time, it's a good spot to take a dip. From there carry on to **Halibut Point State Park,** which has an interpretive center, an old granite quarry (now flooded with water), and an observation tower. Beyond the interpretive center there's an Observation Point atop a cliff above the Atlantic. You can go down to the water, but think twice about going in. The waves and rocks can be very dangerous.

From Halibut Point follow Route 127 around the western side of Cape Ann to Route 128. Then turn right onto Route 133 for a scenic drive up to **Essex,** which is a stopover must if you're in the market for antiques. From Essex it's a short drive to **Ipswich,** where you can feast on clams in one of many roadside eateries. Ipswich is a summer resort town with what many consider one of the best beaches on the Atlantic coast. **Crane Beach,** at the end of Argilla Road on Ipswich Bay, is a 5-mile-long sweep of beach open to the public (you pay for parking).

If you're not pressed for time, carry on to **Newburyport** (picking up Route 1A shortly after Ipswich). Newburyport is a museumlike nineteenth-century town filled with shipowners' and captains' houses overlooking a yacht-filled harbor. There are a couple of museums in town—the Coffin House, Cushing House, and Custom House—worth browsing around if you have the time.

From Newburyport you can easily pick up I–95 and head back to the New York area.

There's More

Antiques. Pickering Wharf Antiques, 69 Wharf Street, Salem, MA 01970; (978) 741–3113. An antiques center displaying the works of more than thirty-five dealers.

Living history. Pioneer Village: Salem in 1630, Forest River Park, Salem, MA 01970; (978) 744–0991. A living-history museum with costumed interpreters.

Whale-watch cruises. Cape Ann Whale Watch operates cruises from Rose's Wharf at 415 Main Street in Gloucester, MA 01930; (978) 283–5110.

Special Events

Last weekend in June. Festival of St. Peter, Gloucester. A four-day-long celebration with sports events, fireworks, and a Blessing of the Fleet.

June. Rockport Chamber Music Festival, Rockport; (978) 546–7391. Recitals are given Thursday through Sunday throughout the month.

Late July. Old Ipswich Days. Arts and crafts shows, exhibits, clambakes, entertainment.

Last week of July. Race Week, Marblehead. Sailing races.

Mid-August. Heritage Days Celebration, Salem. Band concerts, a parade, exhibits, arts and crafts, and food stalls.

Third weekend in August. Waterfront Festival, Gloucester. Arts and crafts show, military reenactment, food, and entertainment.

Labor Day weekend. Schooner Festival, Gloucester. Races, sailboat parade, and maritime festivities.

Other Recommended Restaurants and Lodgings

East Gloucester

Rudder Restaurant, 73 Rock Neck Avenue, East Gloucester, MA 01930; (978) 283–7967. Dinner here is not just a meal, it's a wild party, complete with the zaniest entertainment you may ever see. Closed over the winter months.

Marblehead

Nautilus, 68 Front Street, Marblehead, MA 01945; (978) 283–1198. A waterfront guest house with just four rooms. Summer weekends fill quickly, so call as far in advance as possible.

Seaward Inn, 62 Marmion Way, Marblehead, MA 01945; (781) 546–3471 or (800) 648–7733. Within easy walking distance of the village, this Cape Ann inn (with thirty-six rooms) also offers five-course, home-cooking-style meals.

Salem

Hawthorne Hotel, 18 Washington Street West, Salem, MA 01970; (978) 744–4080. A major Salem landmark, the Hawthorne is within easy walking distance of all of Salem's attractions and restaurants.

Salem Inn, 7 Summer Street, Salem, MA 01970; (978) 741–0680 or (800) 446–2995. Just a short walk away from the Salem Maritime National Historic Site and the city's many attractions, the Salem Inn offers a selection of rooms in three attached town houses that are on the National Register of Historic Places. All three are outstanding examples of Greek Revival architecture.

For More Information

Marblehead Chamber of Commerce, 62 Pleasant Street, Marblehead, MA 01945; (781) 631–2868.

Massachusetts Office of Travel and Tourism, 10 Park Plaza, Suite 4510, Boston, MA 02116; (617) 973–8500 or (800) 227–6277.

North of Boston Convention and Visitors Bureau, 17 Peabody Square, Peabody, MA 01960; (978) 977–7760 or (800) 742–5306.

Rockport Chamber of Commerce, P.O. Box 67M, Rockport, MA 01966; (978) 546–6575. Information Center on Main Street.

Salem Chamber of Commerce, 32 Derby Square, Salem, MA 01970; (978) 744–0004.

Cape Cod

Seascapes and Seafood

3 Nights

Soft breezes off the sea. Acres and acres of salt marshes and cranberry bogs. Clam shacks. For many Cape Cod is synonymous with the word vacation. Indeed it is a vacation land, one big open-air sandbox in which both kids and adults can play.

- ☐ Beaches
- ☐ Antiques shops
- ☐ Seafood
- ☐ Bicycling
- ☐ Boating
- ☐ Boutiques
- ☐ Galleries
- ☐ Whale-watching
- ☐ Nature walks

Though rarely referred to as such, Cape Cod is technically an island, separated from mainland Massachusetts by the Cape Cod Canal. Two bridges span the narrow waters—the Bourne to the south (Route 28) and the Sagamore to the north (Route 6). The Cape, which all writers and just about everybody else who has been there or lives there will tell you, looks like a flexed arm on the map. It's just 70 miles from the mainland to Provincetown but is filled with little galaxies to explore.

Keep in mind that you won't be able to see everything in a couple of days on the Cape. This quick escape is just a glimpse of what it has to offer. You'll spend the first half of the trip working your way up the Cape and then meander back down. As many places on the Cape are open only during the summer, be sure to call ahead if you're traveling during any other season.

Day 1 / Morning

From New York take I–95 north to I–195. Then take Massachusetts Route 25 to Route 6 east. Route 6 runs right up the Cape, most of the time alongside Historic Route 6A. The trip should take between four and four-and-one-half hours.

LUNCH: Chances are you'll want to grab something fast along the way, but if you can hold off until you get to Sandwich on the Cape, you'll find a wonderful historic tearoom right in the heart of the village.

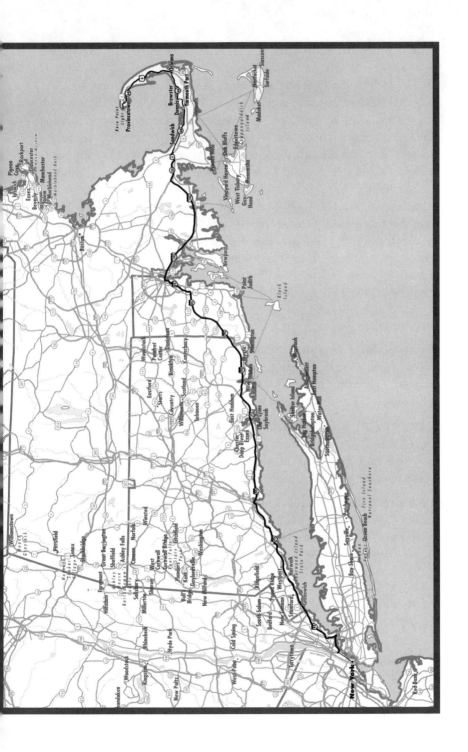

The Dunbar Tea Shop, circa 1740, (1 Water Street, Sandwich, MA 02563; 508–833–2485) offers a "farmer's lunch", a "fisherman's lunch", a "yeoman's lunch" and a "ploughman's" lunch among many other items.

One of the first towns you'll come to is **Sandwich,** which calls itself the "oldest town on the Cape." A lot of people skim right by it, heading for Provincetown. Unless you're tired from the drive up and want to get straight to your hotel for the night, consider stopping for a look around its antiques stores, gracious old houses, and beaches. Sandwich is also home to one of the Cape's top attractions: The **Heritage Plantation,** Grove and Pine Streets (508–888–3300), has seventy-six acres of gardens with museums showcasing antique cars, colonial tools, and a working 1912 carousel. The plantation is open year-round. From May 1 through October 31, hours are 9:00 A.M. to 6:00 P.M. Saturday through Wednesday and 9:00 A.M. to 8:00 P.M. Thursday and Friday. Between November 1 and April 30, hours are 10:00 A.M. to 4:00 P.M. Tuesday through Sunday.

Afternoon

From Sandwich it's a short drive (on historic Route 6A) to **Yarmouth Port,** where you can settle in for the night. Yarmouth Port is home to several old sea-captains' houses that line a stretch of Main Street (which is part of Route 6A) known as the "Captains' Mile."

DINNER: Abbicci, 43 Main Street, Yarmouth Port, MA 02675 (508–362–3501), is just down the road from the Wedgewood Inn. Though it's not a typical Cape restaurant, a meal here is truly worth it. The cuisine is contemporary Mediterranean.

LODGING: The **Wedgewood Inn,** 83 Main Street, Yarmouth Port, MA 02675 (508–362–5157), is a beautiful old house that was built in 1812. All nine rooms are individually decorated with country furnishings. Some have working fireplaces; some have private porches. It's truly a gem.

Day 2 / Morning

BREAKFAST: At the inn enjoy a full breakfast that is included in the room price.

Start the day by taking a walk on the **Nature Trails of the Historical Society of Old Yarmouth.** The trails take you through some of Yarmouth's

Cape Cod offers a huge slice of the good by-the-sea life.

most beautiful land and marshes. Contact the Historical Society of Old Yarmouth, P.O. Box 11, Yarmouth Port, MA 02675; (508) 362–3021.

Then head out of town north on Route 6A to **Dennis.** If the day is clear, or even partially clear, make your way up to the **Scargo Hill Tower** (from Route 6A, turn right onto Old Bass River Road and follow the signs). From the top you can see the Cape stretching out below all the way up to Provincetown.

Brewster is the next stop. Here you'll find two noteworthy attractions. The **New England Fire and History Museum,** 1439 Route 6A, Brewster, MA 02631 (508–896–5711), has one of the world's largest collections of fire-fighting equipment and memorabilia. During the summer, hours are 10:00 A.M. to 4:00 P.M. Monday through Friday and noon to 4:00 P.M. Saturday and Sunday. From mid-September through Columbus Day the museum is open on Saturday and Sunday only from noon to 4:00 P.M.

It's closed the rest of the year. The **Cape Cod Museum of Natural History,** 869 Route 6A, Brewster, MA 02631 (508–896–3867), is a good place to learn all about the Cape's flora, fauna, and ecology. It's open from 9:30 A.M. to 4:30 P.M. Monday through Saturday and from 11:00 A.M. to 4:30 P.M. on Sundays.

A little farther up Route 6A is **Orleans,** which is the midpoint between the Cape Cod Canal and Provincetown. By now it's probably time for lunch and a snooze on the beach or a quick dip in the ocean (bathhouses available and open during the summer).

LUNCH: Stop by a grocery store or deli in Orleans to pick up picnic supplies for the beach.

Afternoon

You can take your pick of beaches in the area. On the ocean side you'll find **Nauset Beach,** a gorgeous beach, with major waves, that stretches on for 10 miles. Over on the bay side **Skaket Beach** is also beautiful but a lot calmer—a good choice for families with young children.

DINNER: Kadee's Lobster and Clam Bar is at 212 Main Street, East Orleans, MA 02643 (508–255–6184). The owners also own the next-door East Orleans Fish Market, which means that you can count on wonderfully fresh seafood here. You can sit outside and feast on a pile of steamers, corn on the cob, and the best lobster ever—and not spend a fortune. Please note that the restaurant is closed during the winter months.

LODGING: Nauset House Inn, 141 Beach Road, East Orleans, MA 02643 (508–255–2195), is just half a mile away from the beach. It's a beautiful country inn with fourteen rooms surrounded by gardened grounds.

Day 3 / Morning

BREAKFAST: Guests have raved so much about the breakfasts at the Nauset House Inn that innkeeper Diane Johnson has printed the recipes up in a booklet. Breakfast is indeed a treat here and is included in the room rate.

Before leaving Orleans pull into the **Bird Watcher's General Store,** 36 Route 6A, Orleans, MA 02653 (508–255–6974 or 800–562–1512). Here you'll find everything on birds and birds on everything from postcards to mailboxes, as well as bins of corn, thistle seeds, and sunflower seeds and a good selection of birdhouses.

Continue up the Cape to **Provincetown** at the very tip. Be fore-warned, however. During summer months traffic can be crazy. Your best bet is to grab the first parking spot you see as you drive in on Commercial Street. Then you can walk the rest of the way into town, passing one lovely shingled house after another. Most of the in-town inns have parking for guests, but you may be too early to check in if you arrive before 3:00 P.M.

P-Town, as Provincetown is locally known, is a very lively community with lots of artist types and writers. Though the town is not big, it's crammed with shops, galleries, restaurants, bakeries, nightspots—you name it. One of its biggest appeals is people-watching. Sit on one of the benches in front of town hall and chances are you'll see more characters in half an hour than some people see in a lifetime. P-Town is a lot of fun, and during summer months it has a tipsy air of carnival. The rest of the year it is con-siderably more serene and is the best time to go if you just want to relax and enjoy the profusion of restaurants, nightspots, and nearby beaches.

LUNCH: Café Blasé, 328 Commercial Street, Provincetown, MA 02657 (508–487–9465), is a good outdoor cafe at which to plant yourself and people-watch. The menu has lots of salads, burgers, and quiches.

Afternoon

You can rent bikes right in town at Arnold's Bicycle Shop, 329 Commercial Street (508–487–0844), and pedal around to some of the nearby attractions. Right off Bradford Street (which runs parallel to Commercial Street), you'll find the town's biggest tourist attraction: the **Pilgrim Monument** and **Provincetown Museum,** High Pole Hill, Provincetown, MA 02657 (508–487–1310). The museum has some Pilgrim exhibits and a potpourri of other collections (including pieces from whaling-ship days, old costumes, World War I mementos). You can climb to the top of the monument for a far-reaching view of the Cape. The museum is open daily from April through June from 9:00 A.M. to 4:15 P.M., July and August from 9:00 A.M. to 6:15 P.M., and September through November from 9:00 A.M. to 4:15 P.M.; closed December through March.

From the monument it's a short, mostly flat or downhill pedal over to **Herring Cove,** where you can get on the **Province Lands Bike Paths,** a webwork of paved trails that take you over the dunes, through pine groves, and alongside the sea. They include the Loop Trail (5¼ miles), Herring Cove Beach spur (1 mile), Race Point Beach spur (½ mile), Bennett Pond spur (¼ mile), and Race Point Road spur (¼ mile).

It's worth pedaling back to Herring Cove for the sunset. On a typical day it's an applaudable extravaganza.

DINNER: There are so many restaurants in P-Town that it all boils down to what you feel like eating. **Café Edwige,** 333 Commercial Street, Provincetown, MA 02657 (508–487–2008), offers both indoor and outdoor dining. The menu is varied and includes lots of healthy dishes such as stir-fry tofu as well as to-die-for crab cakes and native littleneck clams.

LODGING: P-Town has lots of small guest houses from which to take your pick, as well as a handful of hotels. Right in the center of town, the **Brass Key Guesthouse,** 67 Bradford Street, Provincetown, MA 02657 (508–487–9005 or 800–842–9858) has become the place to stay in Provincetown. It recently underwent a multimillion-dollar expansion and now offers thirty-three units that are every-inch luxurious. The service is really top-drawer as well. On top of that, there's an outdoor heated pool and a 17-foot-wide whirlpool.

Day 4 / Morning

BREAKFAST: Follow your nose to the **Portuguese Bakery** on MacMillan Wharf, 299 Commercial Street, Provincetown, MA 02667; (508) 487–1803. Here you can start the day with a pastry and coffee.

If you want to get in a couple of hours at the beach, drive over to **Race Point,** which is part of the **Cape Cod National Seashore.** Sprawling over nearly 44,000 acres, the National Seashore was established by President Kennedy in 1961 to protect the area from commercialization.

Then work your way back down the Cape (you can breeze down on Route 6) to return home. En route, consider detouring over to **Chatham,** which is a beautiful little village with gray-shingled sea captains' houses, shops, restaurants, inns, and beaches.

LUNCH: The **Impudent Oyster,** 15 Chatham Bars Avenue, Chatham, MA 02633 (508–945–3545), which is just off Main Street, serves gloriously fresh seafood (be sure to have some Chatham steamers).

There's More

Nature walks. The Massachusetts Audubon Society, Route 6, South Wellfleet, MA 02663 (508–349–2615), offers naturalist-led wildlife tours, trips to the Monomoy Island Bird Sanctuary, canoe trips, and bay cruises.

Scenic railroad. The Cape Cod Central Railroad, Main and Center Streets, Hyannis (508–771–3800), runs between Hyannis and Sagamore, stopping at Sandwich along the way. There are three departures daily, Tuesday through Sunday, from mid-June to late October and weekends in May.

Whale-watch excursions. Captain John Boats (508–746–2643); Dolphin Fleet Whalewatching of Provincetown (508–349–1900); Portuguese Princess Excursions (508–487–2651). Whale-watching cruises are offered in Provincetown and Barnstable during July and August. From Provincetown there are several excursions a day. From Barnstable Harbor they leave three times a day.

Special Events

Early June. Harbor Festival, Bismore Park on Ocean Street in Hyannis. An annual Blessing of the Fleet, clam-shucking and pie-eating contests, and all sorts of activities take place.

July 4. Fourth of July Parade, on Main Street and Old Colony Way in Orleans. This is a 2½-mile theme parade held every year.

Mid-July through late July. Barnstable County Fair. This annual fair takes place on the fairgrounds (Route 151) in East Falmouth but is sponsored by the Barnstable County Agricultural Society. There are horticultural exhibits, livestock shows, a petting zoo, a horse-and-pony show, and more.

Early August. Cape Cod Antiques Exposition, at the Charles F. Moore Sports Center, O'Connor Way (exit 12 off Route 6). This expo attracts antiques dealers from all over New England.

Late August. Festival of the Arts, Chase Park on Cross Street, Chatham. A juried outdoor event attracting artists from all over.

Late August. Festival Days, Dennis. An annual festival with an antique-car parade, church suppers, crafts fairs, road races, and more.

Early September. Annual Bourne Scallop Festival, Buzzards Bay Park, Buzzards Bay. The largest scallop festival on the East Coast.

Mid-September. Cranberry Festival, Harwich. Races, clambakes, barbecues, a parade—an enormous small-town festival.

Other Recommended Restaurants and Lodgings

Barnstable

Beechwood, 2839 Main Street (Route 6A), Barnstable, MA 02630; (508) 362–6618 or (800) 609–6618. A very elegant Queen Anne Victorian bed and breakfast shaded by beech trees.

Brewster

Chillingsworth, 2449 Main Street, Brewster, MA 02631 (Route 6A); (508) 896–3640. A top-drawer French restaurant. It's one of the Cape's best.

Ocean Edge Resort & Golf Club, 2907 Main Street, Brewster, MA 02631; (508) 896–9000 or (800) 343–6074. Unlike most of the inns you'll find on the Cape, this is a major resort with lots of facilities.

Chatham

Chatham Bars Inn, Shore Road, Chatham, MA 02633; (508) 945–0096 or (800) 527–4884. The doyen of local hotels, the Chatham Bars Inn is a luxury resort gazing out to sea.

Queen Anne Inn, 70 Queen Anne Road, Chatham, MA 02633; (508) 945–0394 or (800) 545–4667. A lovely Victorian inn within walking distance of the beach.

Cotuit

Regatta of Cotuit, Route 28, Cotuit, MA 02635; (508) 428–5715. Housed in a building that dates from 1790, the Regatta has a very sophisticated menu with dishes inspired by the chef's extensive travels.

East Orleans

Ship's Knees Inn, 186 Beach Road, East Orleans, MA 02643; (508) 255–1312. A restored 1790 sea-captain's home.

Falmouth

Coonamessett Inn, 311 Gifford Street, Falmouth, MA 02540; (508) 548–2300. A very relaxed and comfortable historic inn.

Hyannis

Mildred's Chowder House, 290 Iyanough Road, Hyannis, MA 02601; (508) 775–1045. For simple seafood at its best, head for Mildred's. She offers all the favorites: thick clam chowders, creamy oyster stews, steamers with drawn butter, and lobster rolls that blow all other lobster rolls right out of the water.

Orleans

Captain Linnell House, 137 Skaket Beach Road, Orleans, MA 02653; (508) 255–3400. Exceptional seafood and a good wine list.

Provincetown

Lobster Pot, 321 Commercial Street, Provincetown, MA 02657; (508) 487–0842. Here you can feast on fresh lobster and clam chowder on a waterfront deck.

Mews Restaurant, 429 Commercial Street, Provincetown, MA 02657; (508) 487–1500. This is an excellent seafood restaurant with a lovely view of the harbor.

Sandwich

Dan'l Webster Inn, 149 Main Street, Sandwich, MA 02563; (508) 888–3622 or (800) 444–3566. A Cape Cod landmark.

For More Information

Cape Cod Chamber of Commerce, 307 Main Street, Hyannis, MA 02601–0016; (508) 862–0700 or (888) 33CAPECOD.

Massachusetts Office of Travel and Tourism, 10 Park Plaza, Suite 4510, Boston, MA 02116; (617) 973–8500.

Martha's Vineyard

A Carefree Getaway

3 Nights

The Vineyard, as it is locally known and referred to by its fans, lies just off the coast of Cape Cod. It got its name in the early 1600s, when an explorer by the name of Bartholomew Gosnold stepped ashore. Supposedly he, who is said to have had a daughter named Martha, found wild grapes growing, so there you have it! During summer months, the whole island feels like one big open-air party, with vacationers from all over crowding its little streets and duney beaches. Be sure to make hotel reservations in advance.

☐ Beaches

☐ Seafood

☐ Boating

☐ Biking

☐ Historic inns

The island has three main towns: Vineyard Haven is its commercial center and where many of the mainland ferries dock. Oak Bluffs is an old Victorian community filled with gingerbread houses. Edgartown is a museumlike village, with historic houses and inns.

During summer months you must have a reservation to take your car over to the island. A reservation must be made months in advance, especially if it's over a weekend. It's also costly (as much as $110 round-trip in season). The other option is to leave your car on the mainland and rent a car once you get on the island. Either way allow yourself plenty of time to get to the ferry; traffic during summer months can be horrendous. During summer there are more than a dozen ferry trips a day from Woods Hole to Vineyard Haven or Oak Bluffs. The trip takes forty-five minutes.

A trip to Martha's Vineyard can easily be combined with a trip to Nantucket (Massachusetts Escape Five) or to Cape Cod (Massachusetts Escape Three).

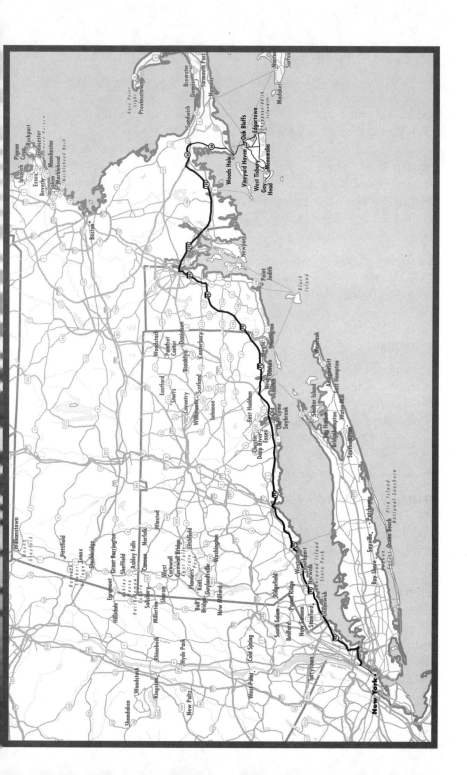

Day 1 / *Morning*

Coming from New York take I–95 north to I–195 to Massachusetts Route 25/28 south, and cross the Bourne Bridge following the signs for Woods Hole. Along the way there are quite a few rotaries, which can get clogged with confused travelers. Take your time.

If you make good time, get your car in line and take a look around **Woods Hole,** which is a mecca for marine biologists. Crowded together near the water's edge are several labs and sea-study centers including the Marine Biological Laboratory, the Woods Hole Oceanographic Institution, the Northeast Fisheries Science Center, and the U.S. Geological Survey's Branch of Atlantic Geology.

LUNCH: If you didn't stop for lunch at a roadside eatery on the way up, head straight for **Shuckers,** 91A Water Street, Woods Hole, MA 02543 (508–540–3850). It's a wonderful little seafood eatery with a raw bar. Try the lobster roll; it's celestial.

Afternoon

Depending on which ferry you get, chances are that once you arrive on the island, you won't have much time left in the day for exploring. Your best bet is to check into your hotel and then head out for dinner and a walk around town. For the first night we suggest staying in Oak Bluffs. If you catch a ferry there, you'll be within easy reach of all the inns as well as the town's attractions. If you take a ferry to Vineyard Haven, it's just a short ride over (signs clearly direct you).

DINNER: Zapotec, 14 Kennebec Avenue, Oak Bluffs, MA 02557 (508–693–6800) in the center of town, serves wonderful Southwestern cuisine. Another good choice is **Jimmy Seas Pan Pasta Restaurant,** 32 Kennebec Avenue, Oak Bluffs, MA 02557 (508–696–8550), where you can take your pick of a wonderful selection of one-pot pasta dishes.

LODGING: Choosing just one place to stay anywhere in Martha's Vineyard is truly challenging. You'll find everything from motel-like accommodations to very elegant inns. One favorite is the **Admiral Benbow Inn,** 81 New York Avenue, Oak Bluffs, MA 02557 (508–693–6825). Just up the road from the center of town, it's a very comfortable inn that's not overly frilly. It's located in an old house that dates from the 1870s.

Day 2 / Morning

BREAKFAST: A full breakfast is part of the room rate at the Admiral Benbow.

After breakfast walk past the row of Victorian seafront houses into town and check out the **Flying Horses Carousel,** 33 Oak Bluffs Avenue, Oak Bluffs, MA 02557 (508–693–9481). Listed on the National Register of Historic Places, it dates from 1876, when the horses were hand-carved in New York. The carousel is open from Easter Saturday through Columbus Day. Hours vary, so call ahead.

From the carousel you can wander over to the **Methodist Camp Meeting Grounds,** just off Circuit Avenue (no phone), which, tragically, many visitors completely miss. Nothing can really prepare you for the sensation of wandering through this community of tiny gingerbread houses painted in every color imaginable. The community originally started as a religious retreat in 1835. Participants stayed in tents clustered together. Many returned year after year and became so passionate about the place that they replaced the tents with more permanent wood cottages. Today it's home to more than 300 cottages, all radiating out from a tabernacle, where there are sing-alongs, religious services, and concerts. There's also a small museum filled with sample furnishings and other bric-a-brac. Do not, under any circumstances, leave the island without seeing this incredible sight. The grounds are open twenty-four hours a day.

Once you've feasted your eyes on the architectural wonders of Oak Bluffs, get back in your car and follow Seaview Avenue around to **Edgartown.** En route you'll pass the State Beach, where you can pull over and take a swim or conk out for a couple of hours.

Your best bet for exploring Edgartown is to, once again, go on foot; in fact there are hour-long guided walking tours. For information stop by the visitors center on Church Street across from the Old Whaling Church or call (508) 627–8619 for information on tours of Edgartown, Oak Bluffs, and Vineyard Haven. The tours take you to the village churches, some eighteenth-century houses, and the **Martha's Vineyard Historical Society,** Cooke and School Streets, Edgartown, MA 02539 (508–627–4441), which has some informative and interesting displays on the island's history.

Once you've seen Edgartown, pick up picnic makings and consider renting a bike (there are a couple of rental shops in town) and taking it over on the ferry to **Chappaquiddick Island** ("Chappy" to those in the

One of the many fancifully designed cottages in Oak Bluffs.

know). It's a mere five-minute ferry ride and costs $5.00 round-trip for both you and your bike and $8.00 round-trip for a car and driver. Call (508) 627–9427 for further information. Once you set foot on Chappy, head straight across the island on Dyke Road to **East Beach.** This beach is beautifully isolated, has substantial surf, and is prime bird-watching territory.

LUNCH: Picnic on Chappaquiddick.

Afternoon

You'll probably get back to Edgartown with just enough time to check into your inn and freshen up for the evening.

DINNER: Edgartown has a handful of exceptionally good restaurants, including **Savoir Fare,** 14 Church Street, Edgartown, MA 02539 (508–627–9864), which has been featured in Gourmet magazine. The cuisine is Italian and Californian.

LODGING: Charlotte Inn, 27 South Summer Street, Edgartown, MA 02539; (508) 627–4751. This is a stunning inn, filled with artwork and antiques. Its restaurant, L'Etoile, serves outstanding French cuisine in a glassed-in terrace or in the garden.

Day 3 / Morning

BREAKFAST: A continental breakfast is included in the price of a room at the Charlotte Inn. A full breakfast is extra, and has many offerings from fresh fruit and yogurt to French toast and eggs prepared any style.

After breakfast set out in your car for **Gay Head,** which is the western tip of the island. Follow West Tisbury Road to Edgartown Road until you reach **West Tisbury.** There you can pause to have a look around **Chicama Vineyards,** Stoney Hill Road (508–693–0309), a thirty-three-acre vineyard. It's open June through October, Monday through Saturday from 11:00 A.M. to 5:00 P.M. and Sunday from 1:00 to 5:00 P.M. (closed July 4th and Labor Day). November through May, call for hours.

From there follow South Road to Chilmark and then turn left onto State Road, which will take you right out to Gay Head. There's not much that's man-made on this end of the island except for some beautiful homes tucked away in the duney landscape. Gay Head is known for its dramatic clay cliffs that plunge into the sea. A whole cluster of tourist shops have colonized the crown of these cliffs, offering the customary tourist crop of souvenirs—postcards, beaded belts, T-shirts.

Once you've walked out to the edge of the cliffs and acknowledged the ocean view, you'll be ready to climb back into your car and continue on. From Gay Head it's a short drive to **Menemsha Harbor,** a small working harbor crammed with picturesque shingled houses.

LUNCH: The **Galley,** right on the water in Menemsha Harbor, Menemsha, MA 02552 (508–228–9641), is a little shacklike building where you'll find excellent lobster rolls. From its back porch you can sit and watch the harbor activity.

Afternoon

After lunch make your way to **Vineyard Haven,** where you can settle in for the night before heading back to the mainland in the morning. Follow North Road to North Tisbury and then turn left following Vineyard Haven Road to Main Street.

DINNER: Chances are that you will have heard of the **Black Dog Tavern,** Beach Street Extension, Vineyard Haven, MA 02568 (508–693–9223), by the time you actually eat there yourself. It's the island's most famous restaurant, understandably so. Not only is the food excellent (lots of fresh seafood, home-baked breads and desserts, innovative dishes), but the view (it's inches from the water's edge) is *very* Vineyard. There's also a Black Dog Bakery just steps away.

LODGING: **Hanover House Inn,** 28 Edgartown Road, Vineyard Haven, MA 02568; (508–693–1066 or 800–339–1066), is a fifteen-room inn half a mile from the ferry.

Day 4 / Morning

BREAKFAST: Homemade breads and muffins (included in room rate) are served each morning at the Hanover House Inn on a sunporch.

Spend the morning hours poking around the shops of Vineyard Haven and then consider picking up lunch at the **Black Dog Bakery** (right near the restaurant). There are sandwiches, wonderful breads, and homemade desserts.

From there you can easily get right on the ferry and head over to the mainland. Once in Woods Hole, retrace your steps back to New York City.

There's More

Fishing. There are several charter outfits around the island, including Big Eye Charters in Edgartown (508–627–3649) and North Shore Charters in Menemsha (508–645–2993).

Golf. The Mink Meadows Golf Course, off Franklin Street in Vineyard Haven, is a public nine-hole course. Call (508) 693–0600 for more information.

Sailing. There are a couple of boats available for chartering in Vineyard Haven, including the clipper schooner *Shenandoah* (call 508–693–1699 for details).

Water sports. There are all sorts of rental shops in the Vineyard towns where you can take your pick of seagoing toys such as Jet Skis and Windsurfers.

Wildlife preserves. There are several nature preserves (for bird-watching and strolling) on the island, including Felix Neck Wildlife Sanctuary between Edgartown and Vineyard Haven, Cedar Tree Neck on the north shore, Long Point on the Atlantic shore, Manuel F. Correllus State Forest in the center of the island, and Cape Poque Wildlife Refuge and Wasque Reservations on the island of Chappaquiddick.

Special Events

June. Illumination Night, Methodist Camp Meeting Grounds, Oak Bluffs, Martha's Vineyard. Every year this Oak Bluffs community strings paper lanterns from Asia throughout the "campgrounds."

Mid-August. Martha's Vineyard Agricultural Society Livestock Show and Fair, at the fairgrounds on State Road. An old-fashioned country fair with crafts, food booths, and exhibits.

Other Recommended Restaurants and Lodgings

Edgartown

Daggett House, 59 North Street, Edgartown, MA 02539; (508) 627–4600 or (800) 946–3400. An antique-furnished inn with thirty rooms.

Harbor View Resort, 131 North Water Street, Edgartown, MA 02539; (508) 627–7000 or (800) 225–6005. Overlooking the lighthouse, this is a lovely spot with a veranda from which you can look out at the water.

Menemsha

Beach Plum Inn and Restaurant, North Road, Menemsha, MA 02552; (508) 645–9454. Set off in a world of its own, this twelve-room inn overlooks Menemsha Harbor, Vineyard Sound, and the Elizabeth Islands. Unlike most of the Vineyard inns, it's surrounded by a substantial amount of property and has its own beach and tennis court. The restaurant, which has a New England menu that changes daily (with an emphasis on seafood) is a splurgey dinner choice.

For More Information

Martha's Vineyard Chamber of Commerce, Box 1698, Beach Road, Vineyard Haven, MA 02568; (508) 693–0085.

Massachusetts Office of Travel and Tourism, 10 Park Plaza, Suite 4510, Boston, MA 02116; (617) 973–8500 or (800) 227–6277.

Ferry Information: For complete, up-to-date fares and schedules, visit the Steamship Authority Web site (www.islandferry.com) or call (508) 477–8600.

Nantucket— With or Without a Car

Cobblestones and Beaches

3 Nights

In many ways Nantucket is the designer-label island of the Northeast, the Ralph Lauren of islands. Absolutely every inch of Nantucket is attractive. The town of Nantucket itself, where the ferry docks, is a webwork of cobbled streets lined with huge old elm trees, gas lamps, and historic buildings. Inside there are art galleries, boutiques, and restaurants run by top chefs.

The rest of the island is made up of rolling moors (punctuated with bayberry, wild roses, and cranberries) and arrestingly beautiful white-sand beaches. More than a third of it is under protection from development. It's a rather small island, 12 by 3 miles, which makes exploring in a couple of days by bike or foot very manageable.

☐ Beaches

☐ Historic inns

☐ Biking

☐ Gourmet restaurants

☐ Bird-watching

☐ Boutique shopping

Like many offshore islands Nantucket has two dramatically different personalities. During summer months the downtown area, as well as many of the island's beaches, is crammed with vacationers. The rest of the year, it's blissfully serene. Do yourself a huge favor and try to go either before June 15 or shortly after Labor Day. That way, you'll be able to enjoy the warm weather without the crowds.

Consider combining an escape to Nantucket with a trip to nearby Martha's Vineyard (see Massachusetts Escape Four) or to Cape Cod (Massachusetts Escape Three). You can easily go over on foot for the day. If you have your own bike, consider taking it along; otherwise, you can rent one.

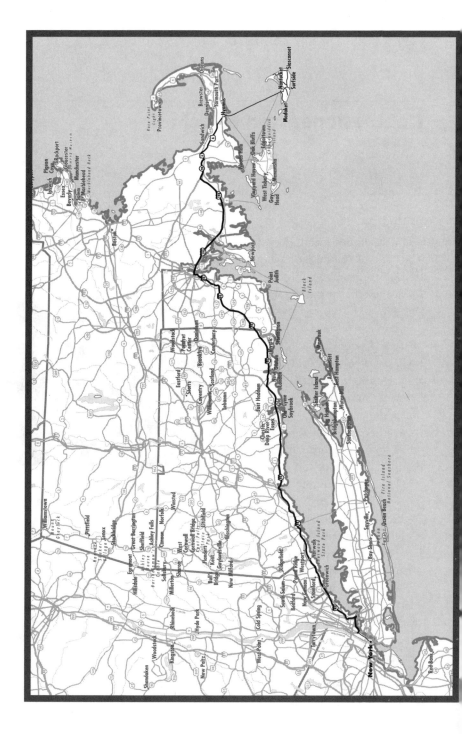

Day 1 / Morning

Consider packing a picnic lunch before you head out. Or, if you think you can hold out, you'll find lots of restaurant choices in Hyannis.

To reach the island you can take a Greyhound Bus (800–229–9424) from the Port Authority in New York to Hyannis. It takes about seven to eight hours. From there you take a ferry over. During summer months ferries run six times daily to the island; other months, they run less frequently. You can also fly Nantucket Airlines over from Hyannis (508–790–0300). If you're driving, from New York take I–95 to I–195. Then take Massachusetts Route 25 to Route 6 east just before the Bourne Bridge. This will take you north and east to the Sagamore Bridge over the canal and right up the Cape. At the rotaries just keep following the signs for Hyannis. Don't even think of taking your car over. It's expensive, there's traffic, and besides, you don't really need one. There's a parking lot right at the ferry docks in Hyannis. During the summer months, the NRTA shuttle operates on the island, providing service to Madaket, Sconset, midisland areas, and Surfside and Jetties beaches. Designated stops are located along the routes. For more information, call (508) 228-7025.

LUNCH: At **Spanky's Clam Shack and Seaside Saloon** (138 Ocean Street, Hyannis, MA 02601; 508–771–2770), lunch couldn't be tastier nor could it be more conveniently located when waiting for the ferry. Here you can get some fish, lobster, fried clams, and other seafood favorites. It's right on Ocean Street next to the ferry docks.

Afternoon

You'll probably catch an afternoon ferry and step ashore sometime just before dinner. Good timing. You can check into your room, which is within walking distance of the ferry, before heading out for dinner.

DINNER: American cuisine—both new and traditional—is what you'll find on the menu at **21 Federal** (21 Federal Street, Nantucket, MA 02554; 508–228–2121). Located in the center of town, it's a popular spot for locals. The fish entrees are especially good.

LODGING: Choosing just one inn in Nantucket is like trying to pick just one chocolate from a sampler. There are many wonderful inns right in town as well as a resort over on the east coast. Prices run the gamut from inexpensive to very expensive. Generally the most expensive ones are very close to the town center. One moderately priced favorite is the **House of the**

Seven Gables, 32 Cliff Road, Nantucket, MA 02554 (508–228–4706), which is about a ten-minute walk from Main Street. It has ten rooms, some with views of the water. Whichever inn you choose, plan to spend all three nights there.

Day 2 / Morning

BREAKFAST: A continental breakfast is included in the price of a room at the House of the Seven Gables and at many of the other inns.

After breakfast set out to explore the town by foot. The biggest attraction is the village itself, which is an official National Historic District. Wander around the cobblestone streets and you'll see beautifully maintained mansions dating from the eighteenth and nineteenth centuries and lots of gardens and window boxes spilling over with fragrant flowers. Consider taking a guided walking tour offered by the **Nantucket Historical Association** (P.O. Box 1016, Nantucket, MA 02554; 508–228–1894). Tours are offered from April through October. The Historical Association owns and runs several historical sites on the island, including the Whaling Museum, Peter Foulger Museum, Hadwen House, Oldest House, Old Mill, Quaker Meeting House, Fire Hose Cart House, and the Old Jail, all of which can be seen by purchasing a History Ticket ($15.00 for adults, $8.00 for children, or $35.00 for families). The **Whaling Museum,** Broad Street, Nantucket, MA 02554 (508) 228-1736), where history tickets can be purchased, is under the Association's care and tells the story of Nantucket's whaling past. Call for hours and days of operation.

There are also several houses that were built during the island's prosperous whaling days, including the **Three Bricks** at 93–97 Main Street. These three identical redbrick mansions (which are not open for touring) were built between 1836 and 1838 by a whaling merchant for his three sons.

Among the properties owned and managed by the Nantucket Historical Association are the **Hadwen House,** 96 Main Street, Nantucket, MA 02554 (508–228–1894), a Greek Revival mansion built in 1845–46 that is now a house museum; the **Old Gaol,** 15R Vestal Street, Nantucket, MA 02554 (508–228–1894), a jailhouse dating from 1805; the **Old Mill,** on South Mill Street, Nantucket, MA 02554 (508–228–1894), a Dutch windmill; and the island's oldest house, Sunset Hill, Nantucket, MA 02554, which dates from 1686.

For the best view of the island, head for the **First Congregational Church,** 62 Centre Street, Nantucket, MA 02554. It's a ninety-two-step climb to the top of the tower.

Gas lamps and cobbled streets grace Nantucket's charming Main Street.

LUNCH: The **Espresso Cafe,** 40 Main Street, Nantucket, MA 02554 (508–228–6930), right in the center of town, is a good choice for a simple soup-and-salad lunch. Try to get one of the tables in the garden out back.

Afternoon

After lunch either poke around the shops and galleries on Main Street or consider riding a bike to the beach. If you need to rent a bike, you'll find several rental places right in town by the wharf. **Surfside,** on the southern coast, is within easy riding distance (about 3 miles) of town. It's a popular beach with a lunch bar, lifeguards, and a changing facility. If you're up for a longer ride, consider heading out to **Madaket** (12 miles round-trip), at the western tip of the island. The beach here is nonpareil: big white dunes, Atlantic waves, and fewer footprints than at Surfside. It's also prime sunset-viewing territory.

If you decide to browse around the shops, check out the Nantucket Lightship Baskets. The weaving of these baskets, which started back in the nineteenth century, is a real art. They come in all sizes, from small purses to huge picnic baskets. They can be round or oval, open or covered. Many are adorned with scrimshaw and intricately carved and shaped handles. Prices can run anywhere from a couple of hundred dollars for a very simple small basket to several thousands for one decorated with fine scrimshaw.

DINNER: Reservations are a must at **Company of the Cauldron,** 7 India Street, Nantucket, MA 02554 (508–228–4016). Fixed-price dinner is offered with only two seatings, at 7:00 and 9:00 P.M. The menu is table d'hôte, so make sure that you ask what's cooking when you call.

LODGING: Your best bet is to stay put in the inn you chose the night before.

Day 3 / Morning

BREAKFAST: At the inn.

Your destination today is **Siasconset** (pronounced "Sconset") on the southeastern side of the island. It's a 7-mile bike trip on bike paths from Nantucket town. As you drive along, you'll pass moors carpeted with blueberry bushes. The blueberries are usually ripest in late July or early August. The village itself is tiny and very Nantucket. You'll find a post office, a rotary, a cafe, a restaurant, and several private homes.

LUNCH: Stop in the **'Sconset Cafe,** Post Office Square, Nantucket, MA 02564 (508–257–4008), to get a picnic lunch for the beach. They make all sorts of unbelievably delicious sandwiches with sprouts and dressings you'll want the recipe for.

The beach is just minutes down the road from the village. There are no changing facilities.

Afternoon

The beach here is so wonderful, you'll probably want to stay for a good chunk of time. Afterward head back the same way you came or consider taking the long route up to the Quidnet area and then follow the signs back along the northern shore.

DINNER: The **Boarding House,** 12 Federal Street, Nantucket, MA 02564 (508–228–9622), has a wonderful patio that's great for people-watching and has excellent cuisine. The fare is generally international with Asian and Mediterranean accents.

LODGING: Same inn as the previous two nights.

Day 4 / Morning

BREAKFAST: Though breakfast is included in the price of a room, consider getting a muffin or a scone and coffee at the **Nantucket Bake Shop,** 79 Orange Street, Nantucket, MA 02564 (508–228–2797).

Before heading back to the mainland, you can take some time to pick up souvenirs or gifts in town if you didn't get a chance earlier.

Once back on the Cape, retrace your steps to New York City.

There's More

Fishing. Several charter companies sail out of Straight Wharf every day in season. Bluefish and bass are the main catches.

Golf. Miacomet Golf Club (508–325–0333) and Siasconset Golf Club (508–257–6596) are two public golf courses with nine holes each.

Water sports. The Sunken Ship (corner of Broad and South Water Streets (508–228–9226) rents scuba, fishing, and snorkeling gear. It also offers scuba lessons.

Nantucket Community Sailing at Jetties Beach (508–228–5358) rents kayaks, sailboards, sailboats, and more. Sea Nantucket, on Francis Street Beach off Washington Street (508–228–7499), rents kayaks.

Special Events

Late April. Daffodil Festival. This spring festival has a parade of antique cars and a prize for the best tailgate picnic..

Early December. Christmas Stroll. Tour Main Street merchants and enjoy special entertainment and carolers.

Other Recommended Restaurants and Lodgings

Nantucket

Brass Lantern Inn, 11 North Water Street, Nantucket, MA 02554; (508)

228–4064. Located in the historic district, this inn is within easy reach of the sites of town and the ferry.

House of the Seven Gables, 32 Cliff Road, Nantucket, MA 02554; (508) 228–4706. Within about a ten minute walk from town, this inn has ten guest rooms.

Jared Coffin House, 29 Broad Street, Nantucket, MA 02554 (508) 228–2400. Located right in town, in the historic district, this is a Federal-style brick house, built by a wealthy shipowner.

Siasconset

Chanticleer, 9 New Street, Nantucket, MA 02564; (508) 257–6231. French cuisine in a rose garden. What could be more romantic?

Wauwinet

Wauwinet, Wauwinet Road, Nantucket, MA 02584; (508) 228–0145 or (800) 426–8718. Off in a little world of its own, this resort is spectacularly situated (surrounded by ocean and harbor beaches). Every inch of it is elegant, and its restaurant, Topper's, is perhaps the best on the island. It's a full-service resort but small (only twenty-five rooms plus five cottages). There are tennis courts and all sorts of sports facilities plus jitney service for getting around the island.

For More Information

Massachusetts Office of Travel and Tourism, 10 Park Plaza, Suite 410, Boston, MA 02116; (617) 973–8500 or (800) 227–6277.

Nantucket Island Chamber of Commerce, 48 Main Street, Nantucket, MA 02554; (508) 228–3643.

Nantucket Information Bureau, 25 Federal Street, Nantucket, MA 02554; (508) 228–0925. Hours are from 9:00 A.M. to 6:00 P.M. daily in summer and from 9:00 A.M. to 5:30 P.M. Monday through Saturday, off-season.

Ferry Information: For current fares and schedules, visit the Steamship Authority Web site (www.islandferry.com) or call (508) 477–8600.

Boston—
With or Without a Car

Exploring the Hub

2 Nights

A college crew team muscling up the Charles. A mime surrounded by a crowd of eager viewers at Faneuil Hall Marketplace. A fragrant basement bakery on Beacon Hill. Like any major city, Boston has its share of famous historical and architectural attractions, but the little things give it its rich flavor. These are the things that will come to mind years later when you think of Boston.

☐ Museums

☐ Restaurants

☐ Colonial history

☐ Universities

☐ Performing arts

You'll find history with just about every step you take, and you'll be taking many. Boston is very manageable on foot, so we've designed this itinerary predominantly as a walking tour. To reach the different neighborhoods, you can hop on the "T," the city's subway.

Three days is just enough time to sample the city's pleasures as well as make a quick visit to next-door Cambridge.

Day 1 / Morning

To reach Boston from New York, you can take Amtrak (800–872–7245) directly from Penn Station to South Station in about five hours. If you're driving, you can motor up to Boston in less than four hours from Manhattan. Take Route 684 north to Route 84 east. Then take Route 90 ("The Mass Pike") east and get off at the Prudential Center exit, which will get you right into the midtown area, near your hotel. Your best bet is to "pak the caah" in the garage of your hotel when you arrive. Be sure to wear reliable walking shoes.

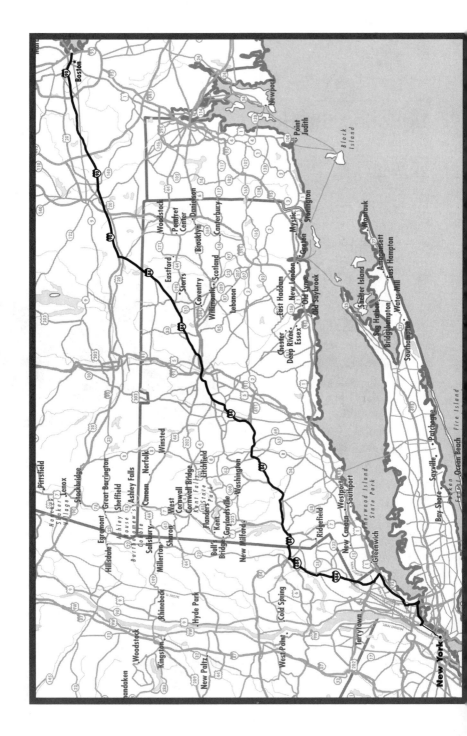

Start by strolling through the **Boston Common** (take the Red or the Green Line to Park Street), which used to be the colonial town's common pastureland and is now the city's most popular park. Make your way up the slope to **Beacon Hill,** where you'll find the **Massachusetts State House** (you can't miss it; it's topped by a golden dome). This building was designed by Charles Bulfinch and was built in the late 1700s.

To the rear of the State House, you'll find **Mount Vernon Street,** which is lined with meticulously maintained brick Federal-style houses. Follow Mt. Vernon Street to **Louisburg Square,** which was laid out in the 1840s. The centerpiece of this incredibly beautiful square is an oval park. By now you're probably starved, and the timing for lunch couldn't be better.

LUNCH: A couple steps away from the State House is the **Black Goose** (21 Beacon Street, Boston, MA 02108; 617–720–4500), which specializes in provincial Italian cuisine.

Afternoon

One block over from Louisburg Square is **Acorn Street,** the street every Boston resident brings out-of-town visitors to when they want to show off. It, too, is lined with brick Federal-style row houses.

From Acorn Street wander back to Park Street, taking Chestnut (yet another picturesque street) to Walnut Street and then Beacon Street alongside the Common. Continue on to Park and turn right, following Park briefly to Tremont. On the corner of Park and Tremont stands **Park Street Church,** a major Boston landmark that was built in 1809. When you leave the church, turn left and walk along Tremont Street to the **Old Granary Burying Ground.** Some major American Revolution figures were buried here including Samuel Adams, John Hancock, and Paul Revere.

Continue northeast on Tremont to School Street, where you'll see **King's Chapel,** which dates from 1754. John Winthrop was buried in the Burying Ground, right next to the chapel. A little farther along School Street is a **Statue of Benjamin Franklin** (though he made his fame and fortune in Philadelphia, Franklin was born in Boston). Keep going on School Street and you'll come to the **Old Corner Bookstore,** which was a gathering place for American authors in the nineteenth century. Turn right and walk a block to the **Old South Meeting House,** 310 Washington Street, at the corner of Milk Street (617–482–6439). It was from here that a group of Colonials set out to throw the Boston Tea Party back in 1773. The house is now a museum, open April through October from 9:30 A.M. to 5:00 P.M.

daily and November through March from 10:00 A.M. to 4:00 P.M. daily. Just around the corner on Milk Street is **Benjamin Franklin's Birthplace,** which is marked by a plaque on the side of a high-rise.

Backtrack on Washington, past the Old Corner Bookstore, to reach the **Old State House,** 206 Washington Street (617–720–1713), which dates from 1713. The Declaration of Independence was read to Bostonians from its balcony in 1776. Follow Court Street and State Street to Congress Street, to the **Boston Massacre Site.** About half a mile away is **Faneuil Hall,** which was originally erected in 1742 as a public meeting hall and marketplace. It's now one of Boston's most popular attractions and is crammed with snack shops, chowder houses, cafes, bakeries, restaurants, and all sorts of boutiques.

DINNER: **Legal Seafoods,** 26 Park Square, Boston, MA 02116 (617–426–4444), is an absolute must. A Boston institution, it's famed for its decently priced, spanking-fresh seafood. Expect to wait for a table.

LODGING: Like any big city, Boston has several major downtown hotels. If you want to stay in a grand old Boston hotel (and feel like splurging), choose the **Fairmont Copley Plaza,** 138 St. James Avenue, Boston, MA 02116 (617–267–5300 or 800–441–1414), right in the heart of the city, facing Copley Square.

Evening

If you want to see a show while in town, arrange for theater tickets in advance or keep your fingers crossed and call Bostix (617–482–2849), which sells day-of-show tickets, often at a discount.

Day 2 / Morning

BREAKFAST: Rather than spend a wad on breakfast at your hotel, consider heading over to one of the coffee shops along Boylston Street.

Then wander around midtown, checking out **Trinity Church,** 206 Clarendon Street, Boston, MA 02116, a hauntingly beautiful French-Romanesque building and the **Boston Public Library,** 700 Boylston Street, Boston, MA 02116 (617–536–5400).

Then head over to **Newbury Street** if you want to do some shopping, or hop on the "T" (take the Green Line's E trolley outbound and get off at Ruggles/Museum) to go to the **Museum of Fine Arts,** 465 Huntington Avenue, Boston, MA 02115 (617–267–9300). The museum specializes in Impressionists, Egyptian artifacts, and Asian art. Visiting hours are from 10:00 A.M. to 4:45 P.M. Monday and Tuesday; 10:00 A.M. to 9:45 P.M. Wednesday, Thursday, and Friday; and 10:00 A.M. to 4:45 P.M. Saturday and Sunday.

LUNCH: There's a pleasant cafe at the Museum of Fine Arts.

Afternoon

If you're up for some more walking, consider taking the Green Line up to Government Center (this will get you back to the Faneuil Hall Marketplace) and exploring the streets of Boston's North End. Among the attractions here are **Paul Revere's House,** 19 North Square, Boston, MA 02113 (617–523–2338), which is open from 9:30 A.M. to 4:15 P.M. from November through mid-April and 9:30 A.M. to 5:15 P.M. from mid-April through October; **Old North Church,** 193 Salem Street, Boston, MA 02113 (617–523–6676), in which the code "one if by land, two if by sea" was created; and **Bunker Hill,** which marks the spot where the Battle of Bunker Hill took place on June 17, 1775.

DINNER: Another Boston institution is **Durgin Park,** North Market Building, 340 Faneuil Hall Marketplace, Boston, MA 02109 (617–227–2038), where dining is communal. There are seafood and steak dishes.

Day 3 / Morning

If you're driving, take the "Mass Ave" bridge over the Charles River to **Cambridge** and head right to **Harvard Square.** Pull into any of the parking garages you see or park on a back street and walk a few blocks—or take the subway right to Harvard Square.

BREAKFAST: Mama Gaia's Café, 401 Massachusetts Avenue, Cambridge, MA (617–441–3999) is a great place to start the day. Menu items include morning burritos, egg sandwiches, and seven-grain toast with strawberry jam. It's a friendly and affordable cafe that prides itself on its earth-friendliness (*Gaia* is the name of the ancient Greek goddess of the earth and of a modern hypothesis in environmental science).

After breakfast get in on one of the free student-led tours around Harvard. Tours leave from the **Harvard University Information Center** (617–495–1573). Check beforehand for departure times; they vary. In an hour's time you'll see the Yard and the exterior of the university's magnificent buildings and surrounding museums. Afterward spend some time in the museums (the Busch-Reisinger, the Fogg Art Museum, the Sackler, and the Harvard University Natural History Museums are the biggies) or the **Harvard Coop,** 1400 Massachusetts Avenue, Cambridge, MA 02138, where you can buy anything from underwear to Frisbees, all emblazoned with the Harvard logo. There are many other shops to explore in Cambridge. You'll be tempted to extend your stay.

LUNCH: Henrietta's Table, at the Charles Hotel, 1 Bennett Street, Cambridge, MA 02138 (617–864–1200), prides itself on fresh food. It specializes in American bistro cuisine and is famed for its brunches.

Afternoon

Head back to New York via Amtrak or the Massachusetts Pike, Route 84, and Route 684, or take I–95 down the coast.

There's More

Harbor sight-seeing. Several companies offer Boston harbor sight-seeing cruises, including Massachusetts Bay Lines, 60 Rowes Wharf, Boston, MA 02110 (617–542–8000) and Boston Harbor Cruises, One Long Wharf, Boston, MA 02110 (617–227–4321).

Jogging. Jogging is one of the most popular pastimes in Boston. Running paths line both banks of the Charles River. For information on races contact the Boston Athletic Association (617–236–1652).

Trolley tours. If you're not up for sight-seeing on foot, consider climbing into a trolley for a Boston tour. Boston Trolley Tours (73 Tremont Street, Boston, MA 02110; 617–742–5905) is one of several companies that offer trolley tours. They have a large fleet of handcrafted trolleys that run year-round. There are well over a dozen boarding stops scattered around the city. The narrated tour lasts about two hours (though you can get on and off at any boarding stop).

Walking tours. In addition to the Freedom Trail, there are a variety of walking tours in Boston.

Concerts by the Boston Pops are held in the Hatch Memorial Shell.

Black Heritage Trail (617–742–5415) is a ninety-minute walk taking you to the city's nineteenth-century black community landmarks. You can opt for a guided tour or pick up a map and brochure and follow it on your own.

Victorian Society in America (617–267–6338) takes you to the city's Victorian sights.

Women's Heritage Trail (617–522–2872) focuses on the lives of twenty women who made significant contributions to the city.

Whale watches. The A.C. Cruise Company (617–261–6633), Boston Harbor Cruises (617–227–4321), Massachusetts Baylines (617–542–8000), and the New England Aquarium (617–973–5200) offer whale-watch cruises.

Special Events

April. Boston Marathon. Takes place on the third Monday every April. Runners run from Hopkinton to the Prudential Center.

July. Esplanade Concerts. Musical programs by the Boston Pops in the Hatch Shell on the Esplanade.

July 4th weekend. Harborfest. A seaside celebration with fireworks, chowder contests, boat races, historical reenactments, and a performance by the Boston Pops Orchestra.

October. Charles River Regatta. One of the rowing world's biggest races is held the third Sunday in October every year.

December. First Night Celebration. Boston Common on New Year's Eve.

Other Recommended Restaurants and Lodgings

Boston

As with all major cities, there are dozens of hotels and restaurants to choose from in Boston. Here is a handful of some of the city's finest:

Boston Harbor Hotel, 70 Rowes Wharf, Boston, MA 02110; (617) 439–7000 or (800) 752–7077. A beautiful harbor hotel with a European accent.

Four Seasons Boston, 200 Boylston Street, Boston, MA 02116; (617) 338–4400 or (800) 332–3442. Overlooking Boston Common and the Public Garden, this hotel is wonderful in every way.

Ritz-Carlton Boston, 15 Arlington Street, Boston, MA 02117; (617) 536–5700. If you're in the mood for all-out luxury, you'll love it here. This *grande dame* hotel recently reopened after a major restoration to its classic grandeur.

Cambridge

Charles Hotel at Harvard Square, One Bennett Street, Cambridge, MA 02138; (617) 864–1200. A full-service luxury hotel with an attached health spa.

Inn at Harvard, 1201 Massachusetts Avenue, Cambridge, MA 02138; (617) 491–2222. Cambridge's newest hotel is adjacent to Harvard Yard.

For More Information

Greater Boston Convention & Visitors Bureau, 2 Copley Place, Suite 205, Boston, MA 02116; (617) 536–4100 or (888) SEE–BOSTON.

Massachusetts Office of Travel and Tourism, 10 Park Plaza, Suite 4510, Boston, MA 02116; (617) 973–8500 or (800) 227–6277.

NORTHERN
NEW ENGLAND
ESCAPES

Vermont's Northeast Kingdom

Scenery and Then Some

3 Nights

Nearly every inch of Vermont is New England just as you pictured it—covered bridges, immaculate dairy farms, steepled villages, and sagging old farmhouses where big-pawed golden retrievers sleep on front porches. Add to that the fact that every season has its own appeals, and choosing exactly when to go and just where to go can be a happy dilemma.

☐ Mountain scenery

☐ Picture-perfect villages

☐ Boutiques and antiques shops

☐ Ben & Jerry's ice-cream factory

☐ Distinguished inns

☐ Autumn-leaf viewing

☐ Winter sports

Fortunately, you can't go wrong in Vermont. In the fall the Crayola colors are everywhere (especially early to mid-October). At that time of year, the weather is often phenomenally beautiful, with flawless blue skies and plenty of sunshine. During winter the hills are alive with skiers and snowshoers. When the snows thaw, the landscape awakens into a profusion of blossoms and green. There's green everywhere, getting greener and greener each day as the state warms into summer.

Northern Vermont is perhaps the state's most sensationally scenic area (though many may argue that). There are miles and miles of cattle-dotted farmlands, silent lakes cupped in the hills as if precious jewels, and streams that really do sparkle. Add to that the backdrop of looming mountains, and you're looking at not just the state's but some of our country's most beautiful scenery.

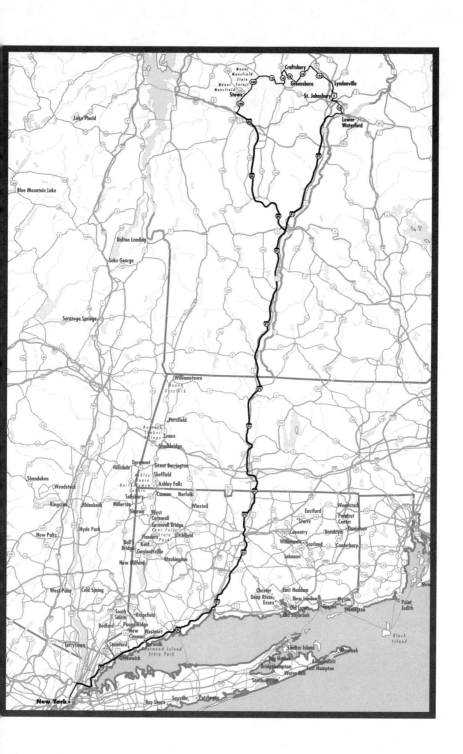

Day 1 / *Morning*

One of our longest escapes, this drive focuses on the northern woods and mountains of Vermont. Do yourself a favor: Head out early in the day so that you can take some time to relax once you get up there. It can take about six hours to get to Stowe, which is your first stop. From New York City head east, picking up I–95. Take that to I–91 north and stay on that until you reach I–89 north. Stowe is only ten minutes from I–89. Get off at exit 10 and follow Route 100 10 miles into town.

On Route 100, you'll pass right through **Waterbury,** where you'll find the legendary **Ben & Jerry's** (802–882–1240) ice-cream factory. It's close enough to Stowe, so if you're too tired to visit now, keep in mind that you can stop by later during your stay. There are tours, exhibits, a gift shop, and an all-around air of carnival. Across the street is the **Cold Hollow Cider Mill,** (802–244–8771) where you can watch cider being pressed and see films on how cider and maple sugar are made.

LUNCH: Chances are you'll be starved well before you reach the Stowe area, so your best bet is to either pack picnic lunches or pull off to a roadside eatery. If you can last until Waterbury, make your way to the **Mist Grill** (92 Stowe Street, Waterbury, VT 05676; 802–244–8522). There are some pleasant lunch dishes on the menu, including a curry chicken salad, portobello burger, and flat-bread chicken pizzarino. The Mist Grill is also great for brunch (on Saturdays and Sundays), bistro dinners (Thursday through Saturday) and what they call the "Sunday Supper."

Afternoon

Carry on a short distance past Waterbury and you'll come to **Stowe,** where you can settle in and take an afternoon hike (or go skiing, if it's winter) and follow it up with a great dinner. In winter this beautiful town is a mecca for skiers, with its daredevil trails, its exuberant aprés-ski life, and its lodges that look like Austria. Stowe is dominated by **Mount Mansfield,** Vermont's highest mountain (4,393 feet). But when the lifts are closed, Stowe is just as appealing. In town there are all sorts of wonderful little emporiums that sell everything from Christmas ornaments to handmade sweaters that look too pretty to wear. There are also several antiques shops to poke around.

DINNER: Depending on what you're in the mood for, Stowe has many dining options. A special treat, however, is dinner at **Edson Hill Manor**

(1500 Edson Hill Road, Stowe, VT 05672; 802–253–7371 or 800–621–0284), which offers fine regional American cuisine.

LODGING: **Trapp Family Lodge** (Trapp Hill Road, Stowe, VT 05672; 802–253–8511 or 800–826–7000) is an Austrian-style lodge propped up on a hilltop with far-reaching views. It's set on 2,000 acres and has hiking and cross-country skiing trails, an indoor-outdoor pool, and a fitness center. Book a two-night stay.

Day 2 / Morning

BREAKFAST: A full hearty breakfast is served in the dining room at the Trapp Family Lodge.

Stowe's natural beauty is its strongest appeal. Give yourself the entire day to dip into its treasures. Though you can drive around and see plenty (in fact, you can drive to the top of Mansfield), consider taking time out to explore by foot. Much of the landscape is part of Vermont's **Mount Mansfield State Forest.** There are many hiking trails, camping areas, and picnic spots. Another way to enjoy the area's scenery (in warm weather months as well as winter) is to ride the gondola to the top of Mount Mansfield. For the ultimate view, climb into a glider at **Stowe Aviation** (802–888–5453). For twenty minutes—or more, depending on which flight you opt for—you'll soar over the peaks and valleys like weightless birds. You can easily fill two days exploring Stowe, so allow enough time.

LUNCH: If the weather's nice, consider stopping by the **Harvest Market** (1031 Mountain Road, Stowe, VT 05672; 802–253–3800) where you can get a gourmet lunch-to-go for a picnic. Or choose one of the small eateries or bistros in town.

Afternoon

Spend the afternoon doing the things you weren't able to squeeze into the morning.

DINNER: For a French meal try the **Isle de France** (1899 Mountain Road, Stowe, VT 05672; 802–253–7751). Another option is the **Cliff House Restaurant,** which is located atop Mount Mansfield, Stowe, VT 05672 (802–253–3000) and is reached by gondola.

LODGING: Return to the Trapp Family Lodge to relax and unwind for the rest of the evening.

Day 3 / Morning

BREAKFAST: Breakfast at the Trapp Family Lodge.

Before setting out consider stopping in town to get picnic lunches. You can pick up the necessities at the Craftsbury General Store (118 South Craftsbury, Craftsbury Center, VT 05826; 802–586–2811). Then head north on Route 100 and then turn right onto Route 15 in **Morrisville.** The landscape here is densely scenic. You'll pass huge red barns with silver silos, old farmhouses settled into the contour of the land, and fields full of cows and sturdy ponies with tangled manes. You'll see fishermen wading in rivers and thousands of white birch trees that look like fish bones against dark pine forests.

In **Hardwick** take Route 14 up to **Craftsbury** (you'll see signs), a Grandma Moses kind of village with crisp, clean white buildings, a billiard-green square, and flawless white fences all around.

LUNCH: If you're ready to dig into that picnic lunch, this is a good place to park yourself.

Afterward, consider stopping in at **Craftsbury Center** (follow the signs on the dirt roads), a camp—for both kids and adults—that is devoted to the graceful sport of sculling. In winter it turns into a cross-country ski center. For information, call (802) 586–7767 or (800) 729–7751.

Afternoon

From Craftsbury follow the road to **Greensboro** (it's southeast of Craftsbury), which is home to **Willey's General Store,** (Main Road, Greensboro, VT 05841; 802–533–2621), an attraction in itself. Here you'll find everything from parts for balsa-wood planes to farm equipment. Then carry on to **Lyndonville,** where there are five **covered bridges** (one dating from 1795) within the town's limits. Follow Route 16 north and then make a sharp right onto Route 122.

From Lyndonville head south on Route 5 to **St. Johnsbury,** which has some beautiful Victorian buildings along with an art gallery and a museum where you can learn all about the production of maple syrup. About fifteen minutes away is **Lower Waterford,** where you can settle in for dinner and the night (head east out of St. Johnsbury on Route 2, then south on Route 18).

DINNER: The French/American meals at **Rabbit Hill Inn** (Route 18 and Pucker Street, Lower Waterford, VT 05848; 802–748–5168 or 800–762–8669) are candlelit and gourmet.

LODGING: Rabbit Hill Inn (Route 18 and Pucker Street, Lower Waterford, VT 05848; 802–748–5168) is a white Federal-style house full of romantic details and a rabbit theme throughout. Some of the rooms have fireplaces, some have Jacuzzis.

Day 4 / Morning

BREAKFAST: The Rabbit Hill Inn serves a full breakfast buffet and is included in the room rate.

After breakfast and maybe a brisk walk, make your way back to New York City by following I–91 south and retracing your steps.

There's More

City exploring. Vermont's largest city, **Burlington,** is situated on the shores of Lake Champlain, not far from the Stowe area. Consider spending some time exploring downtown, a small enough area to negotiate on foot. Its centerpiece is the **Church Street Marketplace,** a 4-block stretch of Church Street closed to traffic, with sidewalk cafes, benches, and all sorts of street performers.

Winter sports. There's no end to the amount of winter sports you'll find in this part of the world, including alpine and cross-country skiing, snowmobiling, snowboarding, skating, and sleigh riding. Contact Ski Vermont for complete information (see "For More Information" at the end of this chapter).

Special Events

January–February. Stowe Winter Carnival, throughout Stowe; (802) 253–7321. Gala parties, ice sculptures, snowshoe races, fireworks, and more.

June. Green Mountain Regatta, Stowe; (802) 253–7321. Remote-controlled model sailboat racing.

September. For Art's Sake/A Taste of Stowe, Stowe; (802) 253–7321. More than eighty artists display their works, which are for sale.

Northeast Kingdom Annual Fall Foliage Festival—Marshfield, Walden, Cabot, Plainfield, Peacham, Barnet, Groton, St. Johnsbury; (802) 563–2472.

Other Recommended Restaurants and Lodgings

Small, distinguished inns can be found all over Vermont—tucked away in forests, set on farmlands, prominently situated in villages, you name it. A complete list of inns (and many bed and breakfasts) is published by the Vermont Chamber of Commerce. For a copy write to P.O. Box 37, Montpelier, VT 05601 or call (802) 223–3443.

Craftsbury Center

Inn on the Common, Craftsbury Common, VT 05827; (802) 586–9619. Sixteen antique-furnished bedrooms located in three buildings. Dinner and breakfast are served for guests (outside guests with reservations only).

Greensboro

Highland Lodge, 1608 Craftsbury Road, Greensboro, VT 05841; (802) 533–2647. A family-owned inn and Nordic ski center beautifully situated overlooking Caspian Lake.

Highgate Springs

Tyler Place Family Resort, Old Dock Road, Highgate Springs, VT 05460; (802) 868–4000. This is a fabulous family resort that is a more substantial escape than a couple of days. For a future trip, consider booking one of the cottages here. It's a "camp" for both adults and children of all ages where guests can choose from a multipage list of activities every day, including biking, hiking, kayaking, canoeing, waterskiing, tennis—you name it. The kids join their age groups, which meet every day from 8:30 A.M. to 1:30 P.M. and again from 5:30 to 8:30 P.M. for everything from pony and boat rides to pajama parties and campouts.

Manchester Village

Equinox, Historic Route 7A, Manchester Village, VT 05254; (802) 362–4700 or (800) 362–4747. If you want to break up your trip to northern

Vermont, consider overnighting at the Equinox, a grand historic hotel within easy reach of many factory outlet stores.

Montpelier

The Inn at Montpelier, 147 Main Street, Montpelier, VT 05602; (802) 223–2727. This historic inn has two stately Federal buildings, both built in the 1800s.

Smugglers' Notch

Smugglers Notch, 4323 Vermont Route 108 South, Smugglers' Notch, Vermont; (802) 644–8851. For a return trip that's a little bit longer than a weekend, consider going beyond Stowe to "Smuggs," a ski area that prides itself on its family-friendliness. During the summer months it's just as much fun, with all sorts of outdoor activities and kids' programs.

Stowe

Topnotch at Stowe Resort & Spa, 4000 Mountain Road, Stowe, VT 05672; (800) 451–8686 or (802) 253–8585. In addition to accommodations and fine dining, Topnotch has a complete spa and more than a dozen tennis courts.

For More Information

Stowe Area Association, Inc., P.O. Box 1320, Stowe, VT 05672; (802) 253–7321 or (877) 467–8693.

Vermont Department of Tourism and Marketing, 6 Baldwin Street, Montpelier, VT 05602; (802) 828–3236.

Vermont Ski Areas Association, (Ski Vermont), 26 State Street, Montpelier, VT 05601; (802) 223–2439.

The Mountains of New Hampshire

Fresh-Air Beauty

2 Nights

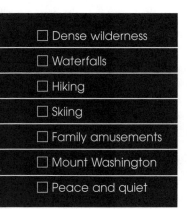

- ☐ Dense wilderness
- ☐ Waterfalls
- ☐ Hiking
- ☐ Skiing
- ☐ Family amusements
- ☐ Mount Washington
- ☐ Peace and quiet

If you want to go somewhere where your soul can breathe, where you have a sense of space—choose New Hampshire. This is a state that still has an undiscovered air to it; a state that lives and lets live and doesn't try to impress. It's remarkably beautiful as well, especially along this route. This escape takes you to the Dartmouth-Sunapee Region and then works its way up to the Eastern White Mountains, where the scenery gets more stunning with seemingly every mile you drive north.

Day 1 / *Morning*

It takes about 5 hours to drive to New Hampshire, not counting any stops. The fastest way to make your way to this part of the world is to take I–95 east to New Haven, Connecticut, where you'll then head north on I–91. You'll go through Connecticut and Massachusetts and then enter Vermont. At White River Junction, Vermont, head east on I–89 to exit 18.

LUNCH: If you don't hit traffic, you should be able to make it up to Southern Vermont in time for lunch. Get off at Exit 4 for Putney, where you'll find the **Putney Diner** (Main Street, Putney, VT 05346; 802–387–5433). Here you can have some wholesome, Vermont-style food. If it's nice out, you could also pick up sandwiches at the **Putney General Store** (considered the "Center of Putney"; 802–387–5842) and just sit outside on the bench in front. Afterward walk over to the **Front Porch**

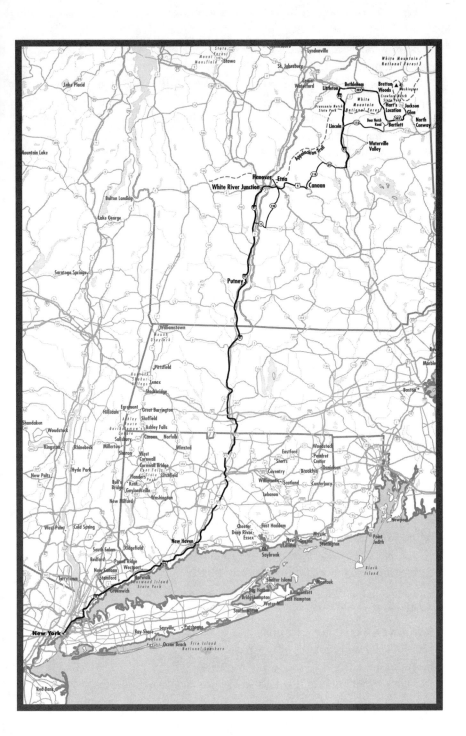

Bakery (133 Main Street, Putney; 802–387–4800), where you'll find a selection of scrumptious baked goods and great coffee.

Get back on I–91 and continue on north. At the risk of tangling you up in directions, we are going to steer you right to Moose Mountain Lodge, which is your home for the night. The owners are the first to say that "getting here is part of the fun." Indeed it is. Get off exit 13 and follow Route 120 north toward Hanover (New Hampshire) for half a mile. Then turn right onto Etna Road, following it for 3.6 miles. Turn left onto Old Dana Road for half a mile to the red barn on the right. Go 100 yards past it. Turn right, following the steep, narrow road for a mile (bearing right twice) to get to the lodge.

Afternoon

Spend the afternoon hiking. Your home for the night, the Moose Mountain Lodge, is set on 350 jaw-droppingly beautiful acres, and the Appalachian Trail cuts right through it. Or you can spend some time poking around Hanover, which is the home of Dartmouth College.

DINNER: Moose Mountain Lodge, P.O. Box 272, Etna, NH 03750 (603–643–3529), prides itself on its excellent homemade food. *Everything* is homemade, and the vegetables are fresh from the garden. Dining is family-style buffet.

LODGING: Moose Mountain Lodge, P.O. Box 272, Etna, NH 03750 (603–643–3529) has lots of return guests, and it's easy to see why. In fact, one guest summed it up wonderfully: "You can go home again . . . it's like visiting perfect parents after a long journey." This is a magical place, owned and run by Kay and Peter Shumway. The lodge was built as a downhill ski lodge in 1938 and has exposed tree trunk timbers throughout. A large double fireplace warms both the dining room and a large sitting room with a piano. The lodge is open from June 15 through mid-October and then from December 26 through early March.

Day 2 / Morning

BREAKFAST: After a leisurely and relaxing breakfast at the lodge, you can do some more hiking or touring in Hanover and then head out for a beautiful drive north to the White Mountains.

Start by taking Route 4 East to Canaan and then go north on Route

Enjoy the natural beauty and solitude in the wilderness of New Hampshire.

118. Then head east on Route 25, following it until you reach I–93, where you'll go north. Along the way you'll see dramatically scenic mountains and waterfalls. Next go east on Route 112, which is the **Kancamagus Highway** that goes through the Franconia Notch. This is considered one of the most scenic highways in the East. Along the way there are picnic sites, trails, and Sabbaday Falls and Rocky Gorge (two short walks). Then cut north on Bear Notch Road which is open only in the summer months. At end of Bear Notch, follow Route 302 to Route 16 and head into Jackson.

LUNCH: The **Thompson House Eatery,** Route 16A, Jackson, NH 03846 (603–383–9341), is attractively set in an old red farmhouse that dates to the early 1880s. The chef has built a reputation for fine food presented in an artful manner.

Afternoon

After lunch have a look around **Jackson,** which is a classic White Mountain village set in the White Mountain National Forest. It is right at the base of **Mount Washington,** the highest peak in the northeast.

Resume your journey by retracing your steps back to Route 302 and following that north to **Bretton Woods,** where you'll find the Mount Washington Hotel.

DINNER: Mount Washington Hotel, Route 302, Bretton Woods, NH 03575 (800–258–0330). Meals are festive occasions here in the Grand Dining Room, with an orchestra and dancing and very formal wait staff.

LODGING: The **Mount Washington Hotel,** Route 302, Bretton Woods, NH 03575; (800–258–0330), is a major White Mountain landmark. A masterpiece of Spanish Renaissance Revival architecture, it was conceived by industrialist Joseph Stickney and first opened its doors in July 1902 after being worked on by 250 master craftsmen. The most luxurious resort of its day, it catered to wealthy guests from Philadelphia, Boston and New York. In 1944 it hosted the Bretton Woods International Monetary Conference at which the World Bank and International Monetary Fund were established. Today it is a grand, full-scale resort with a vast array of recreational activities, from twenty-seven holes of golf, twelve tennis courts, and horseback riding to swimming, hiking, and biking.

Day 3 / Morning

BREAKFAST: A has-everything breakfast buffet (included in room rate) is served in the main dining room of the Mount Washington Hotel as a pianist quietly plays on.

After breakfast consider taking a trip on the **Mount Washington Cog Railway** (round trip takes about three hours), off Route 302, Bretton Woods, NH 03575; (603–846–5406 or 800–922–8825). This train has been making its way to the summit of Mount Washington since the 1860s. Reservations are suggested. It operates Saturday and Sunday in May and daily from June through late October. If you're traveling with kids (or not with kids), consider heading down Route 302 to Bartlett, where you'll find **Attitash Bear Peak** (Route 302, Bartlett, NH 03812; 603–374–2368), offering alpine and water slides, horseback riding, and a chairlift to the top for 360-degree views. It's open daily from mid-June through mid-September and Saturday and Sunday only from mid-September through mid-October.

LUNCH: Stickney's at the Mount Washington Hotel (Route 302, Bretton Woods, NH 03575; 800–258–0330) offers Southwestern fare with wonderful views of the Presidential Range and Mount Washington. During the summer months you can eat outdoors.

After lunch plan to spend the rest of the day returning to New York. You can take Route 302 to Route 3 and pick up I–93 south. Or, if you'd like to gorge yourself on even more beautiful scenery (and possibly get home even faster), consider taking I–93 north to I–91 south.

There's More

Hiking. You'll find ample opportunities to hike in these mountain woods. Be sure to check out Franconia Notch State Park (Franconia and Lincoln, off I–93 about 7 miles south of Route 302; 603–823–5563) and Crawford Notch State Park (Hart's Location, Route 302, about 7 miles southeast of Bretton Woods; 603–374–2272).

Outlet Shopping. There are more than 250 outlet stores in North Conway, including Ralph Lauren, Calvin Klein, and the Gap.

Skiing. For complete information on skiing in New Hampshire, contact Ski New Hampshire, P.O. Box 10, North Woodstock, NH 03262; (603) 745–9396 or (800) 887–5464. Two especially noteworthy ski areas in the eastern White Mountain region are **Waterville Valley** (603–236–8311 or 800–468–2553) and **Bretton Woods** (603–278–3300 or 800–258–0330). Both are especially proud of their family-friendly facilities, staff, and ski terrain.

Theme Park. Story Land, Route 16, Glen, NH 03838; (603) 383–4186. Here you'll find Cinderella and Heidi's grandfather and ride on the Polar Coaster. Open daily from mid-June through mid-September and then Saturday and Sunday only from mid-September through mid-October. Admission is $19 per person and children under four are admitted free.

Special Events

Mid-February. Dartmouth Winter Carnival, Hanover; (603) 795–2143.

June. Annual Fields of Lupine Festival, Franconia and Sugar Hill; (603) 846–5790. Celebration of the wildflowers found around New Hampshire.

July. July Fourth Family Day, North Conway; (800) 367–3364.

August. Attitash Equine Festival, Bartlett; (603) 374–2368.

October. Fall Rail Fans' Day, North Conway; (603) 356–5251.

December. Dickens Holiday Celebration, Hanover; (603) 643–3115.

Other Recommended Restaurants and Lodgings

Bethlehem

Adair Country Inn, 80 Guider Lane, Bethlehem, NH 03574; (603) 444–2600 or (888) 444–2600. This is a spectacular Georgian mansion set on 200 acres with magnificent gardens designed by the Olmsted brothers. Every detail is thought about here, from the feather pillows to the elegant afternoon tea service. Waking up to homemade popovers for breakfast is an extra special plus!

Hart's Location

Notchland Inn, Route 302, Hart's Location, NH 03812; (800) 866–6131. An 1860s granite mansion set on 400 acres and looking out at Mounts Hope and Crawford. All seven rooms and six suites are individually decorated and appointed with wood-burning fireplaces. Dinner is a grand five-course affair served in the elegant dining room overlooking the gardens and the pond.

Jackson

Ellis River House, Route 116, Jackson, NH 03846; (603) 383–9339 or (800) 233–8309. This is an enchanting eighteen-room inn at the base of Mount Washington.

Littleton

Cantina di Gerardo, 363 Meadow Street, Littleton, NH 03561; (603) 444–7700. A dreamy northern Italian restaurant where dinner is served in pans. There's also a take-out menu should you choose to picnic.

North Conway

Cabernet Inn, P.O. Box 489, North Conway, NH 03860; (800) 866–4704. A handsome, red gabled house in the Mount Washington valley, the Cabernet Inn is within easy reach of the 250 outlet stores in North Conway.

Waterville Valley

Valley Inn, P.O. Box 1, Tecumseh Road, Waterville Valley, NH 03215; (800) 343–0969. This is a perfect base for staying if you're skiing at Waterville Valley. You can pick up the shuttle bus to the slopes right in front of the hotel, and you're minutes away from the Town Square and the Nordic Ski Center.

Whitefield

Mountain View Grand, Mountain View Road, Whitefield, NH 03598; (866) 484–3843 or (603) 837–2100. A fully restored 145-room grand hotel with magnificent views, a spa, a pool, and a glorius front veranda.

For More Information

New Hampshire Division of Travel and Tourism Development, P.O. Box 1856, Concord, NH 03302; (603) 271–2665.

White Mountains Attractions Association, P.O. Box 10PM, North Woodstock, NH 03262; (603) 745–8720 or (800) FIND MTS.

The Coast of Maine

The Coast with the Most

3 Nights

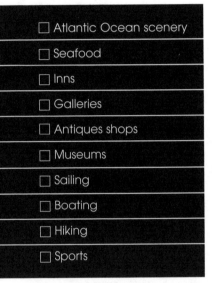

- ☐ Atlantic Ocean scenery
- ☐ Seafood
- ☐ Inns
- ☐ Galleries
- ☐ Antiques shops
- ☐ Museums
- ☐ Sailing
- ☐ Boating
- ☐ Hiking
- ☐ Sports

For more than one hundred years, Maine's coast has been a popular summer vacation area. It's made up of a series of deeply cut coves and narrow peninsulas and has countless offshore islands. Along the way there are dozens of little fishing villages bursting with character. For this particular escape we take you up the Maine coast, from Kennebunkport to Bar Harbor. Keep in mind that many hotels, restaurants, and attractions close during the winter months (sometimes as early as October).

Day 1 *Morning and Afternoon*

To reach **Kennebunkport** take I–95 north of New York City and follow it right up to Maine. Expect the drive to take about five hours. In Maine take exit 3 and head east on 9A to Kennebunkport. You'll see signs for Kennebunk as well—that's the commercial center, whereas Kennebunkport is the port town. The latter is where you'll find most of the tourist activity. Kennebunkport is still known as Bush Country, nicknamed for the first President Bush, whose summer home, Walker's Point, is located here.

LUNCH: Since you will have spent the better part of the day traveling, your best bet is to grab lunch at a roadside eatery en route whenever hunger strikes.

When you reach Kennebunkport, check into your hotel and rest a bit before going out to have a lobster dinner.

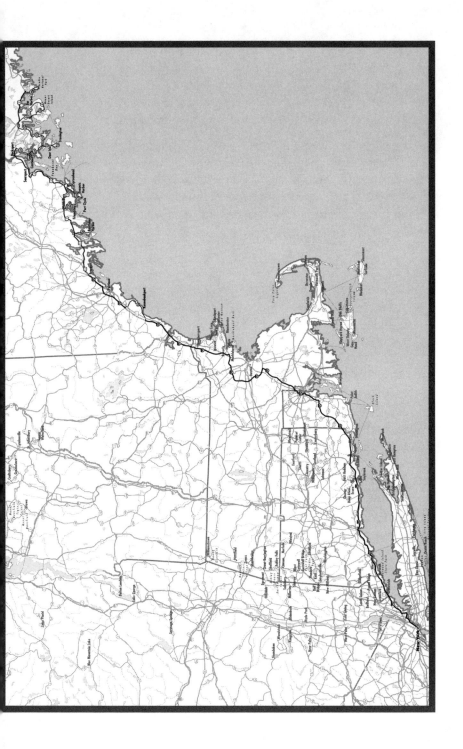

DINNER: The **White Barn Inn** (37 Beach Avenue, Kennebunkport, ME 04046; 207–967–2321) serves impeccably prepared contemporary American cuisine, with a concentration of New England flavors and fresh Maine seafood. A Relais & Château property, it's also wonderful for lodging. On top of that it's New England's only five-star restaurant.

LODGING: The **Captain Lord Mansion,** Kennebunkport, ME 04046; (207) 967–3141 or (800) 522–3141. Designed by Captain Lord, a wealthy merchant and shipbuilder, this is a three-story Federal-style building that dates from 1812. All twenty rooms are beautifully decorated with period-reproduction wallpapers, exquisite antiques, and four-poster beds.

Day 2 / Morning

BREAKFAST: Breakfast at the Captain Lord Mansion is included in the room rate.

After breakfast take time to see the sites in and around Kennebunkport, including **Nott House,** a stately Greek Revival house that dates from 1853 (Maine Street, Kennebunkport, ME 04046; 207–967–2571). Nott House is open Tuesday through Friday from 10:00 A.M. to 4:00 P.M. and Saturday from 10:00 A.M. to 1:00 P.M. Guided tours are available from mid-June to mid-October. Other interesting attractions include mansion-dotted **Ocean Avenue** and the **Seashore Trolley Museum** (Log Cabin Road, Kennebunkport, ME 04046; 207–967–2712), located 3³⁄₁₀ miles up North Street from Kennebunkport. From there drive inland and take an architectural walking tour of **Kennebunk's National Register District** (very noteworthy is the **Brick Store Museum** at 117 Main Street, Kennebunk, ME 04043; 207–985–4802). On Summer Street (Route 35), take a look at the **Wedding Cake House,** an 1826 house covered with white wooden latticework.

Then head up to **Portland,** where you can easily occupy yourself for hours. Tops on our list of sight-seeing attractions in Portland is the **Portland Museum of Art,** 7 Congress Square, Portland, ME 04101 (207–775–6148), which is housed in a striking postmodern building that was designed by Henry N. Cobb of I. M. Pei. It contains extensive collections of Maine-based artists such as Andrew Wyeth, Edward Hopper, and Winslow Homer. Other Portland attractions include the **Wadsworth-Longfellow House,** (489 Congress Street, Portland, ME 04101; 207–772–1807—open daily June 1 to October 31 from 10:00 A.M. to 4:00 P.M.) where the poet spent his childhood, and the **Old Port Exchange,** a six-block area of town (bordered by

The Captain Lord Mansion is a beautifully decorated house that dates from 1812.

Commercial Street next to Casco Bay and Congress Street) lined with restaurants, taverns, and shops that occupy former warehouses and other nineteenth-century buildings, open daily during the summer.

LUNCH: You can grab a light lunch right at the cafe in the **Portland Museum of Art** (7 Congress Square, Portland, ME 04101; 207–775–6148). They serve light sandwiches, soups, and snacks. Or head to **Gilbert's Chowder House** (92 Commercial Street, Portland, ME; 207–871–5636) and get a lobster roll.

Afternoon

About 20 miles north of Portland on Route 1 is **Freeport,** home of L.L. Bean and several brand-name factory outlets (Banana Republic, Brooks Brothers, Polo Ralph Lauren) where you can spend as much or as little time as you please.

Continue up the coast on Route 1 and then take Route 27 to **Boothbay Harbor.** This town started life as a tiny lobstering and fishing community and grew into a tourist mecca of sorts. It's a great place to go with young children.

As you carry on up the coast, you can stop and visit whichever towns appeal, keeping in mind your destination for the night: Castine.

The little village of **Waldoboro** is one of the next towns you'll come to as you continue up Route 1. It has several old homes and a Lutheran church that dates from 1771. Farther out on that peninsula (following Route 220) is **Friendship,** a picturesque lobstering port. You have to go around the inlet and then out to the tip of St. George Peninsula to get to **Port Clyde,** where the mail boat for Monhegan Island runs year-round. You can head out to Monhegan Island from here or take a boat from Boothbay Harbor. On your way back to Route 1, take time out to visit the picture-perfect waterfront towns of **Tenants Harbor** and **Sprucehead.**

Around this point of the coast—at **Penobscot Bay**—you start to see the Maine coast everyone has always raved about. Startlingly beautiful islands rise abruptly out of the choppy waters. Sparkling sailboats gracefully skim about. Most beautiful, though, are the tall-masted windjammers that are famous in this area. You can spend a week on one eating hearty home-cooked meals and flitting about from one drop-dead gorgeous island to another. The main departure points are in the Rockland, Rockport, and Camden areas.

As you continue up the coast, you'll come to **Searsport,** an old shipping port with stately old sea-captains' homes and a multitude of antiques shops. **Bucksport** is next, which is home to the **Fort Knox State Park,** an impressively constructed fort that was manned during both the Civil and Spanish-American Wars.

Castine is the last stop for the day. The town itself is the attraction: A community of eighteenth- and nineteenth-century Georgian and Federal houses standing in impeccable condition. Most of these houses were originally erected in the mid-nineteenth century when Castine was a prosperous shipbuilding town. Many of them have since been restored by people "from away" (in other words, big-city folks with money to invest).

DINNER: **Dennett's Wharf** (Sea Street, Castine, ME 04421; 207–326–9045) is a net-hung, bustling fish house looking out over the harbor.

LODGING: The **Castine Inn** (Main Street, Castine, ME 04421; 207–326–

4365) is a bed and breakfast in town with twenty antiques-furnished guest rooms.

Day 3 / Morning

BREAKFAST: At the Castine Inn enjoy a full breakfast (included in the room rate) of blueberry pancakes, omelettes, homemade granola, corned beef hash with poached eggs and more.

From Castine it's a short, steadily scenic drive over to the village of **Blue Hill,** which is home to seventy-five buildings that are listed on the National Register of Historic Places. Take time out to walk around and poke in the pottery and crafts shops, for which Blue Hill is well known.

Head southwest of Blue Hill and you'll eventually cut through a corner of Little Deer Isle and then climb an arching suspension bridge that takes you over to **Deer Isle,** a wonderful little island almost too beautiful to promote. Don't miss the sweet little town of **Stonington** at the southern tip.

Ever since the mid-nineteenth century, **Mt. Desert Island** has been one of Maine's most popular destinations. Once you cross the bridge connecting it to the mainland, it's easy to see why. The island is home to **Cadillac Mountain,** which, at 1,530 feet, seems to scrape the sky. Looming all around are sixteen other mountains that drop right down into the sea. Fortunately, most of the island (35,000 acres) is under the protection of **Acadia National Park,** which is threaded with miles of hiking, driving, and biking trails. The Park Loop Road takes in the major sights of the park.

The island's main town is **Bar Harbor,** which, back in the late 1800s, was a thriving resort community for wealthy and powerful American families. At present, it's quite a busy tourist hub, with lots of shops, motels, and restaurants.

LUNCH: If you want a quick lunch on the go, you'll find several casual eateries right in Bar Harbor. Consider, too, shopping for picnic items and taking a lunch hiking in the national park.

Afternoon

Divide your day between the natural treasures of the national park with the commercial attractions of Bar Harbor.

DINNER: Jordan Pond House, Park Loop Road, Seal Harbor, ME 04675 (207–276–3316), has wonderful specialties such as lobster stew and baked haddock. It also offers a lovely mountain view.

LODGING: Clefstone Manor, 92 Eden Street, Bar Harbor, ME 04609; (207) 288–8086 or (888) 288–4951. This is a huge mansion that was built back in 1894 as a summer home for James Blair, secretary of the navy under President Lincoln.

Day 4 / Morning

BREAKFAST: At the manor enjoy a three-course breakfast (included in room rate) that starts with fruit or juice, followed by breads and muffins, and then your choice of hot entree.

Take your time leisurely working your way back down the coast before picking up I–95 to return to New York.

There's More

Beaches. The whole coast of Maine is dotted with beaches, most open to the public. Some of the most popular beaches are Ogunquit Beach, Wells Beach, Gouche's Beach (near Kennebunkport), Colony Beach (Kennebunkport), Ferry Beach State Park (between Camp Ellis and Old Orchard Beach), and Crescent Beach State Park (south of Portland).

Gallery hopping. All along the coast of Maine, you'll find galleries displaying works of local painters and sculptors. On Deer Isle you can visit Haystack Mountain School of Crafts (Route 15; 207–348–2306), which attracts artists from around the world who work in metal, textiles, wood, glass, pottery, and paper.

Hiking. In addition to Acadia National Park, the southern coast of Maine has several state parks laced with hiking trails. These include Crescent Beach State Park, Wolf's Neck State Park, Popham Beach State Park, Reid State Park, and Camden Hills State Park, just to name a few.

Island excursion. Consider taking time out to visit Monhegan Island, just off the southern coast of Maine. A mere smidgen on the map (less than 2 miles long and 1 mile wide), it has been known as a popular artists' and writers' retreat for years. The scenery is arrestingly beautiful: steep cliffs, powerful surf, rich, green pine forests, and golden meadows. There's also a lighthouse that dates from 1824. To reach it you can take a boat from either Port Clyde or Boothbay Harbor.

Special Events

January. Winter Carnival, Bangor; (207) 947–0307. Family fun.

June. Annual Windjammer Days, Boothbay Harbor; (207) 633–2353. Windjammer and antique boat parade, concerts, and exhibits.

July. Native American Festival, Bar Harbor; (207) 288–5103. Celebration of Maliseet, Micmac, Passamaquoddy, and Penobscot People of Maine with food, crafts, dancing.

Bangor State Fair, Bangor; (207) 947–0307. A real old-fashioned fair.

Celebration of the Arts, Kennebunkport; (207) 967–0857. Demonstrations and musical performances.

October. Fall Foliage Festival, Boothbay; (207) 633–2353. Craft fair, food, entertainment.

Other Recommended Restaurants and Lodgings

Cape Neddick

Cape Neddick House Bed & Breakfast, 1300 Route 1, Cape Neddick, ME 03902; (207) 363–2500. A beautifully restored Victorian inn.

Deer Isle

Goose Cove Lodge, Deer Isle, Sunset, ME 04683; (207) 348–2508 or (800) 728–1963. A very special inn with cottages and suites for staying. It's set on seventy acres.

Pilgrim's Inn Bed and Breakfast, P.O. Box 69, Deer Isle, ME 04627; (888) 778–7505. Built in 1793, this building, which is on the National Register of Historic Places, has been lovingly restored and meticulously maintained. The fifteen rooms are all beautifully decorated, and some have water views.

East Boothbay

Five Gables Inn, Murray Hill Road, East Boothbay, ME 04544; (207) 633–4551 or (800) 451–5048. A beautifully restored, 125-year-old inn overlooking Linekin Bay.

Portland

Fore Street, 288 Fore Street, Portland, ME 04101; (207) 775–2717. Here is an excellent place for dinner in Portland, with most dishes prepared in wood-fired ovens. Try the Maine crab bake or the spit-roasted pork loin.

Southwest Harbor

Acadia Cabins, P.O. Box 1214, 410 Main Street, Southwest Harbor, ME; 04679; (207) 244–5388. These are adorable cabins peacefully set in a lightly wooded area. This location makes a great base for exploring Acadia National Park, Bar Harbor, and other island attractions.

Wells

Seagull Motor Inn and Vacation Cottages, P.O. Box 338, Wells, ME 04090; (207) 646–5164. Located on Route 1 between Ogunquit and Kennebunkport, this bluff-top inn and cottage colony features meticulously kept rooms and cottages and panoramic views of the Atlantic Ocean.

For More Information

Convention and Visitors Bureau of Greater Portland, 305 Commercial Street, Portland, ME 04101; (207) 772–4994.

Maine Office of Tourism, 59 State House Station, Augusta, ME 04333; (207) 287–5711.

MID-ATLANTIC
ESCAPES

Spring Lake

A Small Shore Town

1 Night

About equidistant from Philadelphia and New York City, you'll find Spring Lake, one of the most pleasant towns on the Jersey Shore. Since the early part of this century, it has been a vacation spot for travelers wanting to get away from both cities. Back then they came by carriage and stayed in what was the grandest hotel (but no longer exists)—the Monmouth House. There are several buildings that do live on from that era, however, including an impressive collection of Victorian "cottages."

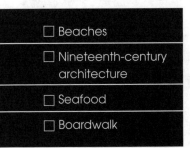

☐ Beaches

☐ Nineteenth-century architecture

☐ Seafood

☐ Boardwalk

For this trip we suggest driving down in the morning (the drive takes not much more than an hour), spending the day and night enjoying the simple pleasures of Spring Lake, and then slowly meandering back to the city, stopping in Red Bank en route.

Day 1 / Morning

Take exit 98 off the Garden State Parkway to Route 34 south. Go 1½ miles to the traffic circle and turn left onto Route 524. Follow Route 524 for about 3 miles, and it'll take you right into town.

One of the best ways to enjoy Spring Lake is to just stroll leisurely. A good starting place is the boardwalk, which stretches 2 miles along the ocean and is not colonized by arcades and the other amusements found at so many other boardwalks.

LUNCH: Right across from the boardwalk is the **Breakers,** Ocean and Newark Avenue, Spring Lake, NJ 07762 (732–449–7700), where you can get a light lunch (sandwiches, salads, burgers).

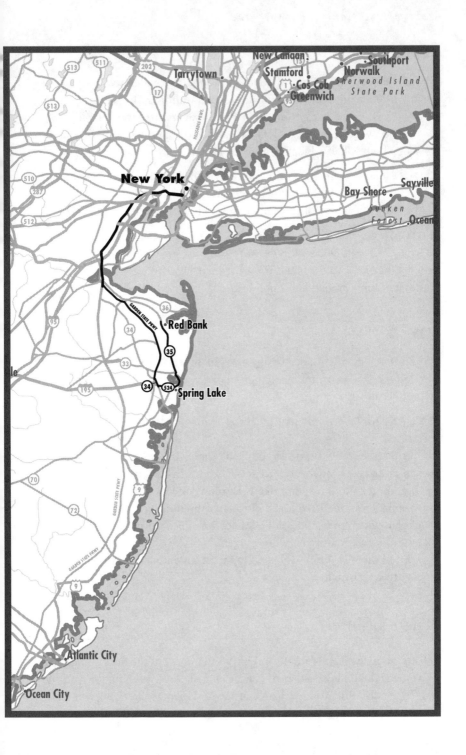

Afternoon

From the boardwalk you can wander through the wide, tree-lined streets of town admiring one beautiful house after another. The lake for which the town is named is right in the center of town, surrounded by a park. Spend whatever time is left swimming or sunning yourself on the beach, which is half a block from your hotel.

DINNER: The **Old Mill Inn,** Old Mill Road, Spring Lake Heights, NJ 07762 (732–449–1800 or 800–803–9031), serves unfailingly good seafood and other American dishes. Many consider it a New Jersey institution.

LODGING: **Sea Crest by the Sea,** 19 Tuttle Avenue, Spring Lake, NJ 07762 (732–449–9031 or 800–803–9031), is an eleven-room Victorian guest house just half a block from the beach. All rooms are handsomely decorated with French and English furnishings from the 1880s.

Day 2 / Morning

If you're a jogger, consider lacing up your shoes and following the paths around the lake or running along the boardwalk, breathing in the invigorating ocean air.

BREAKFAST: Continental breakfast is included in the room price at Sea Crest.

After a leisurely breakfast and some more time spent relaxing on the beach or playing croquet at Sea Crest, head north back toward Manhattan, taking time out to explore **Red Bank.** Poised on the shores of the Navesink River, Red Bank is a historic community with lots of shops. If you're interested in antiques, it's home to a major **Antiques Center,** along West Front Street and Shrewsbury Avenue.

From there you can easily pick up the Garden State Parkway north to return to Manhattan.

There's More

Horse country. Slightly inland and just to the north of the Spring Lake area is a little chunk of horse country. The farms are in full view from the road and are concentrated in a little triangle of towns: Holmdel, Freehold, and Colt's Neck. Many of the farms can be seen along routes 537, 79, 520, and 34.

Spring Lake, New Jersey, has long been a popular shore vacation spot.

Special Events

Summer months. Throughout the summer months, there are model-boat regattas on the lake on Sundays, croquet at Green Gables on Thursdays, and weekly concerts in Potter Park. Check the *Shore Holiday News* for listings.

Other Recommended Restaurants and Lodgings

Rumson

Fromagerie, 26 Ridge Road, Rumson, NJ 07760; (732) 842–8088. This is one of the Jersey Shore's most outstanding restaurants. The food is French, the service very gracious, and the atmosphere elegant. Rumson is a short drive east of Red Bank.

Spring Lake

The Château, 500 Warren Avenue, Spring Lake, NJ 07762; (732) 974–2000 or (877) 974–5253. A renovated Victorian hotel with forty rooms. The beach is 4 blocks away.

For More Information

Eastern Monmouth Area Chamber of Commerce, 170 Broad Street, Red Bank, NJ 07701; (732) 741–0055.

New Jersey Office of Travel and Tourism, P.O. Box 820, Trenton, NJ 08625; (609) 777–0885 or (800) 847–4865.

The Jersey Cape

A Shore Thing

2 Nights

Mention New Jersey and lots of people automatically think of Atlantic City. Indeed, this casino hub has earned its place on the map, but casinos are just part of the picture in this part of the world.

Back in the late 1800s, the Atlantic seashore that runs roughly from just below Atlantic City to Cape May Point was a very popular place to vacation, so much so that after a while, it became too popular and ultimately drove away many vacationers. Attempting to bring back visitors, many towns introduced other activities such as amusement parks and convention facilities. The result, unfortunately, is that many of the lovely shore towns now stand behind boardwalks that are lined with amusement arcades, bowling alleys, pool halls, and fast-food restaurants. On the plus side, the beaches are still there, and the activity makes for good times round the year. The final destination for this escape—Cape May—is a lovely Victorian town where you can settle in for a couple of days.

☐ Shore scenery
☐ Beaches
☐ Seafood
☐ Casinos
☐ Fishing
☐ Golfing
☐ Boardwalk amusements
☐ Victorian buildings
☐ Biking
☐ Bird-watching
☐ Deep-sea fishing

For this escape we suggest making your first stop Atlantic City, then following Ocean Drive (a series of bridges connecting a series of narrow islands that run parallel to the mainland) down the coast to Cape May, making stops along the way.

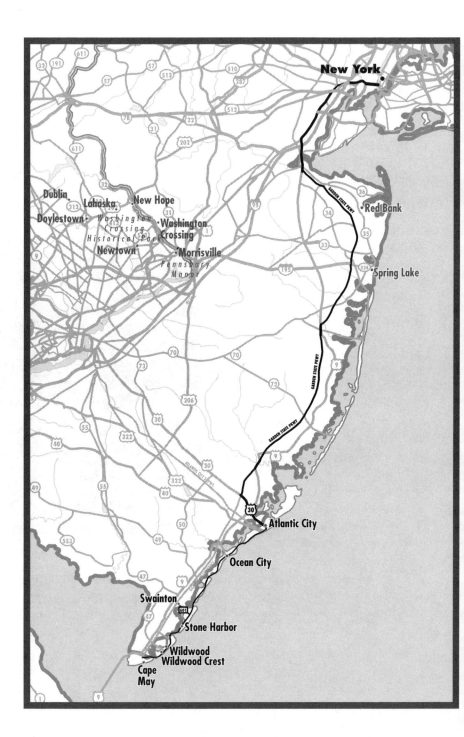

Day 1 / Morning

Set out early from Manhattan, keeping in mind that you can't do everything we suggest and still make it to Cape May in one day. Pick and choose as you go along and what you miss on the way down, pick up on the way back. To reach Atlantic City take the Garden State Parkway all the way south to the Atlantic City Expressway east.

Atlantic City, which was made famous by the board game Monopoly, continues to get national attention every fall when the Miss America Pageant takes place in town. On top of that, Atlantic City is a gambling hub, with thirteen major casinos including Bally's, Caesars, the Grand, Merv Griffin's, and the Trump casinos. These casinos are also famous for their big-name entertainment, world-championship sports, glittery shows, and gourmet restaurants. Atlantic City is also home to a 60-foot-wide boardwalk extending along 5 miles of beaches lined with shops, amusement centers, and food stands. There is also a three-deck shopping complex— the Shops on Ocean One (1 Atlantic Ocean; 609–347–8082)—built to resemble an ocean liner.

LUNCH: While in Atlantic City, you can lunch at one of the casino restaurants (there are dozens) including **Planet Hollywood** at Caesars, Atlantic City, NJ 08401 (609–347–7827).

Afternoon

From Atlantic City head south on Ocean Drive, making your next stop at **Ocean City,** which calls itself "America's Greatest Family Resort." Indeed, there is plenty to do for families on its 2-mile-long boardwalk and 8 miles of beaches. Ocean City prides itself on its wacky and inventive summertime festivals and contests. Every August, for example, there's a Hermit Crab Race and a Miss Crustacean Contest.

If you prefer natural over commercial diversions, continue down the coast to the **Stone Harbor** area, where you'll find **Leaming's Run Gardens** (1845 Route 9, Swainton, NJ 08210; 609–465–5871), one of the finest gardens on the East Coast and the **Wetlands Institute** (1075 Stone Harbor Boulevard, Stone Harbor, NJ 08247; 609–368–1211), an environmental center focusing on coastal ecology. At the latter you'll find an observation tower, a marsh trail, and an aquarium.

Next on the itinerary are the **Wildwoods,** a quartet of shore towns. West Wildwood is a residential area, whereas the other three—North

Cape May's Victorian heritage is preserved in its graceful old buildings.

Wildwood, Wildwood, and Wildwood Crest—are lined with oceanfront hotels and motels. On Wildwood's beachfront you'll find the biggest concentration of amusements including six amusement piers with carnival-like rides.

Less than 10 miles away is **Cape May** (continue down the coast on Ocean Drive), which has been a popular beach resort since the days of the Revolution and, in fact, is the oldest seashore resort in the country that has very successfully preserved its Victorian heritage.

Once you arrive, settle into your hotel (some of the rooms at the Mainstay have parking spots; if yours doesn't, grab the first one you see on the street) for what's left of the afternoon.

DINNER: The **Washington Inn,** 801 Washington Street, Cape May, NJ 08204 (609–884–5697), a former plantation house dating from 1848, is a great spot for seafood and other continental dishes. Especially delicious are the Cape May crab cakes accompanied by a creamy roasted pepper sauce.

LODGING: The **Mainstay Inn,** 635 Columbia Avenue, Cape May, NJ 08204 (609–884–8690), is an Italianate villa with a wraparound veranda. Inside are all sorts of Victorian details. Guests can stay in the main inn or in the more modernized adjacent cottage. Book your room for two nights.

Day 2 / Morning

BREAKFAST: During the summer a light breakfast is served at the Mainstay. The rest of the year, it's a full breakfast and it's included in the room rate.

The heart of town is the Washington Street Victorian Mall, which is a 3-block-long stretch closed to automobiles and lined with shops and restaurants. The real focus in Cape May, however, is the promenade, which runs along the Atlantic and offers a whole host of diversions.

To see the town's historic sites, consider joining a guided Historic District Walking Tour. These tours—which last about an hour and a half— are full of historical insights. Of course, you can also take yourself on a self-guided tour. The Welcome Center, at 405 Lafayette Street, Cape May, NJ 08204 (609) 884–1341, can point you in the right direction and provide you with brochures. Most of the most beautiful Victorian buildings are now inns lined up majestically between the Welcome Center and the beach. These include the **Abbey,** a Gothic Revival house at Columbia Avenue and Gurney Street, Cape May, NJ 08204; **Captain Mey's Inn,** at 202 Ocean Street, Cape May, NJ 08204; the **Mainstay Inn,** at 635 Columbia Avenue, Cape May, NJ 08204; and the **Angel of the Sea,** at 5 Trenton Avenue, Cape May, NJ 08204.

LUNCH: **Water's Edge,** Beach and Pittsburgh Avenue, Cape May, NJ 08204 (609–884–1717), right across the street from the beach, is a good choice for seafood.

Afternoon

Right after lunch, plan to take a tour of the **Emlen Physick Estate,** 1048 Washington Street, Cape May, NJ 08204 (609–884–5404) which is a fully restored eighteen-room Victorian mansion designed by Frank Furness and an excellent introduction to the Victorian era. The estate is also headquarters for the **Mid-Atlantic Center for the Arts** (609–884–5404 or 800–275–4278), which organizes several walking tours (and trolley tours) around town.

If you still have energy left afterward, take a drive out to **Cape May State Park** (follow Sunset Boulevard) for a beautiful walk through one of Cape May's best birding areas. There are 3 miles of trails and a boardwalk that take you over ponds and through wooded areas and marshlands. Then climb the 218 steps to the top of the **Cape May Lighthouse.** Stick around for the sunset, which is astonishingly beautiful from **Cape May Point.**

DINNER: Elaine's Dinner Theater, 513 Lafayette Street, Cape May, NJ 08204; (609) 884–4358. Here you can have a full-course meal and enjoy a live performance. Call ahead for program information.

LODGING: Return to the Mainstay Inn for a good night's sleep.

Day 3 / Morning

BREAKFAST: At the Mainstay Inn.

After breakfast visit the shops in the mall area and near the beach or head back to the beach. The "Cape May diamonds," which you will inevitably see in shops all over town, are actually quartz, rounded by the waves.

Then meander your way back up the New Jersey coast, stopping at those attractions you might have missed on the way down.

There's More

Bicycling. You can rent bikes right in town at the Village Bicycle Shop (at Ocean Street and the beginning of the mall); (609) 884–8500.

Bird-watching. Every fall thousands of migratory birds (including everything from small songbirds to falcons and eagles) stop here on their way south. The best viewing areas are Cape May State Park, the Cape May Migratory Bird Refuge, and Higbee's Beach.

Carriage rides. Carriages leave from Ocean Street and Washington Street Mall for half-hour historic district tours. Call (609) 884–4466 for more information.

Fishing. There are several great fishing areas around Cape May, including the Second Avenue jetty and the World War II bunker by the lighthouse at Cape May Point.

Trolley tours. If you're not up for walking, you can take trolley tours around town. For information contact the Mid-Atlantic Center for the Arts (609–884–5404).

Special Events

April. Tulip Festival, Cape May; (609) 884–5508.

April and November. Cape May Jazz Festival, Cape May; (609) 884–7277.

September. Miss America Pageant, Atlantic City; (609) 272–7242.

October. Victorian Week, Cape May; (609) 884–5508.

December. Christmas Candlelight Tour, Cape May; (609) 884–5508.

Other Recommended Restaurants and Lodgings

Cape May

The Abbey, 34 Gurney Street, at Columbia Avenue, Cape May, NJ 08204; (609) 884–4506. A lovely Gothic-style inn.

Captain Mey's Inn, 202 Ocean Street, Cape May, NJ 08204; (609) 884–7793 or (800) 981–3702. A nine-room inn decorated with Victorian furnishings.

410 Bank Street, 410 Bank Street, Cape May, NJ 08204; (609) 884–2127. This restaurant specializes in Louisiana French cooking. You can sit on the porch or in the garden.

Fresco's, 412 Bank Street, Cape May, NJ 08204; (609) 884–0366. A good choice for Italian cuisine. It's beautifully situated in a vine-covered 1880s Victorian summer cottage.

For More Information

Atlantic City Convention & Visitors Authority, 2314 Pacific Avenue, Atlantic City, NJ 08401; (609) 449–7100 or (888) 228–4748.

Cape May Chamber of Commerce, P.O. Box 556, Cape May, NJ 08204; (609) 884–5508.

Cape May Welcome Center, 405 Lafayette Street, Cape May, NJ 08204; (609) 884–1341.

New Jersey Office of Travel and Tourism, P.O. Box 820, Trenton, NJ 08625; (609) 777–0885 or (800) 847–4865.

Bucks County

A Little Bit of History

2 *Nights*

In the southeast corner of Pennsylvania, Bucks County, which is bounded by Philadelphia County on the southwest and separated from New Jersey by the Delaware River to the east, offers just the right balance between sight-seeing and relaxing. The area was first known to the Lenni-Lenape Indians and later settled by Dutch explorers, followed by Swedes, English Quakers, and Germans.

Today's visitor can dip into a little history, find dozens of antiques shops, sample local cuisine, and stay overnight in historic inns. The centerpiece of the county is New Hope, which has more than 200 properties listed on the National Register of Historic Places.

- ☑ Revolutionary landmarks
- ☐ Antiques
- ☐ Inns
- ☐ Natural beauty
- ☐ Farm country
- ☐ Galleries
- ☐ Fine dining
- ☐ Early Pennsylvania architecture
- ☐ Covered bridges

There's a lot to do in Bucks County. This itinerary takes you to just some of the highlights.

Day 1 / *Morning*

Most of the county's attractions are centered in **New Hope,** which for years has been a magnet for artists and writers. To reach it take the New Jersey Turnpike to exit 10. Then follow Route 287 north to Route 22 west, to Route 202 south. Follow Route 202 over the Delaware River Bridge and then get on Route 32 south. This will lead you right into town. The drive should take about two hours.

If you show up on a weekend, year-round, be prepared for a crowd scene. New Hope gets a lot of day-trippers from Philadelphia, New York,

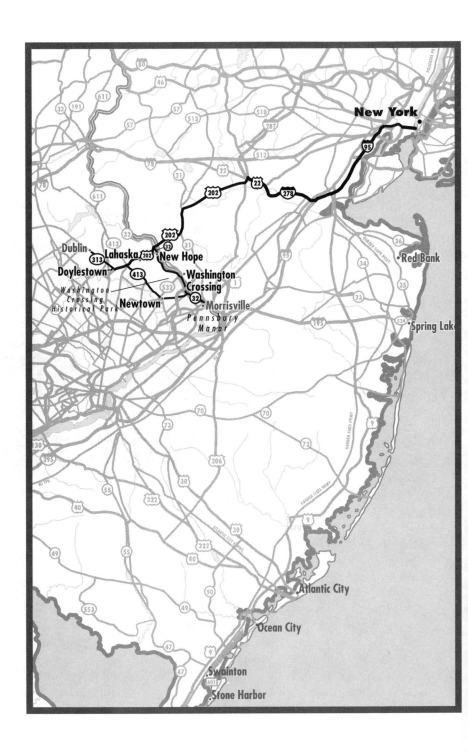

and New Jersey. Its streets are lined with boutiques selling everything from New Age crystals to antique paintings. Your best bet for parking is to drive west of Route 32 and then walk back.

Start by getting yourself a copy of the booklet *The Walking Tour of Historic New Hope,* at New Hope's information center, One West Mechanic Street.

From there walk along Main Street, which has the Delaware Canal on one side and the river on the other, and pop into any shops or galleries that appeal to you. The canal was opened in 1831 to carry whiskey and raw materials between local towns as well as Philadelphia, Pittsburgh, and Lake Erie. Alongside the canal is a towpath, which is used for walking, cycling, and jogging.

One of the highlights of any visit to New Hope is a ride on a **mule barge.** As you slide along the Delaware Canal on a flower-festooned barge, mules pulling alongside, a tour guide fills you in on New Hope's history. New Hope **Canal Boat Company** (149 South Main Street, New Hope, PA 18938; 215–862–0758) rides start on New Street at the southern end of town at noon and 1:30, 3:30, and 4:30 P.M. daily from May 1 through October 31 (plus Friday, Saturday, and Sunday in April). You can also take a ride on the **New Hope & Ivyland Rail Road** (station on West Bridge Street, New Hope, PA 18938; 215–862–2332), a restored steam train, though it's an awful lot to cram into the day. The train runs daily from April through November and on Saturday and Sunday only from January through March.

LUNCH: Karla's, 5 West Mechanic Street, New Hope, PA 18938 (215–862–2612), is a very informal place where you can grab a sandwich, burger, or pasta dish.

Afternoon

After lunch wander over to **Parry Mansion,** 45 South Main Street, New Hope, PA 18938 (215–862–5652). Built by Benjamin Parry in 1784, it now is a museum of decorative arts operated by the New Hope Historical Society. Each room is furnished to reflect a different period from Colonial to American Federal. Tours are conducted on Friday, Saturday and Sunday from late April through mid-December from 1:00 to 5:00 P.M.

Consider returning to Main Street to sample some internationally flavored ice creams (Israel's milk and honey, Ukrainian rose petal, American pumpkin) at **Gerenser's Exotic Ice Cream,** 22 South Main Street, New

Hope, PA 18938 (215–862–2050). Afterward you can burn the calories off by poking around some other shops.

Before the day is over, consider taking a horse and buggy ride from **Bucks County Carriages,** 2586 North River Road, New Hope, PA 18938 (215–862–3582), over to **Phillips Mill,** a gristmill complex built in 1765 by Aaron Phillips. For years it was a political forum and social center for local farm families.

DINNER: **La Bonne Auberge,** Village 2, off Mechanic Street, New Hope, PA 18938; (215) 862–2462. French cuisine served in a historic stone farmhouse.

Evening

After dinner consider taking in a show at the legendary **Bucks County Playhouse,** 70 South Main Street, New Hope, PA 18938; (215) 862–2041. Set on the banks of the Delaware, it used to be a mill but was converted into a theater in 1939.

LODGING: In New Hope, and all over Bucks County, there are many bed and breakfasts. You can take your pick of many inns and hotels. An especially elegant inn is the **Whitehall Inn,** 1370 Pineville Road, New Hope, PA 18938 (215–598–7945), which is about five or six minutes outside of town.

Day 2 / Morning

BREAKFAST: An elaborate four-course breakfast is included in the room rate at the Whitehall Inn.

After breakfast follow the River Road (Route 32) south to **Washington Crossing Historical Park,** routes 32 and 532, Washington Crossing, PA 18977 (215–493–4076). This is one of Bucks County's many beautiful drives, taking you past magnificent homes and river views. The park is divided into two sections. The northern section of the park is dominated by **Bowman's Hill,** which is crowned by a tower commemorating a Revolutionary War lookout point. It's also a **Wildflower Preserve** (devoted entirely to Pennsylvania plants), the only wildflower preserve in North America to be accredited by the American Association of Museums. The lower part, which is 7 miles south of New Hope, is where George Washington and 2,400 soldiers in his Continental Army crossed the Delaware on Christmas night in 1776 to make a surprise attack against the

Historic sites such as Pennsbury Manor abound in Bucks County.

Crown's Hessian mercenaries in Trenton. There are picnic grounds, historic structures (including the old Patriot general store and post office), and the Washington Crossing Memorial building.

Continue down River Road until you reach Morrisville, where you'll turn left and follow signs for **Pennsbury Manor,** 400 Pennsbury Memorial Road, Morrisville, PA 19067, near Tullytown (215–946–0400), which was William Penn's summer mansion built on a bend of the Delaware. Penn's Georgian brick house stands on a multiacre plot of land (originally, it was an 8,400-acre plantation; now it's scaled down quite a bit) overlooking the river where he would travel by barge to and from Philadelphia. It and its many outbuildings (bake and brew house, blacksmith's and joiner's shops) have been totally reconstructed by the Pennsylvania Historical Commission. Costumed guides take visitors through the compound on one-and-a-half-hour tours. The complex is open from 9:00 A.M. to 5:00 P.M. Tuesday through Saturday and noon to 5:00 P.M. Sunday.

From Pennsbury follow the country roads north to **Newtown** (about a twenty-minute drive), the core of which is made up of eighteenth- and early-nineteenth-century houses that were laid out in a plan approved by Penn. More than 225 properties are listed on the National Register of Historic Places. Begin by stopping for lunch and then take your time looking at the different buildings.

LUNCH: Ye Olde Temperance House, 511 South State Street, Newtown, PA 18940 (215–860–0474), has an excellent Sunday jazz brunch with a live Dixieland band and a menu featuring jambalaya, Cajun blackened fish, and smoked-salmon omelettes. Lunch is served every day of the week.

Afternoon

From Newtown follow Route 413 north to Route 202 over to **Doylestown,** your destination for the night.

DINNER: Doylestown Inn, 18 West State Street, Doylestown, PA 18901; (215) 345–6610. Here you can have a hearty basic dinner. Nothing special, but good.

LODGING: Pine Tree Farm Bed & Breakfast, 2155 Lower State Road, Doylestown, PA 18901 (215–348–0632), is one of several very welcoming bed and breakfasts in Doylestown. It's a four-room antiques-furnished stone farmhouse dating from 1730.

Day 3 / Morning

BREAKFAST: Wonderful breakfasts are included in the room rate at Pine Tree Farm.

There's enough to keep you pretty busy all morning in Doylestown. It's home to two castles made of concrete as well as the Moravian Pottery & Tile Works. All three, which are designated as "Mercer Mile," were built between 1908 and 1916 by Henry Chapman Mercer, a local eccentric. **Fonthill,** a fanciful building with turrets, secret rooms, and unexpected stairways, Mercer built as a residence for himself. It's located on East Court Street, Doylestown, PA 18901 (215–348–9461). The hours are Monday through Saturday from 10:00 A.M. to 5:00 P.M. and Sunday from noon to 5:00 P.M. A short walk through the park will bring you to the **Moravian Pottery & Tile Works,** 130 Swamp Road, Doylestown, PA 18901 (215–345–6722), where you can watch tiles being made the same way they were made about a century ago. It's open seven days a week from 10:00 A.M. to 4:45 P.M.; the last tour begins at 4:00 P.M. The other castle, **Mercer Museum,** at 84 South Pine Street, Doylestown, PA 18901, is less than a mile away. Mercer used the latter to house an enormous collection of tools and farm implements that were used by tradesmen in the nineteenth century. It's open Monday through Saturday from 10:00 A.M. to 5:00 P.M. and Sunday from noon to 5:00 P.M.; also open on Tuesday evenings until 9:00 P.M. For information, contact the Bucks County Historical Society, 84 South Pine Street, Doylestown, PA 18901; (215) 345–0210.

Adjacent to the Mercer Museum is the **James A. Michener Arts Museum,** 138 South Pine Street, Doylestown, PA 18901 (215–340–9800), which was named in honor of the famous author, a Doylestown native. In addition to gallery space (which includes a permanent exhibition celebrating Michener's career as a writer, public servant, art collector, and philanthropist), it has a museum shop and a tearoom. Other permanent exhibits include "Nakashima Reading Room," which is filled with furnishings by Bucks County's internationally known woodworker George Nakashima, and "Visual Heritage of Bucks County," which traces the art of the region from colonial times to the present. There are also changing exhibits. Hours are Tuesday through Friday from 10:00 A.M. to 4:30 P.M. and Saturday and Sunday from 10:00 A.M. to 5:00 P.M.; also open Wednesday evenings until 9:00 P.M.

LUNCH: Cafe Airelle, 100 Main Street, Doylestown, PA 18901 (215–345–5930), is a French bistro right on Main Street.

Afternoon

A few miles north of Doylestown at 520 Dublin Road, Hilltown Township (mailing address: Perkasie, PA 18944), you'll find **Green Hills Farm** (800–220–2825), which was Pearl S. Buck's estate. Visitors can tour the 1835 stone house where the author lived when she returned to the United States (after growing up in China with missionary parents) from the age of thirty-two on. When the Nobel and Pulitzer prize–winning author died in 1973, she was buried on the premises. The house is open between March and December. Tours are given Tuesday through Saturday at 11:00 A.M. and 1:00 and 2:00 P.M. and Sunday at at 1:00 and 2:00 P.M..

Return to Doylestown and head east on Route 202 and you'll come to the town of **Lahaska.** On what was the old coach road that connected

Philadelphia with New York, this town used to be home to several chicken farms. In 1962 the farms were transformed into **Peddler's Village,** which began as a collection of shops in reconstructed chicken coops but grew, very tastefully, as shops and restaurants were added. Today there are more than seventy shops (purveying antiques, art, crafts, and other collectibles), several restaurants, and a carousel museum.

From Lahaska return to New Hope and then retrace your steps back to New York.

There's More

Ghost tours. In New Hope tours meet at the cannon on Main Street every Saturday night at 8:00 P.M. from June through November. During October and early November, tours run every Friday and Saturday at 8:00 P.M. Call (215) 957–9988 for more information.

Outlet shopping. Just over the Bucks County border toward Philadelphia is the Franklin Mills Mall (off I–95, exit 22/Woodhaven Road) with about 200 outlets.

Polo. Matches are played from spring through fall at the Bucks County Horse Park on Route 611, between Revere and Ferndale.

Sesame Place. If you're traveling with children, don't miss this stellar attraction. It's located at 100 Sesame Road in Langhorne; (215) 752–7070. Based on the television show, this theme park features water attractions such as Little Bird's Birdbath (with fountains and a water umbrella) as well as parades and shows such as the Big Bird Musical Review.

Wineries. There are several wineries in the area, including the Buckingham Valley Vineyards in Buckingham (215–794–7188), Peace Valley Winery in Chalfont (215–249–9058), Rushland Ridge Vineyards & Winery in Rushland (215–598–0251), and Sand Castle Winery in Erwinna (800–722–9463).

Special Events

Mid-May. Mercer Folk Festival, Mercer Museum, Doylestown.

Early June. Bucks County Antiques Dealers Association Show. More than forty dealers show their collections at Delaware Valley College, at Route 202 and New Britain Road in Doylestown.

Bucks County Balloon and Vineyard Festival, Quakertown Airport, 2425 Milford Square Pike, Quakertown. Hot-air balloons, aircraft, wine tasting, food booths, arts and crafts, and entertainment.

September. State Craft Festival, at Tyler State Park, Route 332, Newtown.

October. Bucks County Artists' Show, Green Hills Farm (Pearl S. Buck's estate).

Late November. Bucks County Antiques Dealers Association Show, held on Thanksgiving Day weekend at Delaware Valley College, Route 202 and New Britain Road, Doylestown.

December. Reenactment of Washington crossing the Delaware. Every Christmas the successful maneuver by George Washington and the Continental Army, which led to a decisive victory for the colonies, is reenacted at Washington Crossing Historical Park, 7 miles south of New Hope. For more information call (215) 493–4076.

Other Recommended Restaurants and Lodgings

Doylestown

Highland Farms, 70 East Road, Doylestown, PA 18901; (215) 340–1354. This stone country house used to be the estate of lyricist Oscar Hammerstein II. It's listed on the National Register of Historic Places.

Inn at Fordhook Farm, 105 New Britain Road, Doylestown, PA 18901; (215) 345–1766. An eighteenth-century house on the National Register of Historic Places.

Lahaska

Golden Plough Inn of Peddler's Village, Route 202 and Street Road, Lahaska, PA 18931; (215) 794–4004. A lovely country inn with sixty-six rooms.

Lumberville

Black Bass Hotel, 3774 River Road, Lumberville, PA 18933; (215) 297–5770. An antiques-furnished inn on the Delaware River.

Cuttalossa Inn, River Road, Lumberville, PA 18933; (215) 297–5082. American cuisine in a very romantic setting.

Newtown

Jean Pierre's, 101 South State Street, Newtown, PA 18940; (215) 968–6201. An exceptionally good French restaurant.

For More Information

Bucks County Conference and Visitors Bureau, 3207 Street Road, Bensalem, PA 19020; (215) 639–0300 or (800) 836–BUCKS.

Pennsylvania Tourism (800–847–4872) provides a booklet for the state.

Lancaster County

Pennsylvania Dutch Country

2 Nights

You don't have to go far from New York to feel as if you're in a foreign country. In Lancaster county, which is less than three hours away, you'll see horse-drawn buggies used as a mode of transportation and farms being worked with horse or mule teams.

Lancaster County is the heart of Pennsylvania Dutch Country, which is home to a large population of "Plain People" (Amish, Brethren, and Mennonite). Most of them carry on their lives as their ancestors did in the seventeenth century, shunning anything modern such as automobiles, electricity, and chemical fertilizers.

In addition to the steadily scenic Amish farmlands for which the area is so well known, there are a whole host of historical attractions including the National Clock and Watch Museum, the Landis Valley Museum, Robert Fulton's birthplace, Wright's Ferry Mansion, and more. There are a number of interesting towns including Lititz, Strasburg (a must for railroad buffs), and the town of Lancaster itself, which contains President James Buchanan's home and other historic buildings.

☐ Farms

☐ "Plain People" communities

☐ Farmers' markets

☐ Traditional home cooking

☐ Auctions

☐ Waterwheels and windmills

☐ Handicrafts

From the eastern edge of Lancaster County to the Susquehanna River on the west, the distance is a mere 45 miles; nevertheless, the area should be explored slowly. Take time to wander down any road that looks interesting. Though all tourist maps will direct you to follow Route 30 in order to see the Amish farms, you'll quickly find that this thoroughfare is painfully overcommercialized and usually a traffic nightmare. Routes 340

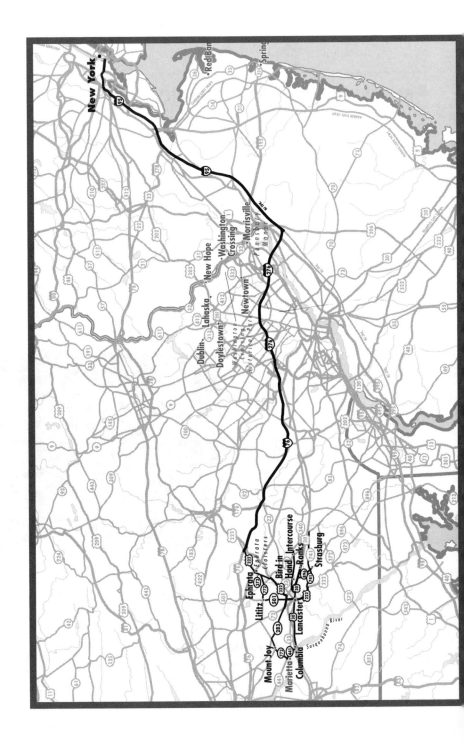

and 772 are better bets. As you explore, enjoy the names of some of the towns—Bird-in-Hand, Blue Ball, Fertility, Paradise, Intercourse.

If you're traveling during a weekend, keep in mind that many of the family-owned Amish shops and services are closed on Sundays. This particular itinerary is set up so that you leave early Friday morning, stay over Friday and Saturday nights, and return on Sunday. Even though the area is so dense with attractions that you could use one inn as your base, we've selected two so that you can have a fuller experience.

A word about when to go: During summer weekends the throngs of tourists in Lancaster can be overwhelming. The best time to go is during the week in spring or fall.

Day 1 / Morning

Driving to Pennsylvania Dutch country from New York is a breeze. You take the New Jersey Turnpike to the Pennsylvania Turnpike west. Then get off at exit 21 and head south on Route 222. About 5 miles south of Lancaster, make your first stop at the **Hans Herr House,** 1849 Hans Herr Drive, Lancaster, PA 17602 (717–464–4438). This is the county's oldest structure and the oldest Mennonite meetinghouse. Back in 1710 a collective of eight Mennonite families bought ten thousand acres of land (for a whopping 25 cents an acre); nine years later the Herr family built their house on the land. Open to visitors from April 1 through November 30 (daily, except Sunday, from 9:00 A.M. to 4:00 P.M.), the house is a beautiful example of steep-roofed medieval German architecture. Guided tours help give you an understanding of how our ancestors lived.

From the Hans Herr House, head east on Route 741 to **Strasburg,** where you can pause for lunch and have a look around the historic railroad and its museum.

LUNCH: Though more popular for its homemade ice cream (in handmade cones and mixed with M&Ms, Reese's Pieces, and other favorites), the **Strasburg Country Store & Creamery,** One West Main Street, Strasburg, PA 17579 (717–687–0766), serves a great "loaf of soup" for lunch—a small, round loaf of bread that is scooped out and filled with the soup of the day.

Afternoon

Strasburg is home to the **Railroad Museum of Pennsylvania,** Route 741, Strasburg, PA 17579 (717–687–8628), and the **Strasburg Rail Road,**

Horse-drawn carriages are a common sight on Lancaster County roads

Route 741, Strasburg (717–687–7522). The latter offers forty-five-minute round-trip rides between Strasburg and nearby Paradise on wooden coaches pulled by steam locomotives.

From Strasburg it's a short ride up to Route 30 (take Route 896) and the **Amish Farm and House,** 2395 Lincoln Highway East, Lancaster, PA 17602 (717–394–6185), which all the tourist brochures, and most guidebooks, will tell you is a perfect introduction to Amish lifestyles. Indeed it is, with its nineteenth-century buildings furnished and decorated as old-order Amish households, waterwheels, windmills, carriages, and sleighs. Conscientious guides take you through the main house, which has been faithfully restored to look as it did in the early 1800s.

From there it's a short drive to the town of **Intercourse,** where you'll find many tourist traps as well as some worthwhile shops and attractions. The name Intercourse is derived from the fact that Route 772 intersects

Route 340 in the village (back in the 1700s and early 1800s, these roads were major commerce routes). If you're interested in learning more about the local quilts (made by the women at quilting bees), don't miss the **People's Place Quilt Museum,** upstairs from the Old Country Store on Route 340 in the center of town, Intercourse, PA 17534 (800–828–8218). Quilts are for sale in the Old Country Store itself.

DINNER: Miller's Smorgasbord, 2811 Lincoln Highway East, Ronks, PA 17572 (717–687–6621), offers a Pennsylvania Dutch smorgasbord. It's very casual and hearty and down-home priced.

LODGING: The **O'Flaherty's Dingeldein House,** 1105 East King Street in Lancaster, PA 17602 (717–293–1723), is a small (four guest rooms) B&B within easy reach of Lancaster's attractions.

Day 2 / Morning

BREAKFAST: A full breakfast, complete with home-baked breads and delicious pancakes, is included in the price of a room at O'Flaherty's Dingeldein House.

After breakfast drive into town (about a mile away), where you'll find plenty of parking in lots and garages. One of the best ways to see the town is to take the ninety-minute **Lancaster Historic Walking Tour,** (717–392–1776), which departs from the Southern Market (call ahead for current tour times).

Lancaster is the county seat, and, back in 1777, for one full day it was home to the Continental Congress when Philadelphia was captured by the British. Its cobbled streets are rich in American history, stories of which are well told by knowledgeable guides.

Lancaster's many attractions include **Wheatland,** the last home of President James Buchanan, 1120 Marietta Avenue, Lancaster, PA 17602 (open April 1–November 30); the **Fulton Opera House,** 12 North Prince Street , Lancaster, PA 17602 (717–397–7133), one of the oldest American theaters; and the **Heritage Center Museum of Lancaster County,** Penn Square, Lancaster, PA 17603 (717–299–6440), which contains examples of early Lancaster arts and crafts and home furnishings. Lancaster is also home to several Georgian churches, Federal-style buildings, and the nation's oldest publicly owned farmers' market, the Central Market on Penn Square. The latter is a huge gabled brick structure filled with produce, crafts, and flower stands.

From Lancaster make your way west to **Mount Joy.** Take Route 283 west; then turn left onto Route 230.

LUNCH: Groff's Farm Restaurant, 650 Pinkerton Road, Mount Joy, PA 17552; (717) 653–2048. Situated in a family-owned farmhouse that was built in 1756, Groff's is widely respected for its "light" Pennsylvania Dutch cooking. The owner, Betty Groff, is the author of several cookbooks.

Afternoon

After lunch follow Route 772 to Marietta and turn left onto Route 441. This will take you along the banks of the Susquehanna River to **Wright's Ferry Mansion,** Second and Cherry Streets in Columbia, PA 17512 (717–684–4325). In 1738 this was the site of an important river crossing for early settlers on land owned by Susanna Wright, an English Quaker. The house, a magnificent example of an early English Georgian Pennsylvania country mansion, is filled with eighteenth-century furnishings. It's open from May through October on Tuesdays, Wednesdays, Fridays, and Saturdays.

Also in Columbia is the **National Watch and Clock Museum,** 514 Poplar Street, Columbia, PA 17512 (717–684–8261), with more than eight thousand time-related pieces. The museum is open Monday through Thursday from 8:00 A.M. to 5:00 P.M. and Friday from 8:00 A.M. to 4:00 P.M.; closed Saturday and Sunday.

From Wright's Ferry Mansion take Route 30 to Route 272, which will get you to the **Landis Valley Museum,** 2451 Kissel Road, Lancaster, PA 17602 (717–569–0401), a complex of nearly two dozen original buildings dating from the mid-1800s. The museum is open from 9:00 A.M. to 5:00 P.M. Monday through Saturday and noon to 5:00 P.M. Sunday.

Make sure you save enough time to visit **Lititz,** a beautiful town first settled by Moravians. Lititz is home to a tree-lined main street, well-preserved eighteenth-century houses, a church built in 1787, and the oldest girls' boarding school in the country, Linden Hall. For many, however, Lititz's biggest attraction is the **Sturgis Pretzel House,** 219 East Main Street, Lititz, PA 17543 (717–626–4354), which was the first U.S. commercial pretzel bakery (established in 1861). Visitors can learn all about the pretzel-making process and try their hand at twisting some. Open daily 9:00 A.M. to 5:00 P.M. except Sunday.

Carry on to **Ephrata** (Route 772 east to Route 272 north), your home for the night.

DINNER: Doneckers, 409 North State Street, Ephrata, PA 17522; (717) 738–9501. This elegant, supremely sophisticated French restaurant is highly respected by gourmets.

LODGING: 1777 House, 409 North State Street, Ephrata, PA 17522; (717) 738–9502. A beautifully restored clockmaker's house filled with antiques and hand-cut stenciling.

Day 3 / Morning

BREAKFAST: A continental breakfast is included in the room rate at the 1777 House.

Start the day by going to the **Ephrata Cloister,** 632 West Main Street, Ephrata, PA 17522 (717–733–6600). Here you'll find a collection of half-timbered and stone buildings, with steep Germanic roofs, which were originally erected in 1732 in a religious experiment by Conrad Beissel, a German Seventh-Day Adventist. Living as a recluse, he started a community of recluses, and by 1750 there were 300 members. Many of them died from typhus, which they contracted while nursing the sick and wounded after the Battle of Brandywine. The rest died off because celibacy was a requirement of their order.

After a serene saunter around the Cloister, consider heading back to Lancaster, where you can outlet-mall hop (Rockvale Square and Millstream are the biggies). They're open daily from 9:00 A.M. to 5:00 P.M. and on Sundays from noon to 5:00 P.M. If you prefer, you can skip the shopping and simply retrace your steps back to New York City.

There's More

Antiques. Throughout the year the Adamstown Antique Market takes place every Sunday from 8:00 A.M. to 5:00 P.M.

Markets. You'll find farmers' markets at various locations on Tuesdays, Fridays, and Saturdays throughout the year:

Roots Country Market takes place Tuesdays on Graystone Road near the intersection of Route 72 near Manheim.

In Lancaster the farmers' market takes place at Central Market (Queen and King Streets) on Tuesdays and Fridays and on Saturday mornings.

Green Dragon Farmers' Market and Auction starts at 10:00 A.M. and goes to 10:00 P.M. every Friday on Green Spot Road, north of Ephrata off Route 272.

Special Events

Early March. Gordonville Fire Co. Auction. A huge auction featuring quilts, farm equipment, and animals.

Mid-May. Carriage and Sleigh Auction. This annual event takes place at Martin's Sales Pavilion in the town of Intercourse.

Late May. Spring Craft Show. An annual Lancaster event.

Early June. Craft days at Landis Museum Valley in Lancaster. Crafts, crafts, and more crafts in Lancaster.

Early July. All-American Ragtime Festival and Contest in Strasburg.

July 4. Fourth of July celebration in Lititz. Thousands of candles are lit and reflected in the narrow waterways in Lititz Springs Park.

July-Labor Day. *Vorspiel* performances at Ephrata Cloister in Ephrata. Every Saturday night, a musical drama about life at the cloister takes place. For information call (717) 733–6600.

Mid-September. Annual Strasburg Heritage Day Antique & Craft Show. Held at the Strasburg Playground. More than fifty antiques dealers and dozens of craftspeople.

Late September. Street Fair in Ephrata. One of Pennsylvania's biggest street fairs.

Annual Harvest Festival. Held at Kitchen Kettle Village on Route 340 in Intercourse. A celebration of the fall harvest season including strolling musicians, baked goods, and regional foods.

Early October. Harvest Days at Landis Valley Museum, 2451 Kissel Hill Road, Lancaster. Food booths, craft demonstrations, harvest activities.

Second week of December. Christmas at the Cloister. An annual concert that takes place at the Ephrata Cloister. For information call (717) 733–6600.

Late December. Christmas Candlelight Tours. At the Ephrata Cloister; (717) 733–6600.

Other Recommended Restaurants and Lodgings

Lititz

General Sutter Inn, 14 East Main Street, Lititz, PA 17543; (717) 626–2115. A landmark inn with twelve rooms decorated with antique country and Victorian furniture.

For More Information

Pennyslvania Dutch Convention and Visitors Bureau, 501 Greenfield Road, Lancaster, PA 17601; (717) 299–8901 or (800) 723–8824.

For statewide information call (800) 847–4872.

Capitalizing on the Capital Area

History and Heritage

2 Nights

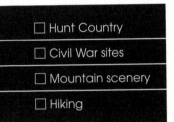

☐ Hunt Country

☐ Civil War sites

☐ Mountain scenery

☐ Hiking

This escape takes you to the countryside west of Washington, D.C., taking in some of the highlights of Virginia, West Virginia, Maryland, and Pennsylvania, all in a matter of a couple of days. Consider combining a visit to the capital itself, visiting some of the museums and attractions.

Day 1 / Morning

Pack a picnic lunch to bring along as you head down the highway. The best way to reach this area from New York is to take I–95 down the coast. When you get to the D.C. area, head southwest on I–495 and take Exit 13 for Route 193 west. Follow that for about 4 miles and then turn onto Route 738 and continue to Great Falls Park.

LUNCH: Great Falls Park is a great place to have your picnic lunch. Here you can hike up to 15 miles of trails (from easy terrain to somewhat rugged) and see the swirling Great Falls of the Potomac River.

Afternoon

From Great Falls Park go through the town of Great Falls and then get on Route 7 north at Dranesville. Follow that to **Leesburg,** which is in the heart of Virginia's Hunt Country. This trip should take about 4½ hours. For a bit of history on the area, have a look around the **Loudoun Museum** (16 Loudoun Street SW, Leesburg, VA 20175; 703–777–7427) and take a walk around the historic district. Also worthwhile (especially for the horsey set) are the **Museum of Hounds and Hunting** and the **Morven Park International Equestrian Institute** in Morven Park,

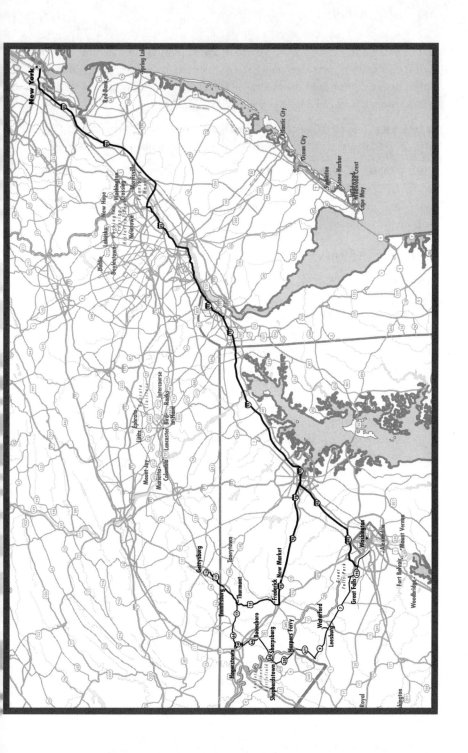

about a mile north of town. **Morven Park** (which sprawls over 1,500 acres) also includes a twenty-eight room mansion, a carriage museum with more than one hundred horse-drawn vehicles, and boxwood gardens. For more information call Morven Park, (703) 777–2414.

DINNER: Green Tree (15 South King Street, Leesburg, VA 20175; 703–777–7246) prides itself on its authentic eighteenth-century recipes.

LODGING: Norris House Inn (108 Loudoun Street SW, Leesburg, VA 20175; 703–777–1806 or 800–644–1806) is a six-room inn that was built in 1760. It has a lovely veranda overlooking the gardens and tasteful antique furnishings.

Day 2 / Morning

BREAKFAST: A full breakfast is included in the room rate at the Norris House Inn.

The countryside surrounding Leesburg is beautiful in every direction, with rolling hills, Thoroughbred horse farms, and beautiful rural villages. To the north (Route 662) is **Waterford,** an eighteenth-century Quaker village, designated a National Historic Landmark. Six miles south of town (on Route 15) is **Oatlands,** (20850 Oatlands Plantation Lane, Leesburg, VA 20175; 703–777–3174), a 261-acre estate that used to be the center of a 5,000-acre plantation. Spend the morning exploring.

Then carry on, making your next stop **Harpers Ferry,** West Virginia. Because of its strategic location, it was a town that changed hands many times during the Civil War. It was also the site of the U.S. arsenal captured by abolitionist John Brown in 1859. To reach it, take Route 9 from Leesburg to Route 671. You're now at the junction of the Shenandoah and Potomac Rivers, where West Virginia, Virginia, and Maryland meet. The whole area (covering more than 2,200 acres) is a National Historical Park. There is a Visitor Center, just off of Route 340, where tours begin. From Harpers Ferry go west on Route 340 for about 2 miles and then turn right onto Route 230 toward Shepherdstown. Cross the Potomac River into Maryland and follow Route 34 to **Sharpsburg.** Just north of town you'll find **Antietam National Battlefield,** (301–432–5124), where one of the bloodiest battles of the Civil War took place on September 17, 1862. At this site more than 23,000 men were killed or wounded when Union forces blocked the first Confederate invasion of the North. There's a self-guided auto tour of the major landmarks.

LUNCH: **Old South Mountain Inn** (6132 Old National Pike, Boonsboro, MD 21713; 301–432–6155). This historic inn/restaurant serves lunch only on the weekends—Saturday from 11:30 A.M. to 2:30 P.M. and Sunday brunch from 10:30 A.M. to 2:00 P.M.

Afternoon

Emmitsburg (which is just south of the Pennsylvania line) is your next destination. The drive—through Maryland's Blue Ridge region—is lovely. You pass through mountain scenery (the Appalachian Trail cuts through this area). Take Route 34 from Sharpsburg to Boonsboro. Then follow Route 66 north to Wagners Crossroads and continue north on Route 40 to Hagerstown. From there head east on Route 64 and then 77 to Thurmont (consider pausing for a picnic at Cunningham Falls State Park or in Catoctin Mountain Park just before reaching Thurmont if you skipped lunch earlier). Then turn left onto Route 15 and follow it for about 9 miles to **Emmitsburg.**

As you approach Emmitsburg, you'll come to two of the area's most famous attractions. First, the **National Shrine Grotto of Lourdes,** (Mt. St. Mary's College and Seminary, Emmitsburg, MD 21727; 301–447–5318), which is a replica of the French shrine (one third the size of the original) and then the **Shrine of St. Elizabeth Ann Seton,** (333 South Seton Avenue, Emmitsburg, MD 21727; 301–447–6606), the first American-born saint. Emmitsburg itself is listed on the National Register of Historic Towns. If you're in the market for antiques, check out the **Emmitsburg Antique Mall** (One Chesapeake Avenue, Emmitsburg, MD 21727; 301–447–6471), which has more than 120 dealers displaying their collections.

Your hotel (and restaurant) for the night is actually 10 miles east of Emmitsburg, on Route 140 in Taneytown.

DINNER: **Antrim 1844,** 30 Trevanion Road, Taneytown, MD 21787; (410) 756-6812. Here the menu offers both French and American specialties.

LODGING: **Antrim 1844,** 30 Trevanion Road, Taneytown, MD 21787; (410) 756-6812 or (800) 858–1844. An antebellum plantation house (1844) on twenty-five acres with fourteen antiques-furnished rooms, some with balconies.

Day 3 / Morning

BREAKFAST: At the Antrim 1844, which is included in the room rate.

From the hotel backtrack to Emmitsburg via Route 140 and then head north on Route 15 to Route 134 across the Mason-Dixon Line into **Gettysburg,** where the Civil War's most decisive battle was fought between July 1 and 3, 1863. The **Gettysburg National Military Park** (717–334–1124 for visitor information) has more than 35 miles of roads through 5,700 acres of battlefield area. You can tour the sites with a **Battlefield Guide,** licensed by the National Park Service, or venture out on your own.

Afternoon

Retrace your steps back to Thurmont on Route 15 and then continue south on Route 15 toward **Frederick.** Founded in 1745, this lovely Colonial town is famous for its numerous eighteenth- and nineteenth-century houses along tree-lined streets. It's a town rich with history, having been the home of Francis Scott Key, author of "The Star Spangled Banner," Chief Justice Roger Brooke Taney (who issued the famous Dred Scott decision), and Barbara Fritchie, the ardent Unionist immortalized by Whittier's poem. Several historic buildings are open for touring including the Barbara Fritchie House (154 West Patrick Street); Schifferstadt (Rosemont Avenue and Second Street), a farmhouse built in 1756; and the Roger Brooke Taney and Francis Scott Key Museum (121 South Bentz Street). Also worthwhile: Trinity Chapel (where Francis Scott Key was baptized), the Mt. Olivet Cemetery (monuments mark the graves of Francis Scott Key and Barbara Fritchie), the Historical Society of Frederick County Museum, and Monocacy Battlefield (3 miles south of town on Route 355).

About 7 miles east of Frederick (take I–70) you'll find the town of **New Market,** which is rife with antiques shops. From there, continue east on I–70 toward Baltimore and then head north on I–95 back to the New York area.

There's More

Outdoor Sports. There are all sorts of outdoor activities you can do in this part of the world, including fishing, boating, and—come winter—cross-country skiing.

Special Events

April. Leesburg Flower and Garden Show, Leesburg, Virginia; (703) 737–7154.

September. Great Frederick Fair, Frederick, Maryland; (301) 663–5895.

December. Old Tyme Christmas, Harpers Ferry, West Virginia; (800) 848–8687.

Other Recommended Restaurants and Lodgings

Harpers Ferry

The Mountain Lake Lodge, 141 Lakeside Drive, Harpers Ferry, West Virginia 25425; (866) 655–6343 or (304) 725–8459. Here you can rent a cabin with wonderful views of the valley, a private lake or the Shenandoah River. Most of them have fireplaces, feather beds, and other luxurious amenities.

Sharpsburg

Historic Jacob Rohrback Inn, 138 West Main Street, Sharpsburg, Maryland 21782; (301) 432–5079 or (877) 839–4242. An historic bed and breakfast circa 1800 with four guest rooms. A multi-course breakfast is included in room rate.

For More Information

Maryland Office of Tourism Development, 217 East Redwood Street, Baltimore, MD 21202; (800) 634–7386.

Pennsylania Office of Tourism, 400 North Street, Harris, PA 17120; (717) 787–5453 or (800) 237–4363.

Virginia Division of Tourism, 901 East Byrd Street, Richmond, VA 23219; (804) 786–4484.

West Virginia Division of Tourism & Parks, 90 MacCorkle Avenue, South Charleston, WV 25303; (800) 225–5982.

Northern Virginia

Past and Present

3 Nights

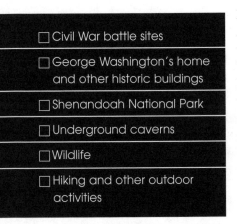

☐ Civil War battle sites

☐ George Washington's home and other historic buildings

☐ Shenandoah National Park

☐ Underground caverns

☐ Wildlife

☐ Hiking and other outdoor activities

Be prepared to soak up lots of American history in a short time when visiting this part of the country. Though not a large area, it's densely historic. Within the span of two days, you can visit several major Civil War sites and tour many historically significant buildings including George Washington's house. The area is also naturally beautiful, holding one of the country's national parks, Shenandoah, which is an Indian word meaning "daughter of the stars."

Like Mid-Atlantic Escape Five, this trip can be combined with a visit to our nation's capital or taken as a trip of its own.

Day 1 / Morning

Set out early from New York, taking I–95 down the coast to the D.C. area. Pick up I–495 heading southwest and then get on I–66 heading west. The drive takes about five hours.

LUNCH: Watch for restaurants located near the highway.

Afternoon

Make your first stop **Manassas National Battlefield Park** (visitor information: 703–361–1339). The scene of two major Civil War battles, this 5,000-acre park has several sites to see, including **Bull Run,** the creek along which the battles were fought. Stop by the Visitor Center (on Henry Hill, just north of I–66 on Route 234), where you can pick up information on self-guided tours (you can take a walking tour and a driving tour of the various areas). Be sure to walk to the top of Henry Hill,

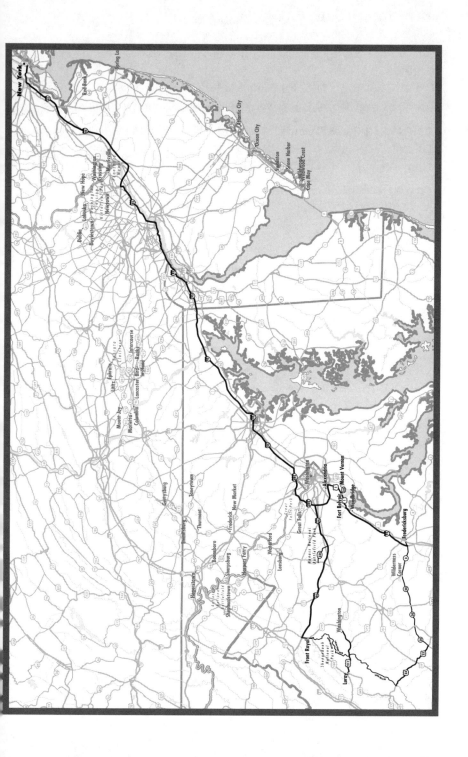

which was a key spot in both battles; from there you can see the entire battle area.

From Manassas National Battlefield Park, continue west on I–66 to the town of **Front Royal,** where you can check into your hotel for the night.

DINNER: Four & Twenty Blackbirds (US 522 and Virginia 647, Flint Hill, VA 22627; 540–675–1111) prides itself on its regional specialties. It's 10 miles south of Front Royal on US 522.

LODGING: Chester House (43 Chester Street, Front Royal, VA 22630; 800–621–0441) is a small (six-room) inn.

Day 2 / Morning

BREAKFAST: A full breakfast is included in the price of the room at Chester House.

Before leaving town, stop at **J's** (206 South Royal Avenue, Front Royal, VA 22630; 540–636–9293) and pick up a gourmet picnic lunch to take along with you.

Just south of Front Royal, you'll find the start of the **Skyline Drive,** a two-lane scenic highway that runs the length of the **Shenandoah National Park** on the crest of the Blue Ridge. The park, which is 80 miles long and from 2 to 13 miles wide, encompasses some 300 square miles of the Blue Ridge. Along the way, there are about seventy scenic overlooks with outstanding views of the **Shenandoah Valley** below. Most of the area is wooded, with more than 100 species of hardwood trees that are in full glory during the autumn months. The park is also a wildlife sanctuary with deer, bear, fox, and bobcat plus more than 200 varieties of birds.

LUNCH: You'll find plenty of wonderful places to spread out your picnic.

Afternoon

One especially worthwhile detour off the Skyline Drive is the short drive west (turn right onto Route 211 at Thornton Gap) to **Luray Caverns** (970 US Highway 211 West, Luray, VA 22835; 540–743–6551). Here you can go underground to see rock formations and hear the sounds of a "stalacpipe." Hours are 9:00 A.M. to 5:00 P.M. daily.

Plan to spend the day enjoying the numerous outdoor activities in the park. You can hike, fish, horseback ride, bicycle, bird-watch, picnic, and camp overnight. There are also ranger-led nature walks. At the entrance

The gardens of Mount Vernon are a great escape.

station pick up a copy of the *Shenandoah Overlook,* a free newspaper that lists daily activities.

To reach your hotel for the night, take Route 211 east to the little town of Washington.

DINNER: The **Inn at Little Washington** (Middle and Main Streets, Washington, VA 22747; 540–675–3800) offers one of the best dining experiences in the state. The service is impeccable, the atmosphere warm and welcoming, and the food is outstanding.

LODGING: The **Inn at Little Washington,** Middle and Main Streets, Washington, VA 22747; (540) 675–3800. A true find, this Relais & Château inn has just a dozen rooms (some of them are suites), all individually and exquisitely decorated.

Day 3 / Morning

BREAKFAST: Continental breakfast is included in the room rate at the inn.

After breakfast continue south on Skyline Drive and then exit onto Route 33, heading east to Barboursville. From there take Route 20 north through Orange to Wilderness Corner, where you'll turn onto Route 3, which will take you to Chancellorsville and then on to **Fredericksburg.** Four major Civil War battles were fought between December 1862 and May 1864 in this general area. You can tour the sites by car or foot. They include **Wilderness National Military Park, Chancellorsville National Military Site, Fredericksburg** and **Spotsylvania County Battlefields Memorial National Military Park,** and **Fredericksburg National Military Park.** For additional information, call (540) 371–0802.

Plan to spend some time looking around Fredericksburg, which is where George Washington went to school and where his mother and sister lived. Though the city was ravaged during the Civil War, many buildings dating before 1775 still stand and are well preserved. Start by stopping at the Visitor Center (706 Caroline Street), where you can watch an orientation film and then set about on a walking tour. Some of the tour's highlights include the Hugh Mercer Apothecary Shop, an eighteenth-century doctor's office and pharmacy; a tavern that was not only a stagecoach stop but an important social and political center built by Washington's brother, Charles; the Masonic Lodge where Washington was initiated in 1752; and the house he bought for his mother. There are also historic churches, cemeteries, and museums.

Afternoon

LUNCH: The **Ristorante Renato** (422 William Street, Fredericksburg, VA 22401; 540–371–8228) serves Northern Italian specialties.

From Fredericksburg head north on I–95. Get off at Route 1, which is just after Woodbridge. Follow signs to Fort Belvoir. Go past Fort Belvoir and then turn right onto Route 235 and follow signs to **Mount Vernon** (visitor information: 703–780–2000) the home of George and Martha Washington. You can tour the house and grounds and see George and Martha's tomb.

Alexandria, which was a prosperous tobacco port back in the 1740s, is the last official stop for this escape. There are guided walking tours of the cobbled streets of Old Town taking in **Robert E. Lee's boyhood home,** the **Stabler-Leadbeater Apothecary Museum** (the largest collection of apothecary glass in its original setting in the nation), and other historically significant buildings dating from the late 1700s.

DINNER: If you're in the mood for a wonderful French meal, try **La Bergerie** (218 North Lee Street, second floor of Crilley Warehouse, in Old Town Alexandria, VA 22314; 703–683–1007).

LODGING: Morrison House (116 South Alfred Street, Alexandria, VA 22314; 703–838–8000) is an elegant red brick building furnished completely in the Federal style. There are forty-five rooms.

Day 4 / Morning

BREAKFAST: Breakfast at the Morrison House is not included in the room rate. Choose either Continental or American for an additional charge.

If you're eager to get back to New York, get on I–495/95 and head north, or if you have more time, drive into D.C., which is just 7 miles away.

There's More

Carillon concerts. On Saturday nights all summer long, there are free carillon recitals at the Netherlands Carillon on the grounds of the Iwo Jima Memorial in Arlington, Virginia, from 6:00 to 8:00 P.M. For more information, call (202) 619–7222.

Special Events

January. Lee Birthday Celebrations, Alexandria; (703) 548–1789.

June. Alexandria Red Cross Waterfront Festival, Alexandria; (703) 549–8300.
Annual Fredericksburg Arts Festival, Fredericksburg; (540) 374–5040.
Martha Washington's Birthday, Mount Vernon; (703) 780–2000.

July. Annual Scottish Games, Alexandria; (703) 838–5005.

October. Alexandria Wine and Arts Festival, Alexandria; (703) 838–5005.
Outdoor Antiques Fair, Fredericksburg; (800) 654–4118.

November. Annual Crafts Show, Fredericksburg; (800) 654–4118.

December. Anniversary of the Battle of Fredericksburg, Fredericksburg; (800) 654–4118.

Annual Scottish Christmas Walk, Alexandria; (703) 838–5005.

A Victorian Christmas, Fredericksburg; (800) 654–4118.

Christmas Candlelight Tour, Fredericksburg; (800) 654–4118.

Christmas Parade, Fredericksburg; (800) 654–4118.

Mount Vernon by Moonlight, Mount Vernon; (703) 780–2000.

Old Town Christmas Candlelight Tour, Alexandria; (703) 838–5005.

Other Recommended Restaurants and Lodgings

Alexandria

Geranio (722 King Street, in Old Town Alexandria, VA 22314; 703–548–0088) is an Italian restaurant specializing in veal, seafood, and pasta.

Union Street Public House (121 South Union Street, between King and Prince Streets, in Old Town Alexandria, VA 22314; 703–548–1785) serves up apple-smoked barbecue pork ribs, linguine with lobster and smoked scallops, and delicious grilled seafood.

Villa D'Este (818 North St. Asaph Street, Alexandria, VA 22314; 703–549–9477) serves Northern Italian specialties.

Stanley (near Luray)

Jordan Hollow Farm Inn (Route 2, Stanley, VA 22851; 540–778–2285 or 888–418–7000) is a converted forty-five-acre horse farm with twenty-one guest rooms. To reach it head south on Route 340 from Luray, then east on Virginia 624, north on Virginia 689, and then east on Virginia 626.

For More Information

Virginia Division of Tourism, 901 East Byrd Street, Richmond, VA 23219; (800) 932–5827 or (804) 786–4484.

INDEX

ABOUT THE AUTHOR

Susan Farewell first started exploring the areas around New York City as a child growing up in South Salem, New York. Back then she traveled with her family, notebook always in hand. She later went on to study at Boston University and then became a travel editor at the Condé Nast Publications. She now writes for dozens of magazines and newspapers around the world, frequently covering the New York and New England areas. She lives in Westport, Connecticut, with her husband, Tom Seligson, and their daughter, Justine.